Positive Negatives

American University Studies

Series VII
Theology and Religion
Vol. 103

PETER LANG
New York · San Francisco · Bern
Frankfurt am Main · Paris · London

Crerar Douglas

Positive Negatives

A Motif in Christian Tradition

PETER LANG
New York • San Francisco • Bern
Frankfurt am Main • Paris • London

BR
128
.D82
D68
1991

Library of Congress Cataloging-in-Publication Data

Douglas, Crerar.
     Positive negatives : a motif in Christian tradition
/ Crerar Douglas.
     p. cm. — (American university studies. Series
VII, Theology and religion; v. 103)
     Includes bibliographical references.
     1. Dualism (Religion)—Christianity—History of
doctrines.   2. Karlstadt, Andreas Rudolff-Bodenstein
von, ca. 1480-1541—Contributions in eucharistic
theology.   3. Hooker, Richard, 1553 or 4-1600—
Contributions in soteriology.   4. Shakespeare,
William, 1564-1616 Winter's tale.   5. Lord's
Supper—History.   6. Salvation—History of
doctrines.   I. Title.   II. Series.
BR128.D82D68   1991   230—dc20   91-31816
ISBN 0-8204-1536-7   CIP
ISSN 0740-0446

Die Deutsche Bibliothek-CIP-Einheitsaufnahme

Douglas, Crerar.
Positive negatives : a motif in Christian tradition /
Crerar Douglas.—New York; Berlin; Bern;
Frankfurt/M.; Paris; Wien: Lang, 1991
     (American university studies : Ser. 7, Theology and
religion ; Vol. 103)
     ISBN 0-8204-1536-7
NE: American university studies / 07

The paper in this book meets the guidelines for permanence and
durability of the Committee on Production Guidelines for Book
Longevity of the Council on Library Resources.

To
Helen Newell Douglas

Acknowledgments

Many people provided assistance to me during the preparation of this book. I am grateful to everyone in my unusually supportive family, and especially to: Helen Newell Douglas, John and Rosalie Douglas, Cameron and Diane Douglas, Albert and Sally Erdman, Robert and Sally Newell, and Amzi and Elma Belle Toops.

I am also very grateful to Mark Chavalas, David Chidester, Märta Cummings, Northrop Frye, Hans-Georg Gadamer, James Goss, Egil Grislis, Dana Hanson, Howard J. Happ, Roderick Hindery, James Kellenberger, J. Louis Martyn, Steven McGarrity, Mokusen Miyuki, Michael Monos, Patrick Nichelson, George A. Riggan, Elizabeth Say, Jack Scherer, Richard B. Sewall, Robert D. Shofner, Emilie Strong Smith, John Macauley Smith, Elizabeth Strong-Cuevas, Richard Torgerson, Richard A. Underwood, and Jeffrey H. Utter for reading and commenting on parts of the manuscript at one or another stage of its preparation. I am especially grateful to my family and to James Goss, Dana Hanson, Howard J. Happ, Mokusen Miyuki, Patrick Nichelson, Michael P. Samartha, Elizabeth Say, Robert D. Shofner, and Richard Torgerson, who have generously shared their ideas with me during discussions which have extended over many years. I am very grateful also to Michael Monos for making available to me his wide range of knowledge in both religious studies and computer science.

Ford Lewis Battles, Olive Brose, Andrew Chiappe, William Theodore DeBary, Ainslie T. Embree, Angus Fletcher, Donald Frame, Egil Grislis, A. Kent Hieatt, Kenneth Koch, William May, LeRoy Moore, Jr., William Nelson, Robert D. Shofner, Richard A. Underwood, and Richard Ernest Weingart are the principal culprits in guiding me to study Christianity in a comparative-religions context. My efforts to understand Karlstadt and Hooker are due especially to the inspiration and guidance of Egil Grislis, and it was Richard A. Underwood who got me so interested, long ago, in the absence of the presence and the presence of the absence. But although I express my heartfelt gratitude to all these teachers, I make no claim that they would endorse the directions I am attempting to take in this volume.

Contents

1

Christianity as a Dualistic Non-Dualism

If I knew how to build a house (and I don't), I would try to build a Victorian house. Instead, however, I have been trying to live for some time as one of the borders in a Victorian theology called ethical monism built in 1893 by Augustus Hopkins Strong (1836-1921). But it is not easy to live in a hundred-year-old theology, especially if you know almost nothing about how to fix things when they break. What has happened is that I spend more and more time outside the house, in a little tent I have put up. I have rigged up the tent to look as much like the house as possible, only smaller—something I can afford and maintain. The tent is called dualistic non-dualism, which, I insist, does not sound too much odder than ethical monism. In fact, I think it sounds rather zany. In the tent I imitate the house in every way I can. Some of the fixtures are original Victorian, but most of the stuff is admittedly pretty cheap modern gadgetry that I have learned, by watching various Saturday TV shows, how to fix up to look Victorian-*like*. The tent is no mansion, but it is mine, and it is fun. It is very exciting to get even this close to a real Victorian theology. I find I can sleep well in it, and that means quite a bit.

In this first chapter I would like to start by giving you a little tour of the real thing, Strong's ethical monism mansion. You will be amazed. Next, I will briefly confess how the dualistic non-dualism tent differs from the mansion; and, finally, I will take you on a little tour of the tent itself, so that at the end of the chapter you can, if you enjoy this kind of thing, compare the mansion to the tent and see what you think. Keep in mind, though, that a lot has happened in the last hundred years, at least to me. I know you will understand. In any event, you need to understand both the mansion and the tent before you get into those hope chests full of linen which are the book's remaining chapters. Otherwise, you will get hopelessly confused. And you will find, incidentally, that I do quite a bit of this type of primitive joking around, or at least I try to. That can also get a little confusing, if not downright tiresome, people tell me. And it does not always seem very religious. But I guess that is why I do it. One last prefatory remark. I hope it is obvious that *Positive Negatives* is not a book about Strong as such. It is Ersatz Strong. It is a birthday-party-type effort to think again in the 1990s in the spirit of his expansive insights of the 1890s. From the perspective of late-twentieth-century specialization, there is something scandalously fraudulent about the enthusiasm of Victorian systematizers for stepping across boundaries that are now sacrosanct. We are not sure that there should be such endeavors as "comparative religions" or the amateur study of *belles lettres*. But even if we do think they should exist, we do not think these pursuits should be hurled together with each other, much less with confessional theology and metaphysics, like so much bric-a-brac. In this book I am seeking exactly that kind of scandalous Ersatz-Victorian eclecticism.

So, let us delay no longer. Before turning to the fraudulent tent, let us take a small tour of the monism mansion. Strong developed his ethical monism as a radicalization of the ethical *monotheism* elaborated by such liberal Protestants as Julius Wellhausen, Albrecht Ritschl, and William Rainey Harper; the Christocentric liberalism developed by William Newton Clarke; and the personalism developed by Rudolf Hermann Lotze, Borden Parker Bowne (and, in Strong's later years, Harry Emerson Fosdick, and, after Strong's death, by the most influential American personalist, Martin Luther King, Jr.). Strong's outlook was similar to the views of all these thinkers in that, like them, he accepted the results of Darwinian evolutionary thought and Wellhausenian Biblical critcism while blending those ideas with an emphasis on Jesus Christ as the personal manifestation of God's presence and purpose in the world. Strong's view was more radical than theirs, however, in the mystical and metaphysical role which he gave to Christ. Like the ethical monotheists, Christocentric liberals, and personalists, Strong said that "theology assumes its best historic form as it becomes Christocentric and recognizes that Christ is the truth of God and the life of man," but while his colleagues would have meant that Christ is metaphorically the life of humanity, Strong meant that Jesus Christ is literally the life of humanity.[1] Yet, identifying himself as an Old School Calvinist, Strong was very conscious of being even more conservative on some matters than Jonathan Edwards, Sr., and proud of being more conservative on almost all matters than Jonathan Edwards, Jr., and the New Haven theology. Yet this conservatism coexisted in Strong with highly speculative flights of doctrinal innovation, all of them justified elaborately by him as new ways of seeing the true meaning of the old Calvinist truths. (The fact that Strong eludes such categories as liberal, conservative, and neo-orthodox is surely one reason he is so little known today and one reason he is so interesting.)

In Strong's ethical monism, "since Christ is the principle of revelation in God, we may say that God never thought, said, or did anything except through Christ. What is more commonly recognized as true with regard to providence and redemption, is also true with regard to creation—it is the work of Christ" (2). To be sure, this view was not so different from that of ancient Christian tradition, but the liberals of Strong's day, believing in the division of labor, were inclined to leave creation to God the Father and redemption as a separate activity to God the Son. By stressing that Christ himself is the creator of the universe, Strong was symbolically linking creation and redemption, ecology (we would say) and history, space and time, concept and action. The mystical, or "monistic," dimension of this idea came to fruition in Strong's claim that "creation, then, is the externalization of the divine ideas through the will of Christ" (3). The "ethical" side of ethical monism referred to the fact that in monism there is usually no moral foundation transcendent to nature on the basis of which ethical absolutes can be elaborated. Christianity, Strong argued, should be different from other monisms in that it should be an *ethical* monism, providing a personal moral absolute in the living Christ, who, though manifest in all of nature, transcends nature as the mind transcends its body.

Strong argued that ethical monism took account of the true insights of idealism and pantheism while at the same time having a God who was more transcendent than theirs: "...the moment we recognize Christ as the principle of self-consciousness and of self-determination in God, we clear ourselves from pantheism as well as from a will-less and soul-less idealism. God is *above* all things as well as *in* all things and *through* all things. This is what pantheism denies" (4). Strong argued that monism is right to see that nature is the externalization of the reason of God, but it fails to see that nature is also the externalization of the *will* of God. As both the reason and the will of God, Christ is "not only wisdom but power. Creation is his free and sovereign act, turning ideas into realities, making objective what was only subjective before. While the plan of creation is the product of his reason, the actual world is the product also of his will" (4). A kenotic evolutionism, in which God exhausts his power by pouring himself totally into his creation, so that there is no God apart from creation, would actually be a denial of both God and evolution, in Strong's view. "Unless there are reserves of power, there can be no progress. Evolution, if it is to proceed toward the better and not toward the worse, requires a power and a will which communicate themselves to the system and reinforce it from time to time" (5). So Christ, as God, stands both above nature and in it.

> All nature is a series of symbols setting forth the hidden truth of God. Since Christ is the only being who can reveal this truth, the world is virtually the thought of Christ. Nature is the omnipresent Christ manifesting God to creatures. The sunset clouds are painted by his hand; the sun that lights those clouds is itself kindled by the Sun of Righteousness. When the storm darkens the sky, the Hebrew poet can leave out of mind all the intermediate agencies of moisture and electricity, and can say, "The God of glory thundereth" (7).

Strong himself, however, did not exclude such intermediate agencies in nature as moisture and electricity. Rather, he saw Christ as immediately present in all the intermediate agencies:

> Matter is not the blind, dead thing that it was [formerly thought to be]. Its qualities exist only for intelligence. We do not know it except in connections with the sensations which it causes. Atoms without force can do nothing; atoms without mind can be nothing. Matter, therefore, is spiritual in its nature. By this I do not mean that matter is spirit, but only that it is the living and continual *manifestation* of spirit, just as my thoughts and volitions are a living and continual manifestation of myself. It does not consist simply of ideas, for ideas, deprived of an external object and an internal subject, are left suspended in the air. Matter exerts force, and is known only by the force which it exerts. But force is the product of will working in rational ways, and will is an attribute of spirit. The system of forces which we call the physical universe is the immediate product of the mind and will of God, and since Christ is the mind and will of God in exercise, Christ is the Creator and Upholder of the universe (6-7).

It is Christ in whom all things consist, Christ in whom we know whatever we know. "A rational bond unites the most distant orbs of space. The universe is a thought; behind that thought is a mighty thinker, and that thinker is Christ, the wisdom and the power of God" (10). Strong especially liked a passage in Robert Browning's Epilogue to the "Dramatis Personae," in which after expressing the bereavement of so many in the nineteenth century who had lost their faith in a personal God, Browning sums up his own hard-won confidence that such a God exists in spite of all the reasons for thinking he does not exist:

> That one face, far from vanish, rather grows
> Or decomposes but to recompose
> Become my universe that feels and knows!

Strong quoted Mrs. Orr, Browning's biographer, as follows: "'That face,' said Mr. Browning, as he closed the book, 'that face is the face of Christ. That is how I feel him.'"

> With one qualification and proviso," [said Strong,] we may adopt the view of Robert Browning. Nature is an expression of the mind and will of Christ, as my face is an expression of my mind and will. Rhetorically, I can identify nature with Christ, just as I identify my face with myself. But, then, let us remember that behind and above my face is a personality, of which the face is but the partial and temporary manifestation. And, in like manner, let us remember that nature is but the partial and temporary manifestation of the Christ who is not only in all things, but before all things and above all things (14-15).

After explaining why he thought that "a Christian monism furnishes us with the best solution of the interactions of the physical and the intellectual universe," however, Strong went on to ask: "Does it explain the facts of the moral universe also?" "This," he said, "is the question of questions" (30). "How can there be any finite personality or freedom or responsibility, if all persons, as well as all things, are but forms or modifications of the divine? How can we be monists, and yet be faithful to man's ethical interests?" (30).

Strong pointed to the doctrine of the Trinity as a guide to reflection on this problem of personalities inside a personality: "If in the one substance of God there are three *infinite* personalities, why may there not be in that same substance multitudinous *finite* personalities?" (30)

If consciousness is present in the elements of the nervous tissue apart from the unit consciousness of the organism as a whole, it need not seem so strange that in the one all-including divine consciousness there should be finite consciousnesses quite unaware of their relation to the whole, and even antagonistic to it. If matter, moreover, be merely the expression of spirit, then the body, as an object of consciousness, may well be only the reverse side of what we call the consciousness of the object. Since the all-including consciousness is that of Christ, our very bodies may be manifestations of the thought and purpose of Christ (31).

But all of this still leaves us with the riddle of sin: "How can that which is of the substance of God ever become morally evil? Our only answer is: it was not morally evil at the first" (33).

God has limited and circumscribed himself in giving life to finite personalities within the bounds of his own being, and it is not the fact of *sin* that constitutes the primary difficulty, but the fact of *finite personality*. When God breathed into man's nostrils the breath of his own life, he communicated freedom, and made possible the creature's self-chosen alienation from himself, the giver of that life. While man could never break the natural bond which united him to God, he could break the spiritual bond, and could introduce even into the life of God a principle of discord and evil (33).

Strong saw the history of the universe as a progressive series of limitations which God freely placed on himself. Adding a schematic form to Strong's important sentence, we have: *the universe is*

a graded and partial manifestation of the divine life:

matter being God's self limitation under the *law of cause and effect;*
humanity being God's self limitation under the *law of freedom;*
incarnation and atonement being God's self limitation under the *law of grace* (68-69).

Nothing could or did obligate God to submit himself to the law of cause and effect which made the material world possible; then to the law that his human creatures would be free; and finally to the law that, by his free grace, God would remove and forgive the sin of his free creatures when they misused their freedom. God provided the remedy for sin as soon as he provided the possibility of sin. "But now," said Strong, "I wish to add what has not been clearly perceived in theology hitherto, that Christ's atonement is not made merely when he becomes incarnate and dies upon the cross. That outward and visible union with humanity which brings him to his sacrificial death is only the culmination and manifestation of a previous union with humanity which was constituted by creation, and which, from the moment of man's first sin, brought suffering to the Son of God" (34):

> If God is holy and sin is ill-deserving, then sin on the part of finite creatures must be visited with penalty. The view of Horace Bushnell that Christ suffers in and with his creatures out of merely sympathetic love, ignores the real reason and ground of suffering in God's moral antagonism to unrighteousness. But if God's nature binds him to punish sin, then he who joins himself to the sinner must share the sinner's punishment. Much more must he who is the very life of humanity take upon his own heart the burden of shame and penalty that belongs to his members (35).

Strong argued that infants and people who do not have the mental capacity to understand the Gospel are still saved by Christ because of Christ's "natural union" with the human race. Strong was making a very radical claim in this concept of Christ's natural union with the human race. Words like Hindu, pantheistic, panentheistic, mystical (all of which, for some Christians, are execrations) spring to mind when we think about this idea of Christ's natural union with the human race and, for that matter, with the whole physical universe. Strong was content to call the idea monism. In that way he was saying that the physical universe is the body of God. As Father, God does not have a body. As Holy Spirit, God does not have a body. But, Strong is saying, as Son, God does have a body, and in that body God the Son feels everything, both pleasant and painful, that anyone or anything in the universe feels because the body of God the Son *is* the physical universe.

The physicality of Strong's language is surprising at first. Conservative Baptist Calvinist theologians usually do not go around saying that this little chipmunk over here is part of the body of God. If you hurt that chipmunk, you are hurting God. If the little chipmunk is having fun, God is having fun inside him. *Former* conservative Baptist Calvinists have sometimes been heard to say that (or is it the other way around?), but Strong was determined to be a monist and a conservative Baptist Calvinist *simultaneously*. It was by no means a popular stance. Strong's fellow monists could of course not stomach the Calvinism, and his fellow Calvinists could not stomach the monism. No wonder the man turned feverishly and massively to poetry for consolation, but (he explained in *The Great Poets and their Theology* and *American Poets and their Theology*) not really only for consolation.[2] Strong had actually begun his study of the great poets and their theology before turning to ethical monism. He began by studying Browning in 1885, and in Browning he first found some of the ideas that became ethical monism. Strong looked to poetry to find the language, the images, the conceptual schema, with which to say that Christianity is an incredibly paradoxical thing. Christianity is not poetry in the way many of us superficially understand poetry, as entertainment or verbal muzak. Rather, Christianity is poetry in the sense in which great poetry is great: revealing simple truths about everyday life in a way that puts familiar realities together so shockingly that, when we experience this poetry, we experience as if for the first time these realities, both in their ordinariness and in their newly revealed strangeness. Through its transfiguration of the everyday, great poetry (like Christianity) opens the windows of heaven onto the everyday, so that from this place and this moment unimaginable infinity and eternity shine forth.

Great poetry, then, for Strong, is not optional in religion. It is central to religious discovery. Only art can lay one language world on top of another (say, heaven on earth or Calvinism on pantheism or Jerusalem on Rochester) in such a way as to reveal each for what it is and yet to reveal that hidden correspondence between these worlds which had heretofore been systematically invisible to us. Great poetry, as a form of great art, a product of great and eminently rational imagination, is a gateway to spiritual enlightenment. Poetry is, along with reason and revelation, one of the engines of true insight into reality as it is. Strong knew that by blending Calvinism and pantheism he would win no friends and influence few people. These two language worlds are simply (to all appearances) too incompatible to be worth trying to superimpose on each other. But Strong was convinced that the people who can see that the world is the body of God desperately need the people who can see that God, to be God, must be high and mighty, exalted far above the world as its sovereign judge and redeemer. And the transcendent-God worshippers, in turn, need the immanent-God worshippers just as desperately, or they will fly straight to heaven at once and slip a disk.

Whether or not we choose Strong's own terminology (and, as I will explain, in some ways I do not), we need to confront the problems he confronted. Our culture needs both: a God who suffers in and with his creatures, flesh of their flesh and bone of their bone, and a God who is sovereign creator, lord and master of his creatures, one who intervenes radically in his creatures' lives every day, not only to suffer with them, but also to rescue them from their, often self-chosen, perdition. Today we need to hear about the God who is so ecological that he is in the holy ecology of that nature which we carelessly destroy, so human that he is in those humans who have been cast by the System (a term we use to avoid saying "us") with industrial efficiency into hunger and need food, into nakedness and need clothes, into prison and need friends. We need to hear again that inasmuch as we neglect one of the least of these we neglect God. And simultaneously, no less urgently, we need to hear about that God who cannot finally be destroyed by the destruction we seem to be bringing upon our sacred ecology and upon so many souls in our sacred five-billion member family. We need to hear about the God of the incarnation, who is alive in heaven and alive on earth simultaneously. If God is stuck in heaven or stuck on earth, he is not the God of the incarnation. Just as much as Strong did, we need to bring together the God of nature and the God of history, the God of space and the God of time, God the Mother and God the Father, the God of the East and the God of the Near East.

We need to see that these supposedly mutually negating God-images do not need to be seen as mutually negating. They can be seen as negatives of each other in the sense in which photographs and their negatives are complementary images of each other, and then we can see that the ultimate contribution of the photograph and the negative to each other is not negative but positive. The photographic imagery in this context seems somehow irresistible in light of the fact that Augustus Strong's brother, Henry A. Strong, having early recognized the potential of young George Eastman, served as president of the Eastman Kodak Company for its first forty years. Perhaps there is no overlap in the brothers' vocations. One brother was a capitalist, and the other was a Calvinist. No overlap in those vocations. Surely just a coincidence. But we can agree that Augustus Strong in his theological Light Room was as inventive in developing (if you will pardon the expression) positives from negatives as was Strong the Eastmanite in his Dark Room. What Strong the theologian was saying about poetry, if we can bear with the analogy for a moment longer, was that believers in God must also go into the Dark Room for very long periods of time if they are to get any positives at all from their negatives, even if they are to get their negatives properly clarified, which requires much darkness in the first place.

The positive-negative Dark Room of theology, for Strong, was poetry. But it was not just poetry in the sense of freely diddling around with exotic verses (you express yourself and I'll express mine). Strong was talking about disciplined, large-scale entry into the vast epic worlds of the genius-poets, the indisputably *Great* poets (a concept which of course throws us democratic equalizers of the 1990s into a hopeless tizzy). Great poems are not necessarily large (remember Shakespeare's sonnets), but great poetry is gigantic, towering, a Louis Sullivan skyscraper of human light and darkness (remember Shakespeare's corpus). The poet skyscrapes for you and for me. The poet skyscrapes for the culture we share. It is not just for the sake of admiring the individual genius of the individual poet that we must spend long hours in the haunted skyscrapers of humanity's poetic past, for Strong. It is for the sake of the ethical monism of the poetry, the monism between the ethics of the poet and the ethics of his or her culture, the monism of shared images by which, in its greatest poets, the culture discovers its horrors and aspirations, its negatives having been clarified and positived in the Dark Room of the poetic skull. We need the poets monistically, then, for individual healing and then for social healing and then, since the great poet never knows when to stop, for cosmic healing (this is sounding Californian), and thus (to put individual, social, and cosmic into a single word) we need the great poets for *theological* healing.

Our great poets are spider-mothers secreting that language web which is the house of our collective, ethical, monistic being (Heidegger had to be dragged into this *somehow*), and so we are irresponsible as ethicists, cosmologists, and people who believe in God if we do not go into the Dark with great poets for long periods of time on behalf of our common culture, jamming into confrontation with each other language-worlds (like, say, Calvinism and pantheism—how the hell could Jonathan Edwards and Ralph Waldo Emerson be related to each other anyway? and why *should* they be?) that do not appear to be mutually confrontable, dipping our language-negatives now into this weird-smelling potion, now into that one, now into another, frantically baptizing our language-worlds in the waters of strange metaphor while our language-worlds tenderly hold their noses. Then we hold our language-worlds up to the light; we hold them up to the dark, and emulsify them again, silverizing, focusing, enlarging, microscoping, trimming, pasting them, and starting over again, until we finally stumble out at dawn, exhausted and changed. That Poetic Dark Room Work, Strong is saying, is not optional for believers in God. It is mandatory.

So Strong's language about God is indeed stridently physical, but at the same time he is not Walt Whitman either, or, to be more precise, Strong is only half Walt Whitman. He is also half Emily Dickinson, never happy until the paraodox is jarring enough. Unlike the vast majority of Christian thinkers, Strong (speaking of physicality and jarring paradoxes as we were) defended the doctrine, sheer heresy—as he knew very well—that Jesus Christ's physical solidarity with his creation is so great that Christ himself was, like all other human beings since Adam's fall, born sinful when the good Virgin Mary gave birth to him.[3] That is not a doctrine calculated to make you popular at religious Christmas parties. Go back to the Dark Room, Strong! We don't want to see you again until at least February.

Strong thought Christ was born sinful in the sense that he had from before the foundation of the world taken upon himself the guilt of human disobedience as thoroughly as if it had resulted from his own disobedience, and in that act Jesus Christ took upon himself the pain of all creatures' (both human and non-human) physical suffering, not *as if* it were his own, but *because* it was his own. This was what it meant to say that God had from the outset decreed to provide a remedy for the sin which he knew his human creatures would freely choose to commit. God did it when he decreed it. He did not decree it and then sit around waiting for several thousand aeons, as we would, before getting started on it. God's word was God's deed. In Christ, God himself provided the remedy for sin by taking the guilt of it upon himself even before the sin had been committed. Psychologically, Christ was separate from Adam. Adam freely sinned. But physically, Christ and Adam were, like Eve and Adam, flesh of each other's flesh and bone of each other's bone.

Physically, Christ *had* to experience the pain and suffering which Adam's sin brought into the world. "It must needs be that the Son of Man should suffer." If we and God are (in the body of Christ, which is the physical universe) in a state of true physical solidarity with each other, as Strong believed (and that is exactly what he meant by the monism that binds God and us into one physical entity), then as soon as one of God's creatures suffers, God suffers—physically—and, because Strong accepted evolution, he knew that there had been creaturely suffering for many aeons before Mr. Adam and Mrs. Eve had started sinning. So Christ must have already taken upon himself the pain caused by sin long before there had been any human sin, just as non-human creatures had started suffering the pain caused by sin long before there had been any human sin. Hence, bearing the consequences of human sin was nothing new to Jesus Christ when he was born on the first Christmas Day.

Once Christ became a human being, as a baby, Christ could not (Strong believed) really be human unless he carried in him (without, obviously, understanding why) the same physical consequences of the guilt for human sin which you and I bear. Those physical consequences involve, as I hardly need to tell you, such things as anxiety, alienation, pain, fear, dangerous ignorance, everything that only a downright Kierkegaardian psychological analysis of guilt would reveal to be concomitant with the state of *being* (not just *feeling*) actually guilty. As a human baby born into a world that is held captive to human guilt, Jesus, said Strong, was also necessarily captive to that state of guilt. Otherwise, he would not really have taken our condition upon him. He would not really have been tempted in all things just as we are. Jesus was born as much a victim of the human race's guilt problem as you and I were. A most uncomfortably paradoxical way to put it, from the standpoint of the orthodox. But Strong seems to have thought a little paradox now and then was good for the orthodox.

Christ bore since his infancy the *guilt* of human sin, but since Christ is God, Christ was under no obligation to pay the *penalty* for human sin. *As a mature, rational human being,* Christ freely (i.e., humanly, anxiously, with much severe temptation to do otherwise, culmintaing in the Garden of Gethsemane on the night before the crucifixion) chose to take upon himself the penalty for the whole human race's sin, thus perfectly doing what only God could do and only humanity could do. On the cross of Jesus Christ, then, the physical solidarity between God and his creatures was consummated, because here we see the consequence of Jesus' freely choosing to do what, for his own sake, he did not need to do. We are accustomed to hearing that Jesus chose to die for *us*, and Strong says that too, but Strong also insists on stressing the less democratically attractive ancient concept that Christ chose to do what he chose to do because his Father said to. We would much rather think that spontaneous, creative young Jesus just came up with this sacrifice-idea on his own, as a favor to spontaneous, creative young us. We hate to think that God the Father would have been so paternal as to demand that the young man do this thing. Surely God the Father would not send God the Son to die on a cross!

Could the Father *make* him choose it? No. Did the Father talk him into choosing it? No. Did the Father assure him that everything would be fine, and he'd come out like a champ if he did it? No. The Father does not seem to have said too much about it at all. But Jesus seems to have figured out what the Father was demanding if the Father really was who Jesus really thought he was. Jesus seems to have decided that night in Gethsemane that if he did not choose to do this particular thing at this particular time in this particular place exactly the way the Father seemed to have been arranging that it should be done, then he, Jesus, was no deliverer, and the world was not going to be delivered at all. If the world was not going to be delivered (we would say) by its own maker, then it is better if there is no God at all. (That is what Strong's own son Charles decided, but Strong forgave him for it, twenty-five painful years later, and assured him that God accepted him in Christ anyway. Strong obviously knew that it was not easy to be the son of Strong. And this discovery in his own life was perhaps one thing that led the elder Strong to think so long and hard about what it had meant to be the son of God, although Strong himself was never so immodest as to put it that way, in so many words. Why am I trying to write about all this? Faulkner, thou shouldst be living at this hour!)

Meanwhile, back at the incarnation, coming into the world with the pain of guilt was, said Strong, not the result of any earthly decision that Jesus made, but going out of the world because of taking the penalty for guilt, a penalty which (if he really was God) he did not need to pay but (if he really was God) only he could pay, that decision was made on a particular night in a particular garden in Israel. That decision (and the act that flowed from it, like the act that had flowed from the Father's decree in the first place, before the foundation of the world, you will recall) was poetry. That decision (and the act on Golgotha that flowed from it) was poetry because, in it, that time and that place were revealing the eternal and the infinite as they really are and thereby revealing that time and that place as they really are, the turning point of human history. The decision and the act were poetry, not by being different from reality or an imitation of reality but by being the revelation of reality. Christ's decision was the essence of a freely chosen, mature, and rational monism (which we call solidarity), and it was the essence of ethics. In Christ God had always taken and always takes upon himself all the pain, alienation, ignorance, anxiety, temptation, despair, and sin of all his creatures because Christ, as God, is absolutely holy and obeys his own holy demand: that we call each other friends and lay down our lives for our each other. This holy way of living issues in love but is not driven by the wayward affections we so often mistake for love. The way of living by which we love our neighbors as ourselves is driven, not by how we feel, but by what God in his inifinite holiness demands.

"The suffering Savior is the life of nature and of man. Through all history he is working out his atonement. The mark of the cross is upon every sun and star, upon every chemical atom, upon the body and the soul of every man" (44). Is salvation, then, universal? Are we puppets on a cosmic salvation-string? Is there no way we can reject Jesus Christ if we choose to? Strong answered by expounding on the verse "There is no other name given under heaven whereby we may be saved": "If we accept him, we become spiritually partakers of the divine nature, and all things are ours. If we reject him, the very stars in their courses fight against us, and the whole universe becomes a cross, to condemn and to punish" (44). Even though we are unconsciously, simply by virtue of dwelling in God's physical universe, accepted and redeemed by Christ long before deciding whether or not to accept Christ's gift, it is still possible to cut ourselves off spiritually from Christ and to reject his solidarity with us and legitimate Lordship over us. But we are still linked physically to Christ, since we are ourselves manifestations of Christ's body, and the result is that if we spiritually reject Christ, we become spiritually like a finger that has a piece of string tightly tied around it. We gradually wither and die spiritually, even when we are part of the very body of the Lord of life. But we must stress here that if we have never really heard Christ's call (as Strong thought happened in the case of his son Charles), that does not mean rejecting Christ. We reject Christ only if we understand exactly what we are rejecting and reject it anyway.

So, since we do have the spiritual independence from Christ to take him or leave him, Strong argues that his monism is still dualistic in certain important ways and that it must be:

> Frankly and bluntly, then, Ethical Monism is dualistic monism. Dualism is a permanent and fundamental truth. If I did not believe that dualism was never to be eradicated from philosophy, never to be escaped by the sober intellect, I would never go on to add to the word "dualistc" the word "monism"; for, of the two, I am free to confess that the more practical, the more valuable, of the two parts of the title is the former. Whatever else we may be, or may not be, we must be dualists through and through, and we must never give up our dualism, because dualism is not only the necessary condition of ethics, but is also inseparably bound up with many, if not all, of those great truths which constitute the essence of the Christian scheme.
>
> But let me define a little more clearly what I mean by dualism. There are two sorts of dualism, and in both of them I most heartily believe. On the one hand, there is the dualism of matter and mind. Matter and mind are two and not one; mind is not matter, matter is not mind; the two are inconvertible. On the other hand, there is the dualism of man and God. God and man are two and not one; man is not God and God is not man; the two are personally differentiated from each

other. These two sorts of dualism, since they both postulate a soul, distinct from matter on the one hand and from God on the other, are only aspects of one truth, and I name that truth psychological dualism (53-54).

The point Strong is making is very important. God is God. Humanity is humanity. I am I. You are you. Even though, in Christ, we are physically united, flesh of each other's flesh and bone of each other's bone, still, psychologically, we are separate entities. Our spiritual union with each other would not be spiritual if it were not freely chosen. We could not freely choose each other if we were not psychologically distinct from each other. So in that respect no matter how monistic the relation between our bodies may be, the relationship between us as total beings, the ethical, spiritual relationship between us, must be dualistic.

I agree, except that I would rather say "dual" than "dualistic." What difference does such a quibble make? To answer that question, I would like to explain how my dualistic non-dualism differs from Strong's ethical monism. I think the term non-dualism would, at least in our time, better convey the idea Strong has in mind when he speaks of a monism that does not exclude dualism. Monism is too static for what he is describing, it seems to me. He means a worldview in which dualism is not the last word, a worldview in which dualism is recognized as important within limits but only after it has been recognized that, beneath our differences, we are in essential non-dualistic solidarity with each other. Monism, it seems to me, over-emphasizes the unity. Strong's explanatory term "dualistic monism" states his paradox more sharply, it seems to me, and I prefer it to the term ethical monism, which seems to imply, on the one hand, that other monisms are not ethical (which may not be the case, since they may have ethics of their own which operate very differently) or, on the other hand, that this ethical monism is, just by virtue of being monism, ethical. So, I prefer to speak of a union of contraries (non-dualism) which is less total and less stable (more dynamic, I hope) than monism.

For the ethical side of the ethical monism paradox, I have some further reflections. First, it seems that Strong started thinking of the unity of Christ with his creatures as an extension of conservative Calvinist William Greenough Thayer Shedd's traducianism, a doctrine more common among Lutherans than Calvinists, according to which original sin is literally inherited rather than being simply legally attributed as a result of the covenant, the latter view being much more common in Calvinism. Traducianism offers, it seems to me, an especially picturesque poetic image of human solidarity, of the unavoidable power over the individual of society's sinfulness. Strong was thinking in this same direction when he added that we also inherit Christ's grace. The presence of sin and the presence of Christ are both unavoidable. Both are part of being a member of the human family. This emphasis on the family may have been partly caused by Strong's effort to explain to his wayward son that Christianity is so all-inclusive that one simply cannot decide to walk out of it any more than one can walk out of the air and expect to keep breathing, but, on the other hand, it may have had nothing to do with that. Strong's effort to maintain conservative, Old School Calvinism's emphasis on the universality of original sin could in itself have been enough to encourage him to follow Shedd into traducianism. Furthermore, Jonathan Edwards had already introduced into New England Calvinism a concern with organic solidarity among creatures and even between creatures and God, which came back to the surface again in the thought of Emerson. Strong was part of that tradition, on the Edwards side, and, in ethical monism, he added the Emerson side. Finally, Strong was enthusiastic about reading German theologians, many of whom were Lutheran and brought with them Lutheran traducianism and Lutheran sacramental concepts of the ubiquity of the glorified body of Christ.

Whatever the causes of Strong's mid-life transition to ethical monism may have been, this turn of interests was accompanied, as we have seen, by his absorption in what he called the theology of the great poets. For me, the importance of ethical monism is not its somewhat typical late-British-Hegelian theology of divine immanence but its poetic character. The other late Hegelians were interested in the immanence of God. Strong was unusual in being interested in the immanence of *Christ*. That idea is more poetic than metaphysical. It is in fact an implicit poetic critique of metaphysics, a poetic re-envisioning of metaphysics. Hymns, prayers, personal experience of the union with Christ, spirituality, even mysticism—these were the stuff of Strong's theology of immanence. And they accompanied a new confidence in Strong that the history of great poetry is itself a coherent narrative, that there is a progress of poetries all over the world gradually revealing more and more about the great moral and aesthetic truths of the universe and, in a hidden, always surprising way, revealing thereby more and more about Jesus Christ. This monism was not so much physical or metaphysical and certainly not (for a Baptist!) sacramental, as it was exactly what Strong called it: "ethical." It was a value-laden, a value-based monism, an ethos of solidarity, an aesthetic of mysterious and meandering long-term redemption. I shall return to the poetic side of Strong's theology in Chapter Two. But I want simply to stress here that although Strong included the concept of a Christ immanent in nature and history, his point was not pantheism but the importance of a personal *unio mystica* with Christ, a theme which was at the center of Calvin's eucharistic theology.

Strong's understanding of the believer's mystical union with Christ comes through clearly in *American Poets and their Theology*, when he is assessing Oliver Wendell Holmes' critique of Calvinism. Strong sums up his defense of Calvinism and critique of Holmes in these words:

> When New England broke away from evangelical theology, no real theology was left to it, and its gravitation was downward. The high Arianism of Channing gave place to the half-fledged pantheism of Parker; and Parker's faith or lack of faith was followed by the full-fledged pantheism of Emerson. More and more the spirit of materialism and agnosticism has taken possession of the Unitarian body, until President Eliot declares that other religions have equal claims with Christianity, and that Christian missions are needless and absurd. This downward progress is equally visible in literary history. The Unitarian poets prove its reality. Longfellow and Lowell succumbed in their later years to the influence of Emerson, and became more or less agnostic; although, as Norton observes, Lowell tried in spite of himself to hold to his old beliefs. But in Oliver Wendell Holmes a new influence was added to the general literary and theological atmosphere of his time, namely, that of modern scientific research. Holmes was a physicist and a physician. The body dominated and explained the soul. Spiritual things were the outcome and efflorescence of the material. And so the theology of Holmes is practically the theology of Herbert Spencer.
>
> Congregationalists furnish still another illustration of this lapse from the true faith. They once were stout opposers of Unitarianism, but they are now on the same road to skepticism. In "The Outlook," Lyman Abbott is asked how a soul seeking after God is to find him. The answer should have been the answer of Christ: "He that hath seen me hath seen the Father"; "I am with you alway, even unto the end of the world"; "I will come to you, and will manifest myself unto you"; "Come unto me, and I will give you rest." In other words, the living and omnipresent Christ is God, manifested in human form, as the object of worship and source of power. But Doctor Abbott apparently sees in Christ no such present Saviour, for he does not point the sinner to Christ, nor urge him

to address Christ in prayer for forgiveness and transformation. In other
writings Doctor Abbott asserts his "faith in Jesus Christ as a giver of life
by his presence and companionship with those who love him and desire
to be like him." But can we rightfully call Christ's presence a personal
presence, without ourselves addressing him and sending others directly
to him? However Doctor Abbott may answer this question, I find in
modern Congregationalists a tendency to look upon Christ as one
outside of us, while Paul regards Christ *in* us as the central secret of the
gospel. [For Dr. Abbott] He is the Way, the Truth, and the Life, only
by proxy—only by being the beginner of these when he was here in the
flesh. Congregationalism is at the parting of the ways. It must either go
forward to Unitarianism and agnosticism, or backward to the
evangelical faith in Christ's deity, omnipresence, and living union with
the believer. This is the essence of Christianity and to give it up is to
give up Christianity itself (344-6).

Thus Strong has no interest in an unparadoxical monism, which would be
pantheism. He is interested precisely in the paradox of a dualistic monism, in
which Christ is free enough as a distinct individual to condemn, punish, and
forgive sinners, who are free enough as distinct individuals to be held
accountable for their actions. The ultimate issue involved in keeping monism
dualistic is thus the ethical issue: individuals' responsibility for the morality of
their actions and inactions.

To bring that ethical concern to a focus in dualistic non-dualism, I
propose that we add one more distinction to our terminology, although I admit
that at first this addition appears only to needlessly and trivially complicate
Strong's already complicated outlook. I suggest that we distinguish between
dualism, in which opposites are seen as antagonistic to each other, and **duality**,
in which opposites are seen as complementary. A fallacy of misplaced dualism
(*pace* Whitehead) occurs when the term dualism is applied to such dualities as
mind and body, self and nature, self and other, time and space, female and
male, rich and poor, homosexual and heterosexual, race and race, language and
language, nation and nation, being and non-being, absence and presence, and
finally even God and humanity. The reason for this distinction between duality
and dualism is that various forms of Christianity have too often introduced an
antagonism between one or another of these paired realities in such a way as to
create a Manichaean metaphysic of opposition where there should have been
instead a more Taoist metaphysic of mutuality. Serious as this dualistic

distortion of Christianity's personalist, Hebraic metaphysic has been, the problem is ultimately not only metaphysical but soteriological.

For the genius of the Christian vision, derived from its Hebraic roots, is its ability to put the antithesis between good and evil in a category absolutely distinct in its seriousness from all other antitheses. When we symbolize mind as antagonistic to body or self as antagonistic to nature, we dilute the seriousness of the antagonism metaphor in the one place where it belongs. We falsely remove the antithesis between good and evil from its proper location at stage center of the human drama. We come to imagine that, by siding with mind against body or body against mind or self against nature or nature against self or one race against another race, we are doing something to help good win over evil. In reality, however, we are doing nothing to help the good when we misplace dualism by imagining a battle where there should not be one. Mind and body, self and nature, self and other self, race and race, are instances of duality, not dualism. Self and other become antagonists only when evil enters their relationship, but in that case it is evil, not duality, that is responsible for the dualism that arises.

I will say what I mean by evil as we proceed, but, for now, the important thing is that the poles of a duality, or polarity, as I am using the concept, have nothing to do with a difference between good and evil. The poles of the kind of duality I have in mind are as complementary and mutual as opposites are in Taoism. To this extent the Taoist metaphysic is a more hospitable home for the Gospel than is the Greek metaphysic because a Christian misuse of the Greek metaphysic has led Christianity into its mind/body, mortal/immortal, divine/human dichotomies. The harmonious co-existence of divinity and humanity in Jesus Christ reveals something a Taoist could understand more readily than an ancient Greek, the complementarity between divinity and humanity, mind and body, mortality and immortality. Many of the differences Christians think they have with Asian religions are not so much differences between Christianity and Asian religions as between Greek philosophy and Asian religions. It is an urgent imperative that Christians not allow their Greek metaphysics to raise a false barrier between the Gospel and non-Greek metaphysics. If Christ is, as H. Richard Niebuhr presented him so memorably, the paradoxical transformer of culture,[4] then we must allow Christ to transform the cultural categories, not only of non-Christian cultures, but also (and especially) of "Christian" culture. Indeed, if Christ is the paradoxical transformer of culture, we should ask whether there ever has been or can be, this side of the parousia, a "Christian culture" worthy of the name. I think the answer is no.

Indeed, the "Christ the transformer" model can be the most anti-Christian of Niebuhr's Christ-and-culture models because, If we misunderstand the category to mean "*Christianity*-the-transformer," we make Jesus Christ into the totem of our own cultural limitations and corruptions. We then see ourselves as Christian conquerors of non-Christian cultures whether by the sword of imperialism or by the more recently fashionable (but not intellectually very different) sword of interfaith dialogue. But "Christ the transformer of culture" should mean humble Christocentrism, not arrogant Christianocentrism. The only culture we are competent to transform is our own, and even here our competence is most doubtful. We are only competent enough to be justifiably held accountable for our incompetence. *Cultura transformata semper transformanda est.* Instead of interfaith dialogue, therefore, I practice interfaith rip-off. I see the encounter between me and a person of another faith as a call to holy larceny. As Saint Jerome justified his rip-off of the pagan rhetoric of Cicero and Vergil by the example of God's command to the Israelites to steal the gold and silver of the Egyptians, so I set about stealing all the non-Christian jewelry my dialogue-partner is wearing. I pin it, paste it, and hook it all over my body. I bring it home to decorate my Christian tent. But, since it is always holy larceny, this larceny carries away only a clone of the original, not the original itself. In fact, spiritual treasures thrive on larceny. The more they are stolen, the more they are appreciated by those from whom they are stolen. The more they are misused by new owners, the more their proper use is purified by their original owners. For spiritual treasures are inherently and inevitably treasures of mutuality. Like mercy, spiritual treasures doubly bless, blessing both the one that gives and the one that takes.

Consequently, if, while I have been stealing scriptures, statues, and temple designs from my non-Christian dialogue partner, the non-Christian has felt inspired to steal something Christian from my jewel box, I feel doubly blessed and doubly virtuous. Some call it syncretism, but I call it fun. I have let someone else discover Christ in my jewel box as the answer to his or her own question, not as the answer to *my* question. And since, as I see it, every spiritual treasure I rip off comes from Christ, I have in the process allowed God to shower yet more blessings on me with every non-Christian gem I have carted away. Now *that* is dialogue.

Too often in interfaith dialogue we share our answer rather than our question. The reason is usually that we have been insufficiently self-critical in our question. We have asked how Christ can help the other person rather than asking what the other person has that may help Christ help me. We have assumed that Christ can come to us only through someone who has stated his or her intention of bringing Christ to us when, if Christ is really the transformer of all culture, Christ tumbles through to us from all cultures, whether those cultures know his name or not. Jesus Christ, as I understand him, is the world's greatest monotheist. Monotheism is a positive-negative bird with (yes) two wings: a non-dualist wing and a dualist wing. The wings ask the following questions:

> The non-dualist wing: *how can peace be regained?*
> The dualist wing: *how can corruption be stopped?*

The non-dualist wing wants to fly backward. It answers its question about peace by flying back to the uncreated non-duality, the non-emergence of the original emergence, the emergence of the non-original non-emergence. The non-dualist wing boggles all oppositions, but at the same time it is not monism. Non-dualism seeks oppositions, but only to boggle them. Non-dualism is the story of the recovery of peace, the waking up which is the deepest sleep, the remembering of all prior lives which is the most blissful forgetting, the gracious recovery of that peace which had seemed least capable of recovery. I am thinking of various kinds of Hinduism, Jainism, and Buddhism, the Indic traditions in general, some being mainly non-dualisms of spirit (Advaita Vedanta), some non-dualisms of matter (Theravada), all being (by intention at least) non-dualisms of the overcoming of the dualism between spirit and matter.

While the non-dualist wing wants to fly backward to the peace before the beginning, the dualist wing flaps forward. Its perception is that corruption is our real danger. Corruption is not an illusion. To fly backward from corruption is to be overwhelmed by it, because corruption is running toward us from out of the future, and the faster we fly away from it, the faster it will engulf us. When Hindus see the snake coiled and hissing down the road in front of them, they discover reality when they discover that the snake (maya) is actually a coiled piece of rope, not a snake. It is not hissing but sizzling in the warm sunshine of reality. The rope will not bite us, but if we treat it as a snake, it may become a snake and bite us. Therefore, we should not seek a battle, but peace, in our relationship with maya. But when the dualist (a Manichee, or a Jewish, Christian, or Muslim fundamentalist) sees the snake, it is really a snake, and it is already striking with the kiss of death. It is the snake of absolute evil. The dualist sees all of reality as a battle between good and evil. The question is: how can corruption be stopped? And the answer is: by doing battle against the corruption and killing it.

I say monotheism has both a non-dualist and a dualist wing because monotheism has the difficult Boeing 767-like task of flying with both a forward-moving wing and a backward-moving wing. Monotheism must ask both: how can peace be regained? (how can we return to the beginning, or, in less linear terms, how can we replace linearity entirely with circularity by denying the distinction between beginning and non-beginning?) and how can corruption be stopped? (how can we fight our way to the end? how can we become more, not less, linear?). Although, for fundamentalists, only the dualist question is valid, Judaism, Christianity, and Islam, in their traditional, non-fundamentalist forms, are based on the proposition that both questions are legitimate and both demand an answer. The problem is that, since there is only one God, both answers must come from the same source and give the same advice. The answer to our two opposite questions must, for the monotheist, be one unified answer. The bird must flap both wings and fly both forward and backward at the same time. A strange bird, monotheism. A wildly impractical and apparently useless dream. But, the monotheist will say, with God all things are possible, and perhaps a way to fly both backward and forward will eventually be found. Meanwhile, how can either the dualist or the non-dualist question be dismissed without an answer?

Not only does non-dualism seek peace while dualism seeks holy war. Non-dualism is more feminizing in its dominant imagery than dualism is. Non-dualist imagery seeks to domesticate the terror of male violence by incorporating that violence in the larger non-violence of (apparently violent) Vishnu and Shiva. The gender-direction of non-dualism is summed up symbolically in the story of the emergence of feminine Kwan Yin from masculine Avalokitesvara. Dualism, on the other hand, is predominantly masculinizing in its imagery. It idealizes the Strong Man, the sword, the imagery of battle and domination. It is so linear as to become ironically non-linear. By symbolizing life as a series of ever more catastrophic battles, dualism breaks the slender thread of historical continuity which makes linearity possible. In Zoroastrian Zurvanism, for example, as in Nietzsche's and Eliade's myth of the eternal return, we see linearity imploding upon itself as every contradiction becomes so much more acute than the last contradiction that there can be no continuity but the continuity of contradiction itself, and so by a most circuitous route our dualist linear history of battles leads us not to a final victory but only to bigger and bigger battles, each future battle being more apocalyptic than the last one.

Progress then equals regress; both the progress and the regress become infinite, and the only meaning is the meaninglessness of both of them and of the distinction between them. So dualism finally destroys itself in a monism beyond the distinction between dualism and non-dualism. Dualism destroys itself by making duality (mutuality) impossible. For mutuality requires continuity. Mutuality requires narrative. There can be no I and Thou without a story which We share. The story and the We mutually entail each other, just as the subject of the story is Thou and I, our Love Story. But even narrative is not enough. Mutuality (i.e. love, dialogue, letting the other be free to be other) requires *true* narrative. Love must be (how nice) *true* love, as all news-stand novels and magazines tell us, or it is no love. Love must be true love because love is the method for uncovering and enjoying the truth. But there is more. Not only must love be true, but truth requires love. The truth can be found only by those who love it. For only in love can we let the other be free to be other, and truth will reveal itself only when it is not coerced, when we love it enough to let it be itself. Truth requires us to confess our non-possession of it. Truth requires us to back off (Take off thy shoes from off thy feet!). Truth requires us to let it unveil itself only in its own time and in its own way. The time and the way of truth's self-unveiling are called by the monotheist historical continuity, the God-us Love Story, the most slender of threads in the world.

For me, that thread is Christ himself as the fulfillment of the messianic shadows, types, and promises of what I still call the Old Testament. When the Old Testament is viewed as the Hebrew Bible (which is a perfectly valid non-Christian way to view it), it is not necesarily a pointer to a Messiah, much less to Jesus as that Messiah. To drag Jesus out of the Hebrew Bible as its secret meaning and culmination is an act of violent and perversely gnostic exegesis. If there had been no New Testament, few of us would have been so grotesque as to attempt to concoct one. But, from the perspective of that Noah's ark which is Christ's church, a miracle has occurred, indeed a whole concatenation of miracles, which I am calling the slender thread of historical continuity. Jesus Christ landed on our planet, and the little Martians who emerged from his windows and doors were hundreds of creeping, crawling saints, apostles, disciples, preachers, nuns, martyrs, monks, priests, missionaries, teachers, ministers, and, o yes, mystics, and all the other washed and unwashed creatures who proclaimed that human history has been transformed by a paradox from both within and without, the paradox of the God-man, King of the Jews. A rip-off if ever there was one!

On Noah's ark, which we see as also Christ's ark, Christ our pilot guides us in the interpretation of his holy Word, and we see the New Testament alive and kicking in the Old Testament like a babe in a manger. Our New Testament and the Old Testament, when interpreted in historical continuity with each other, are a Love Story in which God is the he and we are the she. Sometimes God is called a she in these testaments, but by and large they are (from our late-twentieth-century standpoint) most embarrassingly male-centered documents. They call God she nothing like fifty per cent of the time (nothing like ten per cent). In the overwhelming number of instances these testaments picture God as a he, whether as father, son, husband, king, judge, shepherd, or soldier, or any of a number of other images. Further, in Christian tradition God is represented not only in such scandalously limited and lop-sidedly male categories as these, but, even more outrageously, as covenant-partner of a very small Near Eastern nation. So the testaments confront us with two scandals of particularity: predominantly male images for God and the uniqueness of God's relationship with the Jews. We are rightly shocked by both scandals, and the fact is that the two are related. The ark couples all dualities.

According to Christian tradition, the scandalously small, narrow, and particular history which is the slender thread of Israel's life story is special in all world history and the window onto the meaning of all world history. As special, the history of Israel is not separate from the rest of history. On the contrary, this history of Israel is special precisely in the way in which it is *typical* of the rest of world history, revelatory of its meaning. It is not that in Israel we see what we see nowhere else but that in Israel, seen from the perspective of our faith in her King Jesus, we see precisely what we can learn to see *everywhere*. After the children of Israel lived in exile in Babylon for awhile, they did not say, "Our God is ours only, not yours." On the contrary, the Israelites said, precisely as exiles in a foreign land: "Our God is the God not only of us but of you, too, O Babylonian bastards. You may not know it yet, but it is no less true for all that. The God of Israel is the God of Babylon, like it or not." And they proceeded to rip off the Babylonian myths, symbols, and sacrednesses, translating them into Israelite. The God of Israel, then, became universal not by ceasing to be particular but by intensifying his particularity and expanding it at the same time. We see the culmination and focus of this process of revelatory intensification and expansion in the paradox by which Jesus, precisely as King of the Jews, is Messiah (a word that does not even have a meaning outside Israel's tradition) of all of humanity. Since Israel is Christ's bride, so is everyone else.

As Christians, we must steal the world's symbols to dedicate them to the God of Israel. We need to understand how, through his revelatory relationship with her, God guided Israel's rip-off of the world's power-symbols in such a way as to reveal the paradox of his surprising providence: as a king who orders his people to be free, as a shepherd who seeks lost sheep, a judge who listens, a soldier who lays down his life for his friends, a son who obeys his father, a father who is tender, and a mother who is one tough mother. With similar openness to surprise, we should heuristically fiddle and diddle with all the world's symbols, praying that, through our symbol-centered encounters with other people, God will so transform us that we can discover once again the paradox of his transformative acts. If we use power-symbols unparadoxically, in such a way as to deify the cruelty with which most fathers, sons, husbands, kings, judges, shepherds, and soldiers have ruled this earth, then we are neither propounding a Christlike paradox nor effecting a Christlike transformation. Rather, we are deifying brutality. We are worshipping sin. To say that the God who is Jesus Christ and the Father of Jesus Christ and the Spirit of Jesus Christ is nothing but a typical male is to betray God. To deify malenss is to leave brute force in control of the world, unchallenged, unquestioned, unchanged. It is to flap only the dualist wing of battle and to let the non-dual wing of compassion atrophy in uselessness.

But at the same time we are not being paradoxical enough if, simply translating masculine imagery into feminine imagery, we call God Mother Theresa or Marilyn Monroe. The God of the Old and New Testaments is, to be sure, as merciful as Mother Theresa and as beautiful as Marilyn Monroe, but he is this while at the same time being as scary as Rambo. Now abide Marilyn, Rambo, and Theresa, these three, but the greatest of these is obviously Theresa. Yet it is not enough to say that God is a kind mother. The Bible is making a much more paradoxical statement than that. The Bible, in addition to saying that God is a kind mother, is also saying that the world we have distorted through our collective sin is not a kind or motherly place. The world is violent and armed to the teeth. The world's heart is deceitful above all things and desperately wicked. The God who can subdue and transform such a world must also be violent and armed to the teeth. God is not only non-dualist but also dualist. God is an omnipotent king, but this king (unlike human kings) must also be seen as using his violence to accomplish the very purposes of beauty, innocence, and non-violence which Mother Theresa and Marilyn

Monroe point toward, the non-dual purposes of holy femininity. Both masculinity and femininity are holy. Neither is divine, just as, in Christ, both Jew and gentile are holy, but neither is divine.

God is both as innocent as a dove and as wise as a serpent, as non-dualist as a mother and as dualist as a father. If we see God as only a dove, our symbolism is too non-dualist. If we see God as only a serpent, our symbolism is too dualist. God is both dualist and non-dualist, beyond the distinction between male and female, but I call God father, son, husband, king, judge, shepherd, soldier, and mother because the Bible does. It is the scandal of particularity. I do not seek the God of universal cosmic soup but the God of Abraham, Isaac, and Jacob. When I manipulate imagery and rip off symbols, I do it for the sake of Christian theology, art, proclamation, self-critique. I do it because I am set free by the fact of a revelation which I did not create and cannot manipulate but can only receive and dwell within, the revelation summed up in scandalously particular Jesus, the key to the continuity of world history. Jesus as God's Messiah is the precious thread of historical continuity in a world which does not reveal its continuity apart from him, but, since this thread called Jesus is a mystical thread, with it I can find Jesus everywhere. Jesus himself found faith in himself in the Roman soldier who knew very little about Israel but could see intuitively that he needed Jesus' help. "Not in Israel," said Jesus of the Roman pagan, "have I found such great faith as this." The King of the Jews, then, came to his own, but his own knew him not. Yet knowledge of him grows because of the ability of those who are not his own to know him. Millions know Christ who do not yet know they know him. They bring the King of the Jews to us if we let them, if we rip them off assiduously enough. But we can find Jesus outside Israel only if we learn how to look for him first in Israel. Jesus' story loses its meaning to become only one more story rather than the hermeneutic of all stories if we cut it loose from its historical continuity in the bizarre history of God's Israel. To find Christ beyond Israel, we must first find him in Israel so we will know what we are looking for.

The images by which we know God are mainly dualistic power-images, but the meaning with which God transforms those power-images comes from the non-dualist vocabulary of motherly compassion. So the God-images of the Bible are about the paradoxical transformation of power from domination to liberation. As power-images, the biblical images for God are indeed terrifying and violent. They are negatives, but God's particular and most unworldly way of using his power (a way which comes to clearest focus in Jesus' way of being the Messiah) makes these negatives positive. If we snap the thread of Biblical continuity and switch from calling God he to calling him he/she, she/he, or it, we snap the biblical paradox. We fail to see God dynamically transforming dualism into duality, and we thus fail to see God showing us how power should be used and how he uses it. Finally, if we settle for a unisex God, we lose the ancient Christian tradition of ripping off the Song of Solomon, by which we have used male-female erotic imagery to express our most mystic intuitions about Christ's love for us, his church (female, every one of us, in this most sacred poetry). When the wedding at Cana becomes cosmic, Christ himself gets married, and we become his bride. Then the transforming paradox of the love that binds our Christ and us carries out its miracle. The Great Exchange occurs, and we in our collective femininity become the very body of our Lord.

Remove the sexual imagery, in all the naive beauty of its ancient conventionalism, and you have removed the poetry, the revelation. The temptation to unisexualize God-images is especially strong for my fellow Protestants, many of whom, having thought less than the Christian tradition in general about both mother church and the Blessed Virgin Mary, are of course starving for sacred feminine imagery. They mistakenly conclude that, if only they can unsex God now, their hunger will be satisfied. No to all that! Our motto should be: more sex, not less! Indeed, the eroticism of this male-female Christ-imagery is not what disturbs us today. We worry about the conventionality of the gender roles. Does this image of Christ and his bride not presuppose that the male is necessarily superior in authority to the female? It seems to me, however, that whether or not we accept that assumption in our society (and I do not), we can accept the fact that ancient Israelite society accepted it, and we can appreciate its signifcance within those conventions. Whether or not we believe in monarchy or have any sheep in our neighborhood, we know what a king and a shepherd were. Since we do not believe that males have some inherent authority over females in our society, it becomes all the more urgent to ask whether anyone should ever have authority over anyone else. That requires us to ask whether the mutuality between Christ and us is threatened if we grant Christ authority over our lives. I say no. Christ transforms and fulfills mutuality by being our Lord, not our equal.

Even though we feel that gender is the main problem in our use of power-images for God, I think the truth is the opposite. Our wrestle with gender in theology reflects our discomfort with the very idea of a powerful God. In our quite proper enthusiasm for democracy as the least bad form of government, we forget that it is the least bad only because of human sin. If there were no sin, we would have no problem with the fact that different persons have different amounts of power in different realms. If there were no sin, everyone's power would be for everyone's mutual benefit. When we imagine that there could never be a situation in which power did not corrupt, a situation in which one person's superiority did not threaten another person's dignity, we are taking sin rather than grace as our model for understanding the world, which means taking guilt rather than forgiveness as our model. And that is to commit, not only an error of taste and morality, but also a metaphysical error, because to imagine that there can be no mutuality between unequals is to import an unnecessary dualism (an element of antagonistic evil) into a duality which, in itself, has no necessary relation to dualism.

As often happens when we are trying to think about The Good, we can be rescued by The Beautiful, that most paradoxically transformative symbol of The Good. In other words, thinking about the arts can clarify our thinking about ethics. In the arts, we are all familiar with situations in which someone else has more power than we do and uses that power precisely in such a way as to give us more power than we would otherwise have had. In other words, the artist uses his or her power for a duality of mutuality, not a dualism of antagonism. The phenomenon is called a symphony, a play, a building, a painting, a novel. Artists are by definition people who have superior power in their art. Kindly artists use their power for us rather than against us (although, like God, artists sometimes need to do something against us in order to do something for us). But there is no necessity that artists be kindly, though we always hope they will because power is inherently scary, and we hope against hope that they will use it in such a way as to include us, not exclude us, in other words, letting their mastery of The Beautiful manifest their mastery of The Good. But nothing (except God) can bind powerful artists to be good. Otherwise, they would not really have power in their art. As artists, precisely as symbols of The Beautiful, artists are symbols of The Good, which means, of God. And that means they are both powerful and free. The artists we love are those who use their superior power in a way that creates mutuality, love, sharing, among us. In that way they transport us from *is* to *ought*, from earth to heaven.

There is a certain profound mutuality among Mozart, his performers on the stage, and his listeners in the audience, but the mutuality neither presupposes nor implies that we have as much authority in music as Mozart does. Mozart uses his authority with utter grace, and we delight, not in our equality with him (the question never arises), but in the grace with which he has so disciplined and set free his art that Mozart's power becomes the power of mutuality for all of us: it disciplines and sets us free too, if we creatively submit ourselves to it so that we can grow within it. That is how true spiritual authority operates, on earth as it is in heaven. True spiritual authority liberates duality from dualism. It has nothing to do with equality of power but with mutuality of graciousness. So it is and so it must be with the relationship between Christ and us.

All of this is fine, you might say. We may, for the sake of argument, accept the idea that Christ is an authoritative, tender, and gracious husband (such as the earth has not seen except in him), but are we not thereby implicitly deifying the earthly abuses of male authority? Are we not implicitly saying that Christ can become a wife beater if he ever gets angry enough? To approach that most disgusting of male symbols in a theological context, I need to begin by repeating our distinction between dualism and duality, because it amounts to a distinction between earth as it is and earth as it should be. Earth as it is, is dualism, trapped in the links of its own collective chain of sin. Earth as it should be is duality, a world in which distinctions of power and authority abound (as they do in the concert hall, the gallery, or the theater), but the distinctions lead to mutual sharing and liberation (as they do when both artists and audience know their art). When we make the horrible statement that Christ can use violence against his bride (and has used it and will—though we hope not—use it again), we are saying that only by a tragic, paradoxical, transformative irony can we see any analogy between the symbols we use for dualism and the symbols we use for duality, between the symbols we use for sin and the symbols we use for grace.

The grotesque symbol of Christ as a wife beater shows us why Karl Barth was right to protest so vigorously against the idea that there is any "analogy of being" between heaven and earth, between earth as it should be and earth as it is. When defenders of the analogy of being reply that they never said you can use earthly symbols for heavenly realities (analogy of proportion) but, on the contrary, only heavenly symbols for earthly realities (analogy of proportionality), they are not effectively answering Barth. For the problem is not the gap simply between the finite and the infinite (as in Aristotle) or time and eternity (as in Hegel and Kierkegaard). The problem is the gap between sin and grace, evil and good, what I call dualism and duality. *In God*, there is no infinite gap between the finite and the infinite or between time and eternity (but only mutuality). The infinite gap is between *is* and *ought*, between sin (the only thing God excludes from himself) and grace (the only thing God forces upon his creation). In the dualism caused by sin, there can be no analogy of being but only what Calvin's critics called Calvin's *extra Calvinisticum*, a Logos, a divine reason, which remains divine even in its incarnation in the humanly finite mind and body of Jesus Christ and allows absolutely no basis for the deification (or even the appearance of a hint of an implicit deification) of earthly logos, fallen human reason.

The grotesque symbol of Christ as a wife beater manifests the great divorce between God's grace and our sin, between the realm of *ought* and the realm of *is*. We are dealing with the utter illegitimacy of implicitly justifying sin by moving, without paradox, tragedy, and the total transformation which is Jesus Christ, from human images to divine images. In Christ, and, so far, only in Christ, do we see the one *is* that is *ought*. So the terrible symbol of the violence of Christ, the wrath of God, God's way of making good on his claim to be holy (the ultimate liberation of duality from dualism), comes into focus in the forbidden image of male violence against females but not the way we expect it to. For in The Great Exchange of the cross, Christ took upon himself the life of the oppressed one. Even before we can accuse the Lord of beating us we discover that it is we who are the wife beaters, and it is his body we are raping. (I warned you about the strident physicality of Strongian theology.) Inasmuch as our sin is against Christ's own creation, it is a violation of the very body of Christ himself. Inasmuch as it is our very Noah's ark, our spaceship earth, our five-billion-member family and its sacred ecology that we are violating, it is we who are the rapists. It is we who are the wife beaters. So Christ does not beat his wife. The cross manifests the transformative paradox of Christ's power, by which he is the crucified one, not the crucifier. Christ dwells in the one who is beaten. The beater has sundered his relationship with Christ. Inasmuch as we acquiesce in the beating of one of the least of these victims, we acquiesce in the beating of the body of Christ. In that way Christ holds the mirror up to us. In this world of ours, who is beating whom: Jesus Christ or Christ's people? Christ's determination to be in a gracious relationship of mutuality with us always overcomes our determination to put antagonism where there should be mutuality. Christ's shocking duality always defeats our dualism.

But how does this Oppressed One carry out The Great Exchange when we are so determined to defeat him? We are in imminent danger of bringing nuclear war, nuclear accidents, ecological breakdown, famine, and pestilence to Christ's body in the coming years (even more than we have already), and if we do, we will know that it was we ourselves who did it. Yet we should also know that the human family's collective suffering for the human family's collective guilt on that divine-human collective day will be a visitation by Christ himself, who in his holy Lordship will have decided on that day to tolerate our violence toward each other and toward his creation, toward his very body, no longer. We laugh at the idea of a wrathful God. We shrink from it, but does the goodness of God, the forbearance of God, mean that God endorses sin, that he will never intervene in history on behalf of those in whose oppression we culpably acquiesce? The warnings in Scripture are clear. God in Christ will eventually bring violence to the perpetrators of violence against his people, and his people are all five billion of us, Christian and non-Christian alike (for we are all in the body of Christ whether we know it or not and whether we like it or not). But in our enthusiasm for equality between God and us we try to block those warnings out of our ears.

The threat to our planet is real. The corruption in human society is real. The suffering we both cause and tolerate is real. So, for the Christian, the dualists are right in their perception that there is corruption and that it must be stopped, but they are more right than they want to be: a holy battle is indeed necesary, but not all dualists recognize that the corruption is (because of our non-dualist solidarity with one another) *our own* misuse of *our own* moral freedom, and God's holy battle must be against *us*. It is not easy to see that we have indeed met the enemy, and he is we. We are the rapists of the body of Christ. So, in recognizing our solidarity with all creation (both the good and the bad), the non-dualist also tells us an important moral truth. Prior to the battle, in the beginning, was the peace. Prior to the cutting-down on Arjuna's battlefield is the immortality of the cutter and of the cuttee. But non-dualist cosmogonic consciousness is not only before the battle. Cosmogonic consciousness is before the battle, after the battle, during the battle, the same yesterday, today, and forever. Cosmogonic consciousness is the battle. And the peace. There is no way to regain the original peace because the peace has never departed, only our awareness of it. If our awareness can be clarified, if we can learn by an inward, non-dualist enlightenment to see reality as it is, the peace that has never, *sub specie aeternitatis*, departed will have been (in vision, and vision is essential to the moral imagination) regained.

Both the dualist and the non-dualist, then, have much to teach Christians if we can learn how, not only to convert them, but also to be challenged by them as agents of God himself. We should still preach to them, of course, as to each other, but we must learn how to hear what the non-Christians are saying because they are preaching to us, too, and I believe God is preaching through them. If the logic of monotheistic historical continuity must be (for Christians) not Christianocentric but Christocentric and if Christ is the logic by whom *Christian* culture must be transformed, then we should not go to non-Christian cultures to try to transform them in our own image but, on the contrary, to rip them off, not materially this time around, but spiritually, truly seeking in them for what we can use to make ourselves more human, more aesthetically, ethically, philosophically, and religiously catholic. If Christ is to be the transformer of our "Christian" culture, how can he find a door which we have not already locked shut in Christian xenophobic zeal? One of the best ways Christ can break and enter is through words and symbols that seem to us most *alien*, most surprisingly unchristian. Thus, interfaith rip-off is good, not because there are anonymous Christians, *pace* Karl Rahner, but because there is an anonymous Christ. Both non-Christians and Christians are (often unbeknownst to themselves) bearers of the anonymous Christ. Christ can ride a water buffalo or a camel, a bomb or a daisy. As Luther said, he hides himself behind a mask that appears at first to be the opposite of what we thought he was. Christ is Lord of surprises.

But if Christ and his redemption are so universal, then what is not Christ? What is sin? I am glad you asked. But you deserve to be warned that it will take me the rest of this chapter to answer that question. It is fine to say that the relationship between God and his creatures in Christianity should be one of mutuality, more like the mutuality between yin and yang than the antagonism between Greek mind and Greek body. Does that mutuality between God and creature mean that there must be equality between God and creature? I have tried to tell why I think the answer is no. There is mutuality between Mozart and us, but no equality. Instead, there is a gracious exchange, by which gracious Mozart instills in us, to the extent that we are capable of receiving it, the very power which he has and we lack. Our mutuality with Mozart, then, is like yin and yang only in the sense that there is true mutuality if we submit to the discipline of growing in Mozart's graciousness. With the living Christ, the mutuality between creator and creature is infinitely more intense, but it is no less mutual—infinitely more so. Indeed, since through sin we have lost our capacity to receive Christ, Christ must create the very capacity by which we can thank him for creating the capacity to thank him. The point is that even though in Taoism a mutuality between yin and yang implies something of an equality between them, in Christianity it does not. It implies The Great Exchange, by which our maker and redeemer acts toward us as not only our Lord but also our Friend. Our maker and redeemer washes our feet, gives us his cloak, walks the extra mile with us, lays down his life for us. The point is not equality but mutual respect, mutual love, and so Christ transforms yin and yang as surely as he transformed the ancient Greek mortal-immortal and divine-human categories at Nicaea, Constantinople, and Chalcedon. No cultural categories exist ready-made for Christ any more than any other sinful human capacities are ready, before his transformation of them, for his use. But yin and yang are (in ways that significantly complement Greek categories) susceptible to, and ready for, his entry and transformation. Christianity is for the world, not just for the Greeks, and the same Logos that prepared the Greeks for it has prepared everyone else for it, too. Thus, whether or not you agree, I think you can see what I mean when I claim that yin-yang mutuality between God and us does not, after being paradoxically transformed in Christ, imply equality between God and us, and the inequality, far from depreciating the mutuality, enhances it when the master is, as Christ is, infinitely gracious.

A related and equally important question in all this talk of mutuality, however, is: do you mean that there should be a mutuality between good and evil? Should murder, let us say, be seen as in a relationship of mutuality with peace? Do the two require each other in order to come to their fulfillment? Does good require some evil in order to be good? I want to explain why I say Absolutely Not. I have argued that there is mutuality between all poles in which good and evil is not at stake, but so far I have only hinted at my understanding of evil. I have discussed the non-dualist side of our Christian dualistic non-dualism, but I have not yet probed the dualistic side of it.

What is evil? Evil has two forms: suffering and sin. They are related but different. The Christian life is an effort to live with the claim that suffering is not an ultimate evil. Suffering is not something we are commanded to avoid. The ultimate evil is sin. *But what do I mean by sin?* The essence of sin seems to me to be the infliction of undeserved suffering. What about lust, gluttony, avarice, sloth, wrath, envy, and pride? There is a danger in taking these deadly sins as the model of sin because they can make us look to ourselves in our privacy for the locus of the battle between good and evil, but the battle between good and evil is actually in our relationship to others and to nature (and, through them, to God). We can see how deadly the seven deadly sins are only when we see (what Dante emphasizes) the damage they do to the innocent (including our own innocent minds and bodies). As Dante showed so memorably, the forms of sin are all perversions of the very engine of salvation: the gift of love. Just as love cannot be objectless, then, sin cannot be victimless. Sins cause suffering. Sins are inherently not individual but social. Sin perverts relationship by transforming innocent duality into antagonistic dualism. Sin causes suffering where none (or less) is deserved.

But not all suffering is undeserved, of course. Suffering can be good when it results from mistakes we have made and when we can learn from it, but such justifiable and educative suffering is very different from innocent suffering. In the phenomenon of innocent suffering, good and evil are brought into their most paradoxical possible confrontation. For in this situation "good" seems useless. A good that is doing nothing, and can do nothing, to defend itself against evil begins to seem like such a hopeless good that it is no longer even good. When that happens, evil is apparently winning its most insidious victory. The light is shining in the darkness, and the darkness actually seems to be engulfing it. Then all seems lost, for even darkness loses its character as darkness when there is no light left to engulf. Nor does darkness become luminous when it ceases to be darkness. Darkness without light does not become the morally neutral nothingness of non-dualist Asian mythology (a nothingness which is not evil because this mythology does not presuppose a battle between good and evil in the first place). Darkness without light becomes in dualistic Near Eastern mythology a morally murderous nothingness which is not content to let beings be but must crush them. A Near Eastern darkness which has no light left to engulf is a contradiction with nothing left to contradict. It is both unconceiving and inconceivable. The light must therefore be (inconceivably) prior to the darkness. The positive must be prior to the negative. In the Near East, to be or not to be is indeed the question, and "to be" is the answer, for in the Near East being is prior to and infinitely better than non-being.

The morally neutral nothingness of Asian thought, which can let beings be or let them not be, because it is the very being and not-being of beings, is an example of duality, the creative mutuality of positive and negative. In the Asian traditions, being and nothing engulf each other because prior to the question about which is prior is the priority of their non-priority, the priority of their non-distinction and, even before that, the priority of the non-distinction between distinction and non-distinction. Here the question is not to be or not to be but how to stop making such ridiculous distinctions as that between being and not being. But Near Eastern mythology's Tiamats and Marduks, its Osirises and Isises, Adonises, Abrahams, and Jobs, its Christs and martyrs of Karbala are actors in a very different drama. The Near Eastern myths depict death, destruction, and chaos, not as morally neutral or ambiguous or beyond the distinction between good and evil, but as hideously destructive. The celebrative Chinese dragon and the Near Eastern Leviathan are very different beasts. The former is the happy monster of duality; the latter is the insidious monster of dualism. My argument is that Christians need both the Chinese monster and the Near Eastern monster. The former teaches us about happiness. The latter teaches us about the battle between good and evil. In the phenomenon of innocent suffering, the Near East asks most persistently about its ultimate dragon, and in the language of Christianity that dragon is sin. The question raised in the face of this sin-dragon is: how can the negative of this kind of suffering ever become positive? How can this dualism become a duality? In Israel, the question comes at last into clear focus: if the universe has an omnipotent and wholly good ruler, how can the suffering of the innocent ever be justified?

Innocent suffering is ubiquitous in our daily experience. But why? Why must all the animals and plants suffer? How can the animals ever be compensated for the terror and pain they undergo through no fault of their own, simply as a result of their God-given will to live? Even though their struggle may make possible the upward push of evolution, could there not have been some other way to set up the whole system? If, in the Kingdom of God, the lion will lie down with the lamb and there will be peace on earth, why not now? For Jews and Christians, a locus classicus for the discussion of innocent suffering is the parable of Job. This ancient story has provided a framework within which we have discussed the ultimate dragon for centuries. To explain my understanding of the relation between positive and negative, then, I, too, must devote some attention to Job.

If sin is most fundamentally the infliction of undeserved suffering, must we not say that the God who inflicts suffering on those creatures like Job who do not deserve it is a sinner? The book of Job is, it seems to me, asking exactly that question. It is not only asking why the innocent suffer but, more radically, since the innocent suffer, why should we worship God? Job is asking about the very coherence of the idea of a good God. The first step toward asking that question with Job is to ask how we, Job's friends, can begin even to approach someone who, in his flesh and blood as well as his mind, is wrestling with such a topic on our behalf. The book of Job puts a fence of veneration around the man by showing us two ways *not* to approach him: first, through callous rationalizing and, second, through the worship of suffering.

The first approach is what most of the television Christianity I have seen is urging upon us. According to this approach, suffering is just an obstacle to be overcome by the expert in positive thinking. Positive thinking is presented as a rocket launcher that propels us beyond suffering and our fellow sufferers into a trouble-free world called success. The notion is that Jesus wants us to be successful (and who could quarrel with that?) and, therefore, if you obey Jesus and support the TV program that brings him to you, you will become so successful that you will never need to worry about suffering again.

Under the spell of the religion of positive thinking we can imagine that we would have done a better job of comforting Job than his friends did. Surely we would not, like those buffoons, have bedeviled the poor man for thirty-four chapters with reasons why he must be at fault for his suffering. We hope we would not, and yet we remember how quickly we recoil from those who are in trouble, coming up with reasons why it happened to them instead of us and how, since God is good, their trouble must be their own fault. And we are proud that we and God have made sure that no such disaster can befall us in our uprightness. The problem with a Christianity that offers us nothing but the power of positive thinking is exactly that it allows us to imagine that we have an answer for Job. That vain delusion ruins our ability to be true friends because it makes us more interested in our answer than in our friend. It allows us to feel superior to our friend. It allows us to imagine that to be close to God is to be far from irrationality and pain. But the truth is that God often calls us to walk straight into irrationality and pain, sometimes to help those who are caught there and sometimes for reasons we cannot understand. That is the journey Job's righteous friends were unwilling to make. The book of Job is saying: do not come to this holy man in the supercilious way his friends came to him. So, the first inadequate approach to suffering is that of Job's friends: callous rationalizing.

The second inadequate approach is to make suffering so important that we are actually worshipping it. Shakespeare lampooned this approach in the person of Malvolio, in *Twelfth Night*, who was not having a good time, thank you, and would make sure no one else did either. Sir Toby Belch spoke for all of us when he asked Malvolio, "Dost think, because thou art virtuous, there shall be no more cakes and ale?" Just as callous rationalizing gives us a Christianity that has no lasting joy because of its inability to look suffering in the face, so the nihilisms of our century can also distort our humanity because, in their grotesque melancholy, these counsels of despair can think about nothing but suffering. *This obsession with suffering, which amounts finally to a worship of it, comes in three varieties: exaggerating the power of the devil, exaggerating the power of chaos, and exaggerating the usefulness of sin.*

Exaggerating the power of the devil is the most trivial way to worship suffering. This view says that Satan, not God, was actually responsible for Job's suffering. It appears at first to let God off the hook, but it neglects the fact that God never said to Job, "Sorry, Job, but the devil made me do it." If God could be forced by the devil to do something against his will, would he still be the almighty God whom Job discovered in the theophany at the end of the book? When God tells Job who he is in Chapter 38, God says nothing about sharing power with a malignant demon or with anyone else. Surely Satan did what he did to Job because God decreed to allow him to do it. For reasons unknown to us and to Job, God decreed that Job should suffer. Only to the extent decreed by God does Satan have power over God's creature. We should not give Satan more power than Scripture does.

The second counsel of despair is to exaggerate the power of absurdity. H. Richard Niebuhr said that many of us who officially consider ourselves monotheists are actually polytheists in daily life because we allow ourselves to be pushed and pulled, now here, now there, first by this little god and then by that one, whether power, money, drugs, sex, success, failure, or anxiety.[5] None of us sets out intentionally to worship chaos, but we do sometimes serve chaos in spite of ourselves by belonging to many masters. This way of life results from that counsel of despair which says, "If it feels good, do it." It mistakenly presupposes that we cannot succeed in ordering our lives around the service of the one living Lord. It is true that innocent suffering is, from our human vantage point, an absurdity lodged in the very heart of human existence, but that does not mean that we should worship absurdity. It means that we must find ways to look through the absurdity to something that allows us to treat absurdity as less than ultimate. Treating absurdity as ultimate is in fact a denial of ultimate absurdity becuase in an ultimately absurd universe there could be no un-absurd distinction between the ultimate and the penultimate. Hence, treating absurdity as ultimate rationalizes it and thus makes it less than absurd. Absurdity can only be seen as absurd in the light of that larger un-absurd reality which exposes the absurdity of absurdity.

The third counsel of despair is by far the most subtle and interesting. It exaggerates the usefulness of sin. This approach takes note of the opportunities for spiritual growth and insight which suffering can bring. It concludes that the sin which can lead to such beneficial suffering must ironically be a blessing. This view says that we *should* sin so that we can advance in the knowledge of good and evil, lose our innocence, and grow up, giving God a chance to educate us through suffering. This exaggeration of the usefulness of sin is at first sight one of the most beautiful heresies. It even has a beautiful name: the doctrine of the *felix culpa*, often incorrectly but conveniently translated as the "fortunate fall." It is immortalized in the paradoxical liturgical exaggeration from the Holy Saturday *Exultet*: *O felix culpa quae talem ac tantum meruit habere redemptorem* (O happy fault which merited such and so great a redeemer). As a metaphorical exclamation the doctrine is not a heresy but a statement of exultation about the miracle of Christ's triumph over evil. Christ's triumph is so glorious that it is (sing, shout, dance in exultation!) *as if* the sin over which he triumphed were itself a blessing. The problem comes only when we leave out the singing, shouting, and dancing, the *as if*. For the Christian affirmation is not that good is so good as to make evil good. God brings good out of evil, but that does not mean evil is good or becomes good retroactively. What Joseph's brothers did to him, they meant for evil. The fact that God meant it for good and brought good out of it does not change the fact that abandoning one's brother is evil. Joseph's brothers meant it for evil, and it was evil, even though a gracious God accomplished their complete forgiveness and brought good for many people out of their evil. It is by means of the *felix culpa* metaphor that we call Good Friday good. By calling Good Friday good we are proclaiming that an omnipotently good God brings good *out of* evil. We are not recommending that servants of the Lord be routinely crucified. Nor are we saying evil is good. We are praising, not evil and not the abstract power of the good, but God and God only.

For those who do not like singing, shouting, dancing, metaphors, or exultation in theology, however, the literal interpretation of the *felix culpa* idea is always available. When *felix culpa* is interpreted non-metaphorically, sin and suffering are seen as so important in the process of moral growth, and even in the process of redemption, that in the long run they are good. A literal *felix culpa* doctrine neglects the hard fact that sin and suffering ultimately defy all rationalization. Taken unpoetically, the *felix culpa* theory gives us a God who condones sin and even needs it. It thereby gives us two gods, who must cooperate in the governance of the universe: the good god and the evil god. Christian orthodoxy, on the contrary, holds that God does not need evil to accomplish the good. Rather, God brings good out of evil by defeating evil, making sure it never has the last word. And evil is so real, insidious, and powerful that it captured and killed God himself in the person of God the Son.

So, all three ways of worshipping suffering, the exaggeration of the power of the devil, of the power of chaos, and of the usefulness of sin, fail to deal adequately with the enigma of Job's suffering. How can we deal adequately with it? I would like to make two suggestions. The first is that we must remember the fact that God has given us no explanation of suffering or sin, and the second is that we must remember Jesus.

First, God has given us no explanation. The enigma of sin and suffering remains where the book of Job left it, in the realm of the humanly incomprehensible. God, who knows everything, knows why sin and suffering exist. But he does not choose to tell us why. We may have our favorite theories, but we are not authorized to baptize any of them as the official Christian theory. Christian orthodoxy simply asserts that sin and suffering are unspeakably horrible, that the church exists to minister to those who are caught in the clutches of evil, that the church on earth, though the gates of hell shall not prevail against it, is not exempt from either sin or suffering, and that we will accept no explanation of the enigma short of God's own explanation, which we do not pretend to know. When the tradition says that sin and suffering are universal because of the universal consequences of Adam's sin, it is not giving us an explanation but two imponderables and a key to the solution. The first imponderable is sin itself. Why did the first human beings choose to sin? We are told that it was their fault, not God's, but what finally led them to go beyond the moral status of animals and plants, who live in obedience to their God-given natures, into a willful distortion of their nature through disobedience to their maker? We do not know. Sin remains an imponderable. Equally imponderable, however, is grace. When the story tells us that God had assured his creatures that if they sinned, they would die, we expect God to carry out his sentence. By the imponderable magnitude of his grace, however, God continues to give life to his creatures even when they have chosen death. Why? Again, we do not know. The only thing as incomprehensible as sin is grace. Here again, the tradition is giving us an affirmation but no explanation. And in Christ's condemnation to death on a cross we see God carrying out his promised death-sentence, but he carried it out against one who is both our own substance and God's own substance. Why? We do not know. The magnitude of God's grace is imponderable.

The traditional Christian interpretation of the Garden of Eden gives us a hint of a solution to our problem exactly when it appears to be giving us an intensification of the problem. The hint of a solution is in Paul's claim that all human beings are involved in Adam's fall. This assertion sounds grim to us at first, and it sounds unfair. It is bad enough that I must be my brother's keeper. Does God also expect me to be my father's keeper, and my ancestors' keeper? And does God hold me responsible even for the sin of this ancient Adam, whom I have never met and whose very existence I doubt? In his interpretation of the myth of Adam, Paul is realistically showing us how severe and apparently irrational our human predicament is. We feel relatively innocent. We feel trapped by a demonic logic of sin and suffering which someone else set in motion. We feel quite certain that we did not set it in motion. Yet we feel removed from other people's sin and suffering only because we think our flesh and blood belong to no one but us. We think our flesh and blood are our private property. But Paul is reminding us that our flesh and blood are shared property. We are a human race before we are a human individual. It is the quality of our relatedness that makes it possible for us to be who we are. When that quality is bad, we are bad. When it is good, we are good. When it is mixed, we are mixed. Indeed, we are what we are in our group much more powerfully than in our isolation. Our participation in a group magnifies our power for good, for evil, and for (what is more often the case) a mixture of the two. But the ineluctably social nature of our existence as human beings turns out to be not only our nemesis but also the key to our deliverance.

For Paul goes on to say that if sin could come into our human race through one person, then grace can also come in through one greater person, the new Adam. In that sense the social nature of our existence provides the hint of a solution to the problem of sin and suffering. The righteousness and innocent suffering of God's new Adam overcomes the sin of the old Adam. It is not our social nature that saves us, just as it is not our social nature that damned us. But our social nature, our unavoidable relatedness, is the vehicle both of our perdition and of our deliverance. The origin of our salvation in God's grace is as incomprehensible to us as is the origin of sin in the mind of the first human being. The explanation of sin and grace is unknown to us, but the solution is (for reasons equally unknown to us) new life, both individual and social: it is new life both in Christ and in his church. Instead of an explanation, says Christianity, God gives us a savior. And we affirm that by living with this savior we learn more than we could learn from explanations. Instead of a rocket launcher to catapult us out of suffering, the savior offers us a life in that community which suffers with him, a community so close to him that he calls it his bride and his body. To grow in the knowledge of sin and suffering, then, is not to grow in the knowledge of explanations but of persons, both the persons in Christ's church who commit themselves with us to compassionate lives in Christ and the persons outside the church who need our love and compassion as much as we need theirs.

Many people, of course, both in and out of the church, find no compassion in God's answer to Job. To them, God's assertion of his almightiness seems insensitive. When God says to Job, "Shall a fault finder contend with the Almighty?" is God not being arrogant to his helpless creature? I respond that God's almightiness is our only hope. If the universe is makerless, the good is powerless. If the universe is ruled through shared governance, so that God shares power with the devil or with chaos or with sin, then the good is only uncertainly built into reality. The survival of the good in a humanity in which the good is so inextricably mixed with sin and suffering depends finally on our answer to this question: is the good objectively established in the very heart of things or is it simply a projection of human wishes? When God asserts his almightiness, God is saying that he is the objectively established good at the heart of the universe. God is taking full responsiblity for the whole universe, even for the suffering of the innocent. God is taking upon himself the burden of sin he never committed. When God takes upon himself the burden of sin he never committed, God is saying the buck stops with him. Whether or not we believe there is a God, we can ask whether a God who takes less responsiblity for his universe than Job's God does is worth believing in. If there is a chance (the chance we see in Christ) that such an ultimately responsible God exists, then is not such a chance worth staking our lives on? In Christ's life we see a human being staking his life on precisely that risk. Is Christ's life, with its confidence staked on the almightiness of an ultimately responsible God, an insensitive life? Is it arrogant or domineering? Is it corrupted by its absolute power? The question answers itself.

Hence, the doctrine of God's almightiness leads to my second suggestion: that we remember Jesus when we contemplate the enigma of innocent suffering. For in Jesus we see God taking upon himself both the suffering of the innocent and the consequences of our human rebellion against our humanity. In Jesus, God not only speaks to Job but becomes a Job. In Jesus, God gives up his answers to live in our world without answers. Side by side with us, God in Jesus asks why the innocent suffer and hears only the same exasperating non-answer we hear: that a fault finder should not contend with the almighty. In Jesus, God goes from being the almighty to being the least mighty, and, by virtue of the grace with which God in Jesus lived unmightily, God becomes for us the truly almighty because, in Jesus, God goes beyond the abstraction of our question to ask our question unabstractly, in his own flesh and bone: only in the innocent suffering of God in Christ, the ultimate Job, do we see God's answer to our question about why the innocent suffer. But the answer is his personhood, not his explanation. We legitimately ask why animals suffer. But in the meantime God has become a lamb. As a lamb, God walks blameless to his own sacrificial slaughter, to be executed in order to take away the sin of his executioners. Why do animals suffer? The answer must first of all be a greater question: why does God suffer? But the answer to that question must be an affirmation, that, because Jesus is God's Messiah, the most incomprehensible suffering becomes, not comprehensible, but efficacious.

Here we must pause for a moment to ask why incomprehensible suffering does not become comprehensible in Christ. First, if it did, God would be answering our abstract question with another abstraction. We would then have an abstract suffering-God-principle, called, perhaps, the Jesus principle, which we could plug into all mysteries to dissolve their mystery and thereby remove ourselves from confrontation with the God whose method seems to be the removal of all the abstractions with which we try to remove ourselves from him. Second, if Christ made incomprehensible suffering comprehensible, we would be dealing only with a suffering that is less than ultimate, one whose purpose we could see. We would then be helpless when we encountered that larger suffering whose purpose we could not see. Therefore, we say that Christ makes incomprehensible suffering, not comprehensible, but efficacious. But how can our suffering, which is usually quite useless, be efficacious? Our suffering is made efficacious by our dwelling in Christ, for his suffering is more efficacious than any other act in history.

In God's innocent suffering in Christ, we are present at the birth of a new creation, the new heaven and the new earth. Christ brings us into his new heaven and new earth by making us new creations. He makes all things new. "Trust my almightiness," says the ultimate Job to us, the penultimate Job, "and you will be relieved of the burden of answering my question for me. You will be liberated from your question, so that you can become part of my answer. To be part of my answer," the ultimate Job continues, "you must be willing to risk what I risked: to become human. To become human, you must be willing to go where innocent sufferers go, through the gates of irrationality and pain, where the answers are not abstractions but flesh and blood, where your companions are fellow creatures, not (at first glance) the Creator. You find the Creator only by following his specification that you must first find your creaturehood." This journey to the Jobs is Christ's journey and therefore God's and therefore the church's and therefore ours, since we dwell in Christ by dwelling in his church. The church's invitation to us is to become part of God's answer to Job, to refuse to let that answer be abstract. It is in his church that the efficaciousness of

Christ's suffering becomes tangible. In Christ's church God's answer to Job is creaturely, personal, and yet public: directed to everyone equally. The church's invitation to us in Christ means healing wounds and wiping away tears. The invitation is no less than to participate in Job's theophany, both as Job the victim and as agents of God the healer. In that theophany which is the church, God in Christ is reconciling the world to himself. The church's voyage in Christ is a voyage back to the first creation as God revealed it to Job and forward to the new creation as Christ reveals it to us. It is a sea voyage, and it paradoxically transforms the world, as in a sea change. But the journey forward and back can also be symbolized (by holy rip-off from Sufi Farid Ud-din Attar) as a flight from God to God in God. In the church's journey in Christ, we Sufi Christians can say, the bird of monotheism at last flies both backward and forward at the same time, and that is why Jesus Christ is the world's greatest monotheist.

In Christ the church embarks on the non-dualist flight backward to peace and the dualist flight forward to the heavenly city, to the end of corruption, to the new creation. It is a journey, not an abstraction, but as a journey at the same time back to Alpha and forward to Omega, this Star Trek boggles our linear little minds. But that is good. That is why, in the beginning, God created mysticism. The church's journey back to the original creation and forward to the new creation is mystical, rapturous, and other-worldly, but at the same time creaturely, personal, human, this-worldly, and, though not comprehensible, efficacious. The church's journey backward and forward to creation and new creation is our way of participating in the triumph of Christ's yes over Satan's no, which is the ultimate liberation of duality from dualism.

2

Tragedy as Non-Dualism, Comedy as Dualism

I would like to begin this chapter by telling how I use the important words "religion" and "culture." But since my use of these terms (a usage ripped off, to the best of my ability, from Paul Tillich and Hans-Georg Gadamer respectively) presupposes definitions of a few other terms, I will list my presuppositions about those related terms, as well.

Religion— the depth of culture, the substance of which culture is the form (Tillich)

Culture— the language expressing a people's relation to ultimacy (rigged up by me from a *Horizontenverschmelzung* of Tillich, Strong, and Hans-Georg Gadamer)

Language— the framework of signs and symbols within which people communicate with each other (fairly standard, but pretty much rigged up from Gadamer)

Sign— anything that "stands for" something else in a system of communication (Tillich)

Symbol— a sign that participates in the reality it stands for (Tillich)

Ultimacy— Here I must, for reasons which this chapter will explain, depart from the good Dr. Tillich, for whom ultimacy had to do with being versus not being. Hamlet may have thought that was The Question, but the more common comic view is the one I prefer, according to which The Ultimate Question is: how can we find love and happiness? The elucidation of the difference between The Tragic Question and The Comic Question is the Ultimate purpose of this chapter.

But first we must note that underlying all these definitions is the idea that artists are agents of religion. Artists probe and reveal the depth of culture. When they are good at it, artists swim back up from the depths with stuff that is unbearably sad and funny. Our tears and laughter are the tangible symptoms of the deep-sea spirit-diving which the artist has just done inside us. The intensity (Tillich would say ultimacy) of our concern about those artistic revelations manifests the religiousness of Great artistic production. The artists are prophets, and the prophets are artists. They heal us by both scaring and joking (positive-negatively) the hell out of us. "Poets are the unacknowledged legislators of the world," said Shelley in his *Defense of Poetry*. Augustus Hopkins Strong put it this way:

The poet can express the universal, only as the universal is in him. We must not think of him simply as an individual. He is also a member of the race, with the life of the race pulsating in his veins. When he hears "the still, sad music of humanity," it is because humanity speaks to him and in him. Aye, the greatest poetry expressed a higher life than that of man. David and Isaiah see divinity in nature and in human affairs, because God in them enables them to see God outside of them. This we call inspiration. I do not argue that every poet is inspired, but I do maintain that there are lower as well as higher forms of divine influence, and that the great works of secular literature would never have been possible had not their authors been enlightened by the "Light that lighteth every man."[1]

In writing on *The Great Poets and their Theology*, Strong not only argued that all great poets are inspired by Christ (though on a lower level of inspiration than Scripture) but also that there is a development of doctrine in the history of the development of great poets.

It is not maintained that the poets are conscious theologians. In their vocation as seers, however, they have glimpses of truth in theology, as well as in philosophy and physics....Poetical expressions of these truths are all the more valuable, because they are clothed in the language of feeling, and appeal to our sense of beauty.

The author is inclined to believe that the great poets, taken together, give united and harmonious testimony to the fundamental conceptions of natural religion, if not to those of the specifically Christian scheme. This testimony is cumulative, and it follows the law of evolution, by advancing from vague to clear. Even poets like Goethe, who proclaim another gospel, witness in spite of themselves to the truth as it is in Jesus (vii).

These are weighty assumptions, outlandish, our culture would say. But Strong's volumes on poetry are efforts to explain and defend them. Those volumes speak for themselves. I think they are magnificent. The fact that they have not yet become standard works of literary criticism in the Western canon suggests that they run very much counter to our times, and even to Strong's own time. You know, however, that I think Strong is right in believing that all inspiration is Christ's inspiration, in all cultures, and that although the coherence of all cultural inspirations is not yet evident to us (except symbolically in Christ as the Messiah), there is a coherent order of inspirations in all places and at all times. If I were a Hegelian, I would imagine that we can already see this order in literal detail and describe it. As one whose dialectic does not reach a third, unifying stage beyond the relation of positive and negative, however, I am content to say that we can trust that the coherence of human symbols exists even without our being able to see or say what it is beyond Jesus Christ. We are not yet in heaven, after all. I imagine it will turn out that, beyond Jesus Christ, no further coherence is necessary. But anyway, our presupposition that we share humanity with every human being on earth is itself an implicit presupposition that there is enough coherence of human symbols for us to have a common humanity to share. And that fund of coherence is not small. It is enormous, intricate, cosmic, and shocking. But the coherence-fund hides. It pops into visibility only once in awhile, when it feels like it, when *die Sprache* visibly *spricht*.

One reason we react so negatively to Strong's confidence that Christ speaks through all great poets in all cultures (aside from the fact that we now have no idea what greatness could possibly mean and therefore xenophobically presuppose that it must be something terrible-centric) is that finding Christ all over the world sounds so imperialistic. We are quite properly concerned to let all cultures raise their own questions and seek their own answers in their own way. We resist any meta-narrative that can be imposed on cultures as a whole (not realizing, of course, that our ideal of infinite "individual self-determination" is itself a thoroughly bourgeois meta-narrative that presupposes a steady supply of money, natural resources, health care, and ecological stability to make our ever more individualized quests for self-determination possible). But we are doubly offended when we see Victorian Strong saying not only that all cultures should subscribe to the same Christian meta-narrative but that, lo and behold, they do subscribe to it even though, poor benighted souls, they may not know it. Like Homer, Virgil, and Goethe, the cultures of all the world are just waiting for a kindly Strongian missionary to tell them the many ways in which they have, like St. Paul's men of Athens, been (ignorantly) worshipping the God of Jesus Christ all along. Is that really the best way to be open to a person of another culture, to be ready to hear something truly new and different?

For me, the answer must of course be both positive and negative. Yes, Strong's way is the best way to engage in intercultural and interfaith dialogue, and, no, it is not. I like the distinction Northrop Frye made in *The Critical Path* (written in 1968-69 during the student uprisings) between the myth of freedom and the myth of concern.[2] He thought that in the students' understandable wish to commandeer the university for political purposes that were supposedly revolutionary, the students were acting out the myth of concern but forgetting the myth of freedom. In the myth of concern, our task is not just to study the world but to change it, while, of course, in the traditional liberal myth of freedom we ask no more than to study and attempt to understand the world as it "is." Frye's argument was that we need both myths, and we cannot reconcile them. We can only say that all of us must live in both of them. Each myth has its legitimate claim on us. Responsible social life is a balancing act in which we give the myths of both freedom and concern their due allegiance.

To my knowledge, Frye did not associate this particular dialectic with his dialectic of tragedy and comedy, but it will advance our inquiry if we try to. To begin with, we can connect Frye's freedom/concern polarity with the *forza-froda* polarity which he takes over from Dante.[3] For Dante, human sins could be divided between the sins of violence (*forza*) and the sins of guile (or fraud) (*froda*). Machiavelli said every effective ruler needed a good supply of both, and Frye said that Western culture and (by implication, for monomythical Frye) all cultures have in fact been well stocked with these two handy survival skills, for they are the roots respectively of tragedy (as in violent, tragic Achilles) and comedy (as in wily, comic Odysseus). The tragic plot is a descent, and the comic plot is an ascent. The tragic plot descends into the isolation of the hero, while the comic plot ascends into the kind of reunion celebrated at the end of the Odyssey. In Dante, the two correspond to Dante's tragic journey down into hell and his comedic, divine journey up to Purgatory and then on up to Paradise.

The myth of freedom, it seems to me, is, quite paradoxically, the tragic myth of *forza*. We might expect that force would be associated with the myth of concern, in which someone (say, Lord Cromwell) is so concerned about your well-being that he is willing to use force to assure it, force against *you* if need be. But ironically I think tragedy, the violent mode, leads to the myth of freedom because tragedy violently sets the hero free from illusion. Tragedy makes it possible for the hero to kiss the world good-bye. Tragedy is non-dualist rather than dualist in the sense that it is about transcendence of the horrors of existence *whether or not* the horrors ever get "conquered." Like Arjuna, Gandhi, and so many unarmed, non-violent women both in stories and in the real world, the tragic hero must suffer more violence than he or she wants to suffer. He or she must suffer more violence than he or she is able to give in return. Tragic heroes, even the most vicious, like Othello and Macbeth, are (by the end of their disaster) usually more sinned against than sinning. It is not that they did nothing wrong. It is that, like Job and King Lear, the wrong they did, did not deserve the extent of the pain they suffered in return for it, or, like Othello and Macbeth, they were violent victims of their own naivety. Othello and Macbeth, under the influence of Iago and Lady Macbeth, stepped farther into evil than they would have stepped without such wicked advisers. They were determined to be powerful masters of their situations, and the very excess of that determination made them weak.

The point of the story, however, is not that these tragic heroes fell but that their fall revealed Reality to them. What they finally saw was their true self in its true circumstances. And that made them free. The difference between a disaster story and a tragedy is that the tragedy is a freedom story. It is about a hero's violent liberation from his or her own misunderstanding of himself or herself and of the world. At the end of a tragedy, the hero (though perhaps physically blind and almost dead) can finally see. Therefore, the tragic hero, like Oedipus, can (if he or she lives so long) become, post-tragically, a useful resource to the community as an adviser, a seer, a holy person, a non-dualist *sanyasin*.

Comedy, on the other hand, corresponds, I believe, to *froda*, the myth of concern, and dualism. The fact is that comedians are, like Aristophanes, Juvenal, and Jonathan Swift, often very conservative people, whose chief art is to show how absurd are silly, new-fangled people's departures from traditional law and order. Even comedy in Dante's larger, sacred sense is a growth in freedom only by the route of a growth in penitence on the Mount of Purgatory and a growth in law-abiding, infinitely *concerned* virtue as one ascends the stages of heaven. Dante's heavenly pilgrim must reverse the effects on society of that worst form of sin (*froda*) by redirecting love in such a way as to live as most people only *feign* to live. The heavenly pilgrimage is parodically obsessed with *froda* because it is the story of the exact opposite of that most damaging sin. *Froda* and paradise are each other's Antipodes. Furthermore, as a poet, Dante had to be feigning more and more intensely with every new heavenly plateau he reached because it is easy to write about the hell we have all experienced but very hard to write in a convincing way, and with a straight face (no St. Peter jokes!), about heaven. Finally, comedy is non-violent in the sense that people who slip on a banana peel on the comic stage are never injured. In comedy, people who lose everything they have are to be laughed at because there is always a comic distance between the audience and the stage. We know in a comedy that the pain of the heroes is only fraudulent. That is part of what makes it ridiculous. But the *froda* of the comic stage is actually turned against us in the audience. For the fools we are laughing at are ourselves. What they lose is what we are most *concerned* about losing, and what they are seeking (love and happiness) is what we are most concerned about seeking.

If tragedy is a discovery of the answer to the non-dualist's question (how can peace be regained?), it is by bringing the tragic hero to his or her hard-won enlightenment, to true insight. The hero discovers exactly who he or she has all along *been* and finds peace only in learning to live with that past. Tragedy is, like Job's theophany, a journey back to the beginning, but this time with Insight, Enlightenment, so that, this time, we understand the beginning. If comedy is an answer to the dualist's question (how can corruption be stopped?), it is by showing comic heroes, not who they have been, but how they must act in order to become the person they want to become. In that respect, comedy is about the myth of concern; it is hopeful and future-oriented; it is about discovering the rules of sensible behavior and removing obstructing figures who are unsensible and insensitive. In that respect comedy is about law and order and new beginnings. Comedy is a journey forward to the redeemed society at the end of what we call time. It is about the community's decision to commit itself to healing. Comedy means concern for redemption.

How does this relate to interfaith dialogue? We need to bring both our questions and our answers to interfaith dialogue. Our questions are (following Paul Tillich) existential. I would say they are tragic. They are questions about the ultimate purpose and value of life which all human beings share. We must enter interfaith dialogue as tragic heroes meeting fellow tragic heroes from the alien planets of other faiths. The myth of freedom must prevail here. The purpose of the dialogue is to learn from each other, to let each be exactly who he or she wants to be. Dialogue at this level is not yet friendship. It is encounter. It is the discovery of what Hans-Georg Gadamer calls the alien character of our respective horizons. In tragedy, the hero is finally isolated— and free only by learning to accept and live with that isolation. At this tragic (somewhat *forced*), isolated stage of interfaith dialogue, I think Strong's Christian meta-narrative is not useful. It is a real hindrance to discovering the otherness of the other. And I think Strong would have agreed. His whole life of dialogue shows it.

But if interfaith dialogue should happen to move from a series of strange encounters to a real friendship (or marriage or both), the myth of freedom is not enough. Now comedy sets in. *Froda* goes to work. We start ripping off our dialogue partner, imitating him or her, borrowing, arguing, and committing all kinds of (o no!) syncretism. At this point, it is questionable whether dialogue is even the proper word for the relationship. No-holds-barred-fight would be one word for it. Love Story would be another. Marriage is still probably the best word for it. The point is that when love or friendship or hatred enters a dialogue (any intense manifestation of the mutuality of I-Thou in Buber's sense), we have crossed into the kind of liminality which so perturbed establishment academicians like Frye in 1968. As far as religion is concerned, we have left The History of Religions and entered (heaven forbid!) religiousness. Eighteenth-century, so-called "secular" modern and postmodern universities, which are based only on Enlightenment and Insight, do not know how to handle the confrontationality, the violent and often obscene humor, the infinite concern of religiousness and (what is the same thing) Truly Serious Politics. They do almost all they can to eliminate it as the very enemy of reason. But to do that, is to commit the sin of conservatism. Religious people must insist on their right to speak religiously on eighteenth-century campuses, to disturb the Enlightenment, to raise a little hell in the name of heaven. The isolation of tragedy, the leisure of the myth of freedom, is not enough. On the comic level Strong is absolutely right about interfaith dialogue. On the comic level, we go out into the world, not to find fellow tragic heroes, but to find friends, and friendship is a positive-negative dialectic, in which we discover not only the alienation of our horizons but also, as Hans-Georg Gadamer personally epitomized, if anyone ever did, the *Verschmelzung* of our horizons. Long live tragic alienation. But also long live Hermes and his breezy hermeneuts (that famous sixties rock group). Long live comic *Verschmelzung*, with all its fraud, its interfaith rip-offs, its everlasting, tacky little Love Stories. Comedy and tragedy, like dualism and non-dualism, must dwell together if monism is to be ethical.

Does the dialectic of *forza* and *froda* have a place, not only in the attitudes we bring to interfaith dialogue, but also in the actual relationship between Christianity and other religions? In Chapter One, I suggested that, in general, Eastern religions ask the non-dualist question, while Near Eastern religions ask the dualist question. If, however, religion, as the depth of culture, is really, universally, a Christic positive-negative process by which we move from the tragedy of paradox to the tragedy of transformation, from *forza* to *froda*, from tragedy to comedy, should I not attempt to examine some specific examples of this dialectic in action in non-Christian religions? I propose to look at a few examples from Islam and Buddhism in the light of our dialectic. In the spirit of comedic rip-off, I will examine these religious phenomena, not for their own sake, but for my sake, seeing what I can learn from them about my own faith, what I can find in them that has any analogues in my own forty-six years of Christian experience. I do not need to be told that interfaith rip-off is a very different thing from The History of Religions. I know that. But tell me again if you wish. I am very happy that there are many good Historians of Religions in the world, but they are doing *forza*, and I am doing *froda*. Long live both of us! One more methodological note. Why, when there are so many religions in the world, pick only Islam and Buddhism? The reason is that Islam and Buddhism share with Christianity a history of missionary activity. Unlike some religions, these three are out to change the whole world (although the ironies of disagreement about what that means and how it should be done are infinite in each of these traditions and fun topics for study in their own right). The missionary character of these religions brings into focus the positive-negative dialectic I am especially interested in, the dialectic between paradox and transformation (the paradox that fulfillment has already occurred and the transformation that will be necessary before fulfillment can finally be full).

So, to meander toward Islam and Buddhism, let us check in on Paul Tillich again and see what he is up to. He usually has a conceptual map or two sitting around, and he just might have maps to Baghdad and Kyoto. He will not mind if we rip them off. Tillich was fond of distinguishing between two types of philosophy of religion, the ontological and the cosmological: "the way of overcoming estrangement and the way of meeting a stranger" (289).[4] I would like to include this dialectic also in the moss on our positive-negative roling stone. I will in due time tell why I think the ontological approach is *forza* and the cosmological approach is *froda* and why I think Tillich would have been much wiser to put these two in a positive-negative structure of mutual polarity rather than the structure of mutual antagonism in which he most often put them. Fixing that up for him will be the interest I will pay when I return his maps after we get home from our journey. But first, let us look at Tillich's own discussion of the ontological and cosmological approaches to God. Tillich thought that in the ontological approach we meet ourselves when we discover God. God is identical with ourselves but infinitely transcends us. We can be estranged from him but never separated from him. In the cosmological approach, we meet a stranger when we meet God. We can be provisionally related to him, but he can disappear. Only probable statements can be made about him (289).

Tillich associated the ontological approach with Augustine. He believed that Augustine established the ontological approach by giving the most important answer in the history of Christendom to the problem of the two absolutes. The two absolutes are the absolute being of the Greek philosophers and the absolute God of the Hebrew prophets. The philosophers and prophets used their absolutes to free themselves from domination by the tyrants of mythology: the "half-religious, half-magical, half-divine, half-demonic, half-superhuman, half-subhuman, half-abstract, half-concrete beings" who dominate the lives of people who have no absolute (289). The problem of the two absolutes is: how are they related to each other? "Augustine, after he had experienced all the implications of ancient skepticism, gave a classical answer to the problem of the two Absolutes: They coincide in the nature of truth" (290). God, as absolute truth, is the presupposition of the search for God. God is the truth presupposed in the search for truth. Tillich argued that the Franciscan tradition built on Augustine's ontological philosophy of religion by seeing God as immediately knowable. Bonaventure said that "God is most truly present to the very soul and immediately knowable" (290). God is knowable because he is the principle of knowledge, the first truth, in the light of which everything else is known, as Matthew of Aquasparta says. As such, says Tillich, God is the identity of subject and object. As the truth itself, God is manifest in the ultimate principles of knowledge, which are "independent of the changes and relativities of the human mind." These principles of knowledge appear "in the logical and mathematical axioms as well as in the first categories of thought" (291).

"The fact that people turn away from this thought [this immediate knowledge of God] is based on individual defects but not on the essential structure of the mind" (292). Nevertheless, the individual defects have a history of their own, beginning with the illustrious Anselm of Canterbury, who, in Tillich's view, moves us away from the Augustinian immediacy through his ontological argument for God's existence, an argument which demotes God from *esse ipsum* (as he was for Augustine) to *ens realissimum*, thereby making God not the presupposition of all knowledge but the goal of a process which faith seeking understanding attempts to arrive at (292). The ontological journey from the finite to the infinite is, however, impossible. The thought of the *ens realissimum* simply does not necessarily entail its existence outside of thought. And when the great Aquinas seeks to save God by demoting him yet again, this time from the conclusion of a logical process to the conclusion of an empirical cause and effect analysis, our vision becomes divided between a plodding intellect which shows that we need revelation and a mighty will which bows to the authority of a revelation which is pictured as coming in from outside the soul rather than up from its center. Thereby, says Tillich, the Bible is demoted from the handbook to contemplation which it is for Bonaventure to the book of revealed propositions which it is for Thomas. Revelation and the self become alien to each other, and an authoritarianism, which Tillich calls heteronomy, takes the place of that Augustinian theonomy which Tillich finds in Bonaventure (292-4).

Consequently the risk of faith becomes the risk of believing mightily in propositions which have weak evidence to support them rather than the risk of trusting that "the unconditional element of being itself can become a matter of ultimate concern only if it appears in a concrete embodiment" (299). But how do we know, as good Augustinians, when the unconditional, the ultimate concern, is truly manifest in our midst? "The criterion," says Tillich, "of every concrete expression of our ultimate concern is the degree to which the concreteness of the concern is in unity with its ultimacy" (299).

At this point let us ask how Tillich's schema relates to religions other than Christianity. In Hinduism, for example, it would seem that there can be many, indeed millions, of instances in which the concreteness of ultimate concern is in unity with its ultimacy, as long as no one physical image claims to be the exclusively normative container of divinity. In Buddhism there is more anxiety about physical containers of divinity because of the fear that people who attach themselves to any particular container may also be attaching themselves to their ego, thereby absolutizing the ego and its suffering. Islam, however, shares with Judaism a special distrust of icons and other physical containers of divine power. Islam is even more iconoclastic than Judaism because Islam will not even affirm the notion that a unique covenant relationship with a unique people of God in a unique land can be a manifestation of divinity. For orthodox Islam, only the iconoclasitc Qur'an can be revered with anything like the intensity with which iconic peoples revere their icons, but, even in the case of the Qur'an, the reverence is profoundly paradoxical because what is revered is not the book as a physical container but the words as invisible conveyors of the divine will, and the words make it abundantly clear that God has no truck with icons.

Mecca, formerly the storehouse of the idols of Arabia, could still be revered by Muhammad and his followers, but not, of course, as the storehouse of idols: on the contrary, as the symbol of the destruction of idols, the clustering place of that sacred emptiness which fills the house of the black rock, that rock which (like Islamic revelation) was once on fire with heavenly light but has now cooled, as it were, to become touchable for reverent believers in that God who dwells in light inaccessible. The Qur'an can be revered, but not as an icon: on the contrary, as the abolition of all icons. Muhammad can be revered, but not as a saint or divine person: on the contrary, as a symbol of the sharp dividing line between the divine ecstasy of the revelation which he experienced and the cool and humble obedience which is demanded of his followers. The city of idols has become the symbol of the end of idols, and the sacred book of prophecy has put an end to prophecy. The greatest prophet has put an end to prophets. The Sufis and Shi'ites, of course, have not been comfortable with these sharp dividing lines between Muhammad and us, but the very fact that they have been such controversial communities suggests that something of the genius of Islam depends on that very icon-anxiety which the Sufis and Shi'is are so driven to question, test, and re-interpret.

What Tillich and Augustine are saying about the concrete embodiments of ultimate concern is the opposite of what Islam is saying. John of Damascus, the normative defender of Christian icons from within the caliph's iconoclastic court, would have agreed with Tillich's claim that "the criterion of every concrete expression of our ultimate concern is the degree to which the concreteness of the concern is in unity with its ultimacy." And this criterion, for Tillich as for Augustine and John of Damascus, is manifest normatively in Jesus as the Messiah. Jesus was transparent to the divine ground, which is God; transparent to God's holiness and love. This transparency to the divine love made Jesus the normative mediator of that love, the criterion by whom we decide whether anything else in the universe is really mediating the love of God to us. Jesus is not only the chief of the lights we see but the light in whom we see the only light there is, the one light of the one God who shines through all creation. Therefore, said Augustine, John, and Tillich, let there be images; let there be physical containers of divinity; let there be icons and symbols and sacred histories and rituals which we revere as vehicles, in Christ's light, of that light of God which nothing in God's creation can obstruct, that universal light which can be obstructed only by sin (our creation, not God's, or better, to speak Augustinian, our distortion of God's creation, our pseudo-creation, living like a cancer a chimerical pseudo-life on the host whose blood it devours). Only sin can obstruct the light of God which shines through all creation, until we see that God has graciously acted to remove even sin: in Christ we see the obstructing sin removed; in Christ's transparency to God's purpose all obstructions to God's light are canceled once and for all; in Christ we see that light which transforms the whole universe into a cathedral, diaphanous with the presence of God.

Now this is obviously where official Islam must say NO. The ontological approach of Augustine, John of Damascus, and Tillich must seem to the Muslim like idolatry and self-worship. For the Muslim, the icons of Christ and the Blessed Virgin and the saints must seem like obstructions rather than windows. For the Muslim will accept no normative concrete expression of ultimate concern except that book of law which tells us that God's holiness is so inviolable that he will not imprison it in finite concreteness; and since nothing finite can be the normative manifestation of the ultimate, there can be no chosen people, no Messiah, no unique sacred history, no icons, no fleshly containers of divinity, no immediate knowledge of God, no ontological philosophy of religion. Just as Hinduism, at least in its Advaita Vedanta form, follows the non-dualist path, Islam, at least in its legalist traditions, follows the dualist, iconoclastic path.

Yet one thing that fascinates the Christian in all this is the relentlessness with which God refuses to leave himself without a witness in any place or time, including Islam. Islam, it seems to me, is, in spite of itself, full of icons and saints, cathedral windows shining with Christlike splendor for all the world to see. To borrow another term from Tillich, Islam has thousands of theonomies. I propose to discuss just one of those theonomies of Islam (one which I would call—but Tillich most assuredly would not—a visitation from the anonymous Christ: Abu-Hamid Muhammad al-Ghazali's discovery of the limits of the law). Tillich used to distinguish between autonomy and heteronomy by saying that, in the former, reason follows the reason which the individual finds in himself and in the latter reason follows the reason which the individual finds outside himself. The emphasis is on the claim that both autonomy and heteronomy are searches for reason. They are reason seeking reason, finite reason seeking unconditioned reason, because finite reason is itself a manifestation of that unconditioned reason which it seeks. In both autonomy and heteronomy reason is seeking a norm by which to regulate reason. Reason is seeking that which claims it infinitely because that which claims it infinitely is that from which reason arises.

Tillich argued that autonomy and heteronomy have fed on and generated each other throughout history. He summed up their relationship in a famous passage on pages 85 and 86 of Volume I of the *Systematic Theology* in such a way as to argue that autonomy and heteronomy have reached their fruition in Western culture only in those few moments when they have been united in theonomy ("autonomous reason united with its own depth," a situation in which "reason actualizes itself in obedience to its structural laws and in the power of its own inexhaustible ground"), as among the pre-philosophical Greeks, to some extent in Plato, again in Clement and Origen, and then in Tillich's beloved Bonaventura.[5]

I am not aware that Tillich ever encapsulated Islamic spiritual history in his autonomy/heteronomy/theonomy categories, but I would suggest that it could go something like this: Islamic spiritual history is a struggle between the legalists and the Sufis, the legalists representing a marriage of heteronomous revelation and Greek philosophy (an uneasy marriage, to be sure) and the Sufis representing an autonomous and always more or less blatantly semi-legal apprehension of the immediate presence of God, conveyed eccentrically at times and with dazzling brilliance at times through poetry, painting, music, joke, dance, and enigma. A person in whom this whole struggle was alive and kicking (very much the way the Christian struggle was alive and kicking in Augustine) was Abu-Hamid Muhammad al-Ghazali (1058-1111). Al-Ghazali's first vocation was the study of Islamic law. He became so proficient in that field that he was appointed to the most important legal professorship in the foremost school of the foremost city of the Islam of his day, Baghdad. In many ways this era of al-Ghazali's life can be compared with Augustine's Manichaean era. Al-Ghazali was more famous during this heteronomous, legalistic phase than Augustine was during his Manichaean phase, but the interesting thing is that both began their lives as so many talented youth have done, launched on a Yuppee-like *cursus honorum*, outwardly upholding the law and its righteousness, inwardly yearning on the one hand for a more complete righteousness and on the other hand for liberation from the heteronomous demands of the tyrannical legalism under whose authority they had (for all the wrong reasons) placed themselves.

And then the crisis, the divinely willed collapse, the salvific tragedy, the end of the law. Augustine passed mysteriously from the dualism of the Manichees to the mystical monism of the Neo-Platonists, and al-Ghazali passed from his professorship in law to a loss of his power to speak. He resigned from his teaching position. He left his family, city, friends, and books to join up with non-dualist mystics, the Sufis, who were the object of irate scorn among al-Ghazali's erstwhile colleagues. It was from Yuppee to Hippie at a time when being a Hippie was (if such a thing is imaginable) even more unpopular than it is today. Among the Sufis, however, an amazing thing happened to al-Ghazali. He was gradually healed, in spirit and in body. He regained the power of speech, but more importantly he gained a new insight into Islam. The Sufis taught al-Ghazali to find the experience beneath the words about God. They taught him a personal, ecstatic knowledge of God. And then an equally amazing thing happened. Just as Augustine moved beyond the non-dualist aestheticism of the Neo-Platonists to the rigors of a Christian life, so al-Ghazali left the Sufis for a mind-boggling return to the very Islamic orthodoxy which he had previously abandoned.

Al-Ghazali returned to the orthodoxy of his youth, but this time seeing the kernel beneath the husk, the love which the Sufis had taught him was the essence of all true religion. The Sufis taught al-Ghazali that God's No is grounded in God's Yes, that God's message of judgment presupposes his ultimate purpose of mercy (to translate-rip-off Sufism into Barthianism for the sake of *Horizontenverschmelzung*). And so al-Ghazali taught the law again, but with a new vision of what I would like to call (in borrowed Tillichian terms, *verschmelzen, verschmelzen*) its ontological basis in the immediate presence of the living God. Al-Ghazali now taught the living spirit of the law, not just its letter. And just as Augustine defended the traditions of the church on penance against the rigorist Donatists, who were ultimately schismatic, so al-Ghazali dedicated himself to the refutation of the Isma'ilis, some of the most radical of the Shi'ites, who thought the traditional laws of Islam were too loose and who preferred to rely on rigorist personal authoritarianism. Even more remarkable is the similarity between Augustine and al-Ghazali on the dread topic of predestination. Just as Augustine defended, in his late anti-Pelagian treatises, God's freedom at the expense of human freedom, or rather grounded human freedom in God's prevenient freedom to be gracious, so al-Ghazali tried to show why the great al-Ash'ari had been right to defend predestination against those who thought human justice should be the norm by which to measure God's justice.

Like Augustine, al-Ghazali was always defending the objectivity of God's action in the world, or better, as Tillich would have it, God's priority to any distinction between subject and object, and al-Ghazali made this mighty case for God's priority to our subjectivty by writing the first major spiritual autobiography of his culture. Just as Augustine taught Christendom to look for the God of church and Bible in the center of the individual human soul (which is as large as the circumference of the universe), so al-Ghazali taught his culture how he himself had been most lost when he had thought he was most secure and how he was closest to God the day he woke up alone and destroyed. By analyzing his own personal experience, al-Ghazali had learned the lesson, so monstrous to orthodox Muslim ears, that God can be known immediately, even apart from the holy book, in the self's discovery of the ground of its being (for another Tillichian *Verschmelzung*). But I think al-Ghazali so terrified himself with this discovery that he felt that he had to orthodoxify it somehow. Hence, Augustine and al-Ghazali both went beyond their early heteronomous legalism into middle periods of autonomous, non-dualist mysticism and finally into a third period (are not all important lives neatly divided into Early, Middle, and Late?) of what we might call monotheist, personalistic mysticism (analogous to Ramanuja's personalism in contrast to Shankara's non-dualism), and in this progress Augustine and al-Ghazali became spiritual educators of generations of followers, paradigmatic personalities who, having been pregnant with the future of their whole culture, bequeathed to generations of descendants, not just the results of their pain, but the biographical history of it, an authoritative spiritual birthing how-to guide. Al-Ghazali and Augustine had both passed (I would say) from the *forza* of a tragic, Dionysian, paradoxical, non-dualist, self-discovery (Sufism for al-Ghazali and Neo-Platonism for Augustine) to the *froda* of a new legalism, a new Apollonianism, a new Calvinism (!), a new dualism of transformation. They decided that being free was not enough. Comedically, they went into show biz. They needed to make some laws so that others could also be as free as they now were (*froda, froda*). They passed from the myth of freedom to the myth of concern. By telling their own life stories so paradigmatically, however, Augustine and al-Ghazali (like stars of stage and screen, we Californians say) really made their own life stories into laws. And in that way both of them often had the effect of killing the very theonomy which should transcend non-dual autonomy and dualistic heteronomy. Augustine and al-Ghazali left heteronomy for autonomy and then autonomy for heteronomy in such a way as to leave their followers, not with theonomy at all, but with the heteronomy of the religious establishment, now validated by the now forbidden autonomy of its two now paradigmatic theonomists. This was the tragedy our two comedians bequeathed to us Christians and Muslims, their feuding descendants. And our spiritual heads are still spinning. But now perhaps we can see why our spiritual Tweedle Dee and Tweedle Dum had such similar careers. They were engaged in parallel tasks on behalf of the monotheism bird: al-Ghazali and Augustine were both trying to get the darn bird to fly backward and foward at the same time.

Yet we must not neglect the differences between Augustine and al-Ghazali. The basis of the iconic vision in most Christianity seems to me to be Paul's doctrine of justification, which of course Augustine could presuppose and al-Ghazali could only execrate. This doctrine legitimizes the iconic, I believe, by de-legitimizing the absoluteness of the law. Law tells us that our unworthiness separates us infinitely from God's holy love, and therefore law can tolerate no incarnation of the holy God, no icon, no sacrament, no concrete embodiment of ultimate concern. We, the containers, are too separated from the holy to contain the holy fully in ourselves. In Christ, however, Paul sees both the validation and the relativization of the law. For Paul, Christ both relativizes and demystifies the law. Christ removes the law's impatience with our flesh, putting in the place of that impatience his own perfect flesh, his lawful human flesh, his legitimation of incarnation, his sanctification of the body and the bodily, his proof that human nature is not too separated from the holy to contain the holy fully in itself in the blessed incarnation.

Al-Ghazali, however, good Muslim that he is, will not accept any such doctrine of justification by faith, any such substitutionary atonement, and consequently cannot accept either icons or divine incarnation. But al-Ghazali's discovery of the Sufis' glorious autonomy, their wild claim to immediate experience of God, is (I would say) his Islamic analogue to Paul's doctrine of justification by faith, his tragic break-through. Not the same, to be sure, but an analogue. And, even while disagreeing (at least I would disagree) with al-Ghazali's particular way of re-sanctifying the law, the Christian can rejoice that at least for one theonomous moment in al-Ghazali's conscientious life a hard question had arisen about the all-sufficiency of law, and the Christian can pray that God will lead all of us to that kind of gracious collapse of confidence, a salvific tragedy, a loss of all that we count on for security, so that we, too, can be emptied to start life over again in God.

A further word must also be said about the problematic aspects of Augustine's and al-Ghazali's influence on us. Fazlur Rahman blamed al-Ghazali for the notion that Islamic orthodoxy cannot evolve.[6] We have seen that once al-Ghazali had autonomously validated a heteronomous orthodoxy in the fire of his mystical experience, orthodoxy passed paradigmatically from iron to steel. With all due respect to al-Ghazali, then, Rahman urges Muslims to seek enlightenment, instead, in Ibn-Taymiya, whose orthodoxy was more open to development. Similarly, Augustine has been criticized both as the father of all heresies (because of the suggestive wildness of his passionate formulations) and as the codifier of ecclesiastical conservatism. Many Christians today are restless with the pervasive mind-body dualism in Augustine and (as with al-Ash'ari and al-Ghazali) an eccentrically hard-line predestinarianism in his later writings. When al-Ghazali and Augustine finally crashed through to their spiritual discoveries, they did it with such a gust of wind that, for every theological door they opened, they slammed several shut. It is quite natural that, after a few centuries to catch our breath, we are in our time trying to open some of the authoritatively closed doors for at least a glimpse of what might have been beyond them, for better or for worse. Yet our very restlessness with the formulations of Augustine and al-Ghazali is all the more reason for us to take them seriously again. Like parents, these superstars influence us more than we realize, perhaps (as always with parents) most when we realize it least. Our only hope of becoming adults in our our right is to cope seriously with the adulthood of our forebears. But the most important reason for studying these mediators of the faith is that they can help us avoid the heteronomous excesses that are sure to result from the renewed fundamentalisms of both the Christian and the Islamic communities in our day. Back to the Scriptures indeed! But not by neglecting the hermeneuts like Augustine and al-Ghazali of the centuries between the Scriptures and ourselves. These fellow-adults are neither monsters nor fools. Or, even if they are monsters and fools, Augustine and al-Ghazali are, as our progenitors, mirrors of our own Christian-Muslim monstrosity and folly.

A methodological lesson that I draw from this comparative *froda*-exercise is that Tillich, who was so good at identifying creative polarities of mutuality (such as dynamics and form, freedom and destiny, individualization and participation, self and world), should have put his ontological and cosmological approaches to God into that kind of positive-negative mutuality. Tillich could see only the negative side of the cosmological approach, of heteronomy, and of late medieval thought generally. This imprisoned him in non-dualism. What if God is neither our deepest self (ontological) nor a stranger (cosmological) but *both*? Cosmological (heteronomy) and ontological (autonomy) should be the two poles of theonomy. They are certainly the two wings of the monotheism-bird. In Strong's terms, Tillich is stuck with too much monism and not enough ethics, or dualism. In my terms, Tillich is stuck with too much tragedy of paradox and not enough comedy of transformation. The poor man is trying to fly with just one wing, and he needs our help. Tillich's first mistake was in starting his theology with a self-world polarity instead of a self-self polarity. Tillich starts with the tragically isolated self and its world, and he concludes with the tragically isolated self and its world. How much more joyful, monotheistic, and (I would rashly say) Judaeo-Christian-Muslim Saint Martin Buber is, who starts with self and other self. At the end, Buber's God is a Person, while Tillich's is a Ground and an Abyss. But the living God should actually be seen Tillichian-Buberically as Ground, Abyss, *and* Person.

If there is a link between what I call tragic, autonomous non-dualism and what Tillich calls the ontological approach to God, then there is something tragic in the Franciscan tradition and something comic in the cosmological, Thomist, Dominican approach. Surely this is involved in Dante's way of linking up the Franciscans and the Dominicans in the *Paradiso*. The mutuality of the two approaches is what Dante is emphasizing there. And, in mega-Christian terms, the Eastern Church has pursued the tragic, non-dualist vision, while the Western Church has pursued the comic, dualist vision. Here again, mutuality is the important thing. The Christian bird needs both its Eastern and its Western wings. Think of the peaceful, mature, victorious tragic-hero Christ of the East, enthroned like sagacious Antigone on a cosmic icon which centers the whole universe around itself, compared with the West's hopeful young Jesus, Lord of the Transformation, being transubstantiated on his Western crucifix of Agony. That crucifix is not *froda*, you say. And I agree. But I think that, like Dante's paradise, the crucifix is about *froda* to the extent that it is the systematic Antipodes of *froda*. The crucifix is a statement about *froda* by being the comedic revelation of the *froda* of Christ's crucifiers. The crucifix is also a comedic revelation of the radical transformation of consciousness that is required of us if we are to imagine that young man on that instrument of torture forgiving his torturers as he did. The crucifix is the high drama of duty, of pure virtue, of heteronomy (since it was the Father's will that was being done). It is a drama of concern, in which we discover, not who we have been (as in tragedy) but how we should behave if redemption is to heal our society (as in comedy). The East is concerned with the cosmic *posture* of the peaceful Pantokrator, while the West is concerned with the de-centering, transformative *action* of a youthful invader of Satan's corrupt domain. It seems to me, anyway, that the East stresses the ontological, non-dualist wing, and the West stresses the cosmological, dualist.

But be that as it may, it is fatal to pursue ontological themes or cosmological in isolation from each other or at the expense of each other. Monotheism needs both. But as Tillich sees history, we started sliding down a very slippery slope after the cosmological approach began to become dominant in the Middle Ages. Things are getting worse and worse after Bonaventura. We are getting farther and farther from theonomy. That is clearly not how Dante saw it, much as he loved Bonaventura. Dante would say that a theonomy which, like Tillich's, cannot put St. Thomas in its heaven along with St. Bonaventure is too one-sided. In Chapter Three I will present what I think is a better way of schematizing medieval Christian theology than Tillich's: that of Thomas F. Torrance. We will see Torrance arguing that a schema like Tillich's, which focuses on the image of a container (asking whether the finite can contain the infinite), is too static. A better model is a space-time continuum, in which there are no containers because there is no timeless space at all. Torrance's space and time seen in continuum are in what I call a duality rather than a static dualism or non-dualism. This conception requires us to think in categories of dynamic emptiness rather than static thingliness. In that respect Torrance's view is closer to that of the Kyoto School Buddhism which has recently been so popular in the West than to either Augustine or Tillich. But we shall come to Torrance in Chapter Three.

For now, let us turn to Buddhism for a moment. My suggestion for a little East-West *Verschmelzung* is that perhaps the bodhisattva's discovery of nirvana in samsara is (like the experiences of al-Ghazali and Augustine) a discovery of something analogous to a tragic, non-dual awakening to one's moral accountability in this life which we share (why should I attain enlightenment when some sentient beings cannot yet attain it?—tragic, liberated autonomy) and comic, activist return to society (then I vow not to take my enlightenment until all sentient beings have attained theirs—post-mystical comic heteronomy). If theonomy means simply trusting "God" in an Abrahamic sense, then Buddhist enlightenment is a very different phenomenon. But if theonomy can be understood so as to include the experiences of both Augustine and al-Ghazali, both (as Tillich suggested) the pre-Socratics and Bonaventura, then perhaps it can also be analogous to the experience of some bodhisattvas. And the structure of this theonomous experience would be an incorporation of tragedy (while remaining tragedy) in a larger comic vision, as in Dante's incorporation of hell in his larger experience of paradise, Shakespeare's incorporation of Othello and Desdemona within his larger experience of Leontes and Hermione, Milton's incorporation of *Paradise Lost* within his larger experience of *Paradise Regained*.

Enlightenment, then, in spite of its infinite difference from salvation, would have this in common with it, that enlightenment is a transformation from what Gadjin Nagao calls conventional understanding to what he calls true insight in such a way as to see that the worlds of conventional understanding and true insight are utterly different from each other and yet (when seen from the standpoint of true insight) utterly identical.[7] The infinite difference between salvation and enlightenment is (from my standpoint) the matter of historical continuity. Buddhist enlightenment does not need universal-historical continuity. Christian salvation does. In salvation, the Savior, as the long-awaited King of the Jews, at one point in time (the first Good Friday) at one specific place (on the cross between two thieves at Golgotha), defeated Satan, destroyed sin, killed death, and opened the gates of paradise, while, in enlightenment, such imagery is but imagery. Salvation sees the positive of good as the opposite of the negative of evil, while Enlightenment does not deal with the battle between good and evil but with the complementarity between samsara and nirvana. For enlightenment, the transformation depicted by imagery is real only as that transformation transcends the imagery by being personal, unique, and experiential. In Christianity, the imagery of salvation is not only untranscendable but infinitely more than imagery: it is *history*. In Buddhism, the imagery accompanying enlightenment is transcendable precisely because enlightenment is infinitely more than imagery, while in Christianity also salvation is infinitely more than imagery. But it is more than imagery by being the consummation of the history of the relationship between God and humanity. These two visions are, thus, infinitely different from each other. But are they not also infinitely analogous?

The infinite similarity between enlightenment and salvation is that in enlightenment (as presented by Gadjin Nagao) reality liberates us to see the reality of reality and makes us (even in spite of ourselves and to our utter surprise) into agents of reality in the midst of a world mired in "conventional understanding." Furthermore, this similarity between enlightenment and salvation means that neither enlightenment nor salvation is reducible or translatable into the other. Each is uniquely what it is *in experience.* Anything other than the experience is relatively useless commentary. Yet the commentary is, insists Nagao (following Nagarjuna), only *relatively* useless. The commentary on liberation does have value because liberation so thoroughly links the world of true insight and the world of conventional understanding that, amazingly, we can really talk about the world of true insight in the language of conventional understanding. Just as there is no unifying Other beyond the world of true insight and the world of conventional understanding, there is no unifying Other beyond enlightenment and salvation. Each is only what it is. But what each is, is analogous to what the other is. There is no earthly reason why this should be so. The Buddhist must leave the reason for the analogy to the mystery of enlightenment, and the Christian must leave it to the mystery of salvation. Only by letting unique experience and real difference be humanly ultimate in this way do we remain deconstructionists and avoid a Hegelian monism of philosophical explanation. And certainly we want to avoid that! For now, however, we have at least introduced the possibility that interfaith rip-off can be conducted in a spirit of truly mutual rip-off and that, to do so, we need both the tragic vision and the comic vision, both the *forza* and the *froda*.

To understand the relation between Augustine and Tillich, however, we must say a few things about Luther, who was the most important bridge between Augustine and Tillich. The problem of the apotheosis of being came to the surface in a perhaps surprising way in the case of Luther. A person can be very great and understand most things, even the most important things, and still not understand absolutely everything. May not Martin Luther be a case in point? Luther was a faithful and powerful student of people he admired. That is hardly a fault. Therefore, I do not think it is a fault of Luther's that he read his St. Augustine a bit too well. In knowing a few things about some forms of Buddhism in which nothingness is highly valued, we have a certain advantage, if we are interfaith rip-off artists, that Luther could not have been expected to possess in the sixteenth century. There are some Buddhist ideas which, I think, Martin Luther would have liked very much if he had had a chance to get accustomed to them. (You can tell this is being written in California.) These Buddhist ideas include the notion that we in the West have in many ways forgotten God in our rush to deify being. It is as if we have wanted desperately, as an act of devotion to God, to deify something that is as close to God as possible. So we chose being. And Luther inherited this deification of being from his Augustinian tradition. It is the very heritage Tillich admired so much: the idea that the Hebrews' absolute God was the same as the Greeks' absolute being. It was to prove a fateful (and, I think, fatal) identification.

There is, of course, much to recommend the deification of being, not least the lofty pre-Christian example of the ancient Greeks. Plato, for instance, seems to have been quite depressed by the thought that the most important things in our lives are not things, that what we *are* is a very brief candle indeed in the mind-numbing expanse of endless square miles of cosmic darkness. We might reply that the extent of the darkness that surrounds us was not knowledge available to Plato. True, but he could have seen it in the violence of our short lives, in the hypocrisy of the men of Athens, in the tenuousness of political integrity everywhere, in the massivenss of the suffering of so many of the beings in the world. You reply that Plato definitely saw the darkness which engulfs our lives, and that is why he attached himself so idealistically to Socrates, in whom there was a light of humane understanding of the world, a reasoned confidence in immortality, an awareness of the absolute goodness of being itself. It was Socrates who taught Plato exactly that the most important things in our lives are *not* things, but ideas.

The problem is, however, that since being was the standard by which Plato measured reality, he could give ideas the credit they deserve only by giving them a stake (which they cannot be shown to possess) in absolute, unchanging being itself. In that respect Plato did make his ideas into things, disembodied, unchanging things that are unavailable to our ordinary senses and feelings, but still things. In the process, of course, Plato savagely truncated our humanity, for he made *us also* into things, disembodied, unchanging things called minds, bifurcated from our ordinary senses and feelings. Plato seems to have thought that was the only way he could rescue from annihilation the values that mattered most to him (and note, in passing, the thingliness of the word "mattered" and the unmistakably negative connotation of the word "annihilation": our Greek culture tells us that what "matters" is dualistically antagonistic to the realm of nothingness).

Aristotle rightly challenged Plato's confidence that it means anything significant to say that the good, the true, and the beautiful exist in a realm of absolute being itself, which is a kind of invisible but somehow powerful heaven standing behind or above what is right in front of us. Aristotle, like Aristophanes, thought that if we get too wrapped up in the mental heaven, we just might miss the reality and importance of what is down here beneath the clouds. But when Aristotle proceeded to name everything he could find right in front of him and in front of every other learned person he could query, he followed Plato in failing to take serious account of what is right in front of us but cannot be named, the darkness, for example, which engulfs us. In one place Aristotle momentarily casts a glance at the darkness, when he writes so briefly about tragedy, what makes a tragedy work, why people on the tragic stage, like King Oedipus, arouse such deep pity and terror in us; and how, after all, it is good for us to have those feelings aroused and purged from time to time. But what a momentary glance it is. And, when he discusses, in the *Nicomachean Ethics*, the ideal hero, his "magnanimous man," what an unattractive, humorless, immoral monster the aristocratic wretch is.

You reply that it was not the philosopher's business in ancient Greece to emote about the darkness, the nameless, and the nothing. That was left to the tragedians and, perhaps somehow, the sculptors, dancers, and architects. Fine. We do indeed learn much more about what makes life precious from artists like Aeschylus, Sophocles, and Euripides than from Plato, Aristotle, and Plotinus (in my humble opinion), but the problem is the compartmentalization of this knowledge, the fact that it is too neatly aestheticized, sanitized, as it were, consigned to that realm of *feelings* that Plato and Aristotle thought inferior to the rational *mind*. This model of humanity (we now generally agree) is sick. It cuts the mind from the body, thereby denigrating both the body's knowledge and the mind's feelings because this philosophy assumes that the mind must filter everything sanitarily, wash the fears and delights out of it, wringing the deliverances of our senses thoroughly and hanging them up to dry before taking them seriously. If ever the expression "misplaced dualism" applied aptly to an outlook, it applies to the outlook bequeathed to us by Plato and Aristotle, a view in which there is not a mutuality between being and non-being, self and other, mind and body, but a built-in antagonism, by definition, and this wall of antagonism becomes all the more powerful and sullen as it basks in the sunshine of the highest praise the ancient Greeks could imagine: they called the wall of antagonism "the mind." Our critical faculties, our ability to say Yes or No or both Yes and No, all of these are summarily robbed from us in this lofty appellation, mind. For in that walling-off word, with its implicit contrast to "body," the living organic unity of our moral personhood is cut in two, to die.

Selling our souls to the ancient Greeks is as if we decided that we like ancient Rome so much that, from now on, we will do all our mathematics in Roman numerals. Good-bye electronic hand-held calculators! Good-bye the digital mathematics that makes computers possible. But, most fundamentally, good-bye Zero. To sell our minds to the ancient Greeks and Romans is to refuse to think about The Zero. I have chastized the good Plato and Aristotle for being insufficiently attentive to that tragic awareness that their own playwrights knew so much more about. I am thereby chastizing the ancient Greeks (in spite of the greatness of their tragedians) for their failure to incorporate The Tragic more significantly into their philosophy. But The Tragic is only one way into The Zero. It is a very important way. Probably no one in the Greco-Roman tradition experienced The Zero so thoroughly as the tragic heroes and their creators and, one assumes, at least some members of their audiences. But tragedy is not the only way into The Zero.

Comedy goes there, too. In comedy we discover the zerohood of ludicrous anti-life spoil-sports, the refusers of festivity, the mean authority-figures who try to keep young lovers apart, but, more importantly, in comedy we get jollied up. We clear the air. We open the windows of our spirits. In that way we let The Zero in, the sunshine and fresh air of Holiday. The Tragic takes us to the darkness of The Zero, but The Comic takes us to The Zero of the light, we could say, if we wanted to get overly pretentious about the whole thing, as is, after all, our wont. Zeroes, those wonderful holes in the middle of the wheel, where the axle and all the spokes meet, are not only The Darkness Oedipus sees when he blinds himself but also The Festive Place, the openness, where we meet to debate, to trade, to worship the gods. Zeroes are the gateway to all numbers, positive and negative, rational and irrational, integral and broken. Yet our Greco-Roman heritage was so obsessed with distinguishing between its at least implicilty deified Being and its at least implicilty execrated Non-being that it cared very little about The Zero.

The point is (in case this seems a bit far from Martin Luther) that faithful children of the West (and the diligent Dr. Luther was one of the most faithful) have had a very hard time waking up to the importance, and value, of zero. It has been extremely difficult for philosophical off-spring of Plato and Aristotle to believe that zero is not necessarily negative, which really means (since zero is the gateway to both the positive and the negative numbers) that the negative is not necessarily, well, negative, that the negative can be, well, positive, that The Nothing which King Lear discovers is good for us but also that it is not so different from The Joy that Rosalind and Orlando discover. We fear that if joy is something like nothing, if the comedic is something like the tragic, then joy is profoundly threatened. We want to wall joy off from what King Lear sees. What that means is: we want to Wall Lear Out. The dumb bastard made a mistake. Now let him pay for it!

And of course this is where Israel struts and frets her hour upon the stage. Israel is a prophetic reminder to all who would Wall Joy In and Wall Lear Out that you mustn't try to do that. Not that it won't work (there are many joyful potentates at any given moment who have no Lears in sight). Not that critical intellect doesn't love a wall. Critical intellect loves a wall. But Israel is always tumbling walls down with all her music, praying, shouting, and believing. What Luther knew about Israel, he knew from reading his Christian Bible and Christian commentators. Christians today realize that there was much about Israel that Luther did not know and misunderstood. And some of what he had in his early years understood, he forgot or misunderstood in his later years. There is no excuse for Luther's cruelty to the Jews. There is no excuse, but the reason is that very human sinfulness on which Luther spoke so eloquently and truly. Like Moses, Luther was capable of being very wrong exactly where it mattered most to be right. But Luther was steeped enough in his Christian Bible to have a very healthy critical distance on Plato and Aristotle, especially the latter. If any sixteenth-century Christian tried mightily to develop a personalist, Hebraic worldview rather than an abstract classical Greek one, it was Luther.

Still, the implicit deification or near-deification of being over against non-being which St. Augustine took over from the classical Greeks and Romans infected Luther's ontology, as well. He certainly knew about numerical zeroes, but he does not seem to have poetized about their beauty. He certainly knew about the experience (which I would call tragic) of the utterly negative, of doubt, temptation, despair, fighting with Satan. To call such experiences positive would be to utterly trivialize and betray them. There is nothing positive, for Luther, about *Anfechtung*. But one of the many things for which we are grateful to Luther is that he was willing to tell us, to some extent at least, about these experiences, though never in a tacky, self-aggrandizing or self-abasing way. Surely Plato and Aristotle, even Calvin and Shakespeare, had *Anfechtungen*. But the simple gesture of shared humanity by which Luther could talk about his most negative feelings in a passionate but, we feel, always deeply honest, almost fatherly, way is something we simply cannot expect from Plato, Aristotle, Calvin, Shakespeare. And we can hardly criticize them for that. Why do we have any right to expect them to sit for interviews with the

National Enquirers of their eras? How they felt when their universe imploded on them is none of our damn business. But we are, for that very reason, all the more grateful to Luther and to those who sat with him, writing down his every word as dogs eat bones.

The negative, in Luther, is becoming, not positive, of course, just as yin does not become yang, but the negative is being incorporated, embodied, in a larger life that is positive enough and large enough and alive enough to really take the negative into itself in a way that we feel is (two of our favorite words) healthy and, yes, creative. The jargon of our psycho-bab seems to apply to Luther, not because he is so trivial as that but because his "healthiness" ("wellness?" O! No! Please not that!) and his "creativity" seem accessible to us. And this is much more important than simply satisfying our curiosity about other people's religious fantasy lives. It is a question of validating a range of experience large enough to include the dissonant, the tragic, the profoundly disturbing, the thoroughly questionable. The arts do that and are supposed to. Religion does it but claims (usually) not to. Philosophy of the Greek kind, of course, does not. But the fact that so many modern philosophies have tried to incorporate the negative and the unsettling into their visions is a sign that we are restless with our inherited compartmentalizations of the artistic, the religious, and the philosophcal regions of our brains. We need the kind of personal effort at integration of negative and positive that is Martin Luther. But I want to try to show how Luther could and should have gone even farther in taking the negative into himself in a positive way.

Against the Heavenly Prophets is (to speak psycho-bab) an S.O.S. flare in one of the darkest cosmic nights of Luther's life.[8] If Luther was, as I think, wrong to reject heavenly Müntzer and Karlstadt quite so quickly as he did in that treatise, it is hardly surprising that a person could get a bit confused or over-heated in the inner and outer circumstances of those days. I will not tell again here the long story of all those circumstances. In the vast literature on Luther there is an abundance of excellent descriptions of the context in which Luther wrote *Against the Heavenly Prophets* (to the extent that anyone really understands such mysterious things): how the peasants, having been inflamed with evangelical preaching which they found roughly similar to Luther's, rose up in armed rebellion against their tyrannical land-owners and employers, only to be sorely disappointed when Luther, far from criticizing the bourgeoisie with the vigor he had brought to criticizing the Pope (though he had indeed, long before, warned the landholders to seek more justice fast or else), wrote his notorious *Against the Robbing and Murdering Hordes of Peasants*, in which he recommended that the civil authorities suppress the violent rebellion with state violence.[9] It is natural, from our standpoint, to wish that Luther had supported the peasants. What do we care about the rights of unjust landholders and jaded aristocrats? Did not Luther sell out to them? Is this not just one more proof that the so-called Reformation was really an effort at bourgeois take-over of power—peasants and workers be damned?

We must vent our thoroughly proper democratic rage, as long as we do not stop too long to ask why bourgeois industrialized nations like ours have more right to food and medical care than, say, Bangladesh or Ethiopia. Do we not operate on the assumption that this situation will be O.K. for the foreseeable future? And do we do not assume that nothing will put us into the embarrassing position of announcing our sad social philosophy to the world in a document that everyone will read and remember for more than four hundred years? Luther's unjustifiably conservative political behavior should require us to apply many hot compresses of guilt to both him and ourselves. And then we can begin to ask other questions: what political presuppositions and consequences are involved in the Reformation heritage? how does that political outlook relate to the outlook of Christendom in general? of other religons? of modern secular society? But those questions are, I regret, too difficult for me.

I am only interested in understanding, in the categories of spirituality, how Luther's erstwhile Wittenberg dean and colleague Andreas Rudolf Bodenstein von Karlstadt, to whom Luther gives such a merciless drubbing as a Heavenly Prophet, so exquisitely got Luther's goat and what that little tiff may have portended for the spirtual future of Europe and the world. That's all I am asking about. But even in asking such a modest question as this, I am, I fear, treading near yet another topic (in addition to politics and sociology) about which I know very little: psychology. It has often been argued that Karlstadt simply had a hellish personality (as one's deans and colleagues so often do). There is evidence that Karlstadt was abnormally vain, pretentious, pedantic, and avaricious. Certainly none of us would want to be associated with a person who had *those* personality traits!

In any event, I shall need to leave the social science of the Luther-Karlstadt debate to the social scientists. In the meantime, I am interested in the debate which comes to a focus in *Against the Heavenly Prophets* for one reason. I grew up as a Protestant minority in predominantly Catholic neighborhoods in the United States, and it always seemed to me that the Catholics did something mind-bogglingly different at church from what we did. What is the difference? Does the difference have any meaning? And, quite personally, can a low-church Protestant minority like me have any self-respect when the truly admirable, fashionable, virtuous, intelligent, and well-educated Catholic majority (in whose very bosom I grew up) didn't give my religion no respect? Surely Andreas Rudolf Bodenstein von Karlstadt, the Rodney Dangerfield of Protestant Reformers, will come to my rescue and validate my low-churchliness. All I have ever heard about Christian worship (outside my own little traditons) is the awesome mystery by which Jesus Christ becomes, not only spiritually present to the faithful, but really, physically present on the altar in the bread and the wine, and even (as so many kind priest-friends have tried again and again to explain to me) how "we" offer once again in the eucharist the sacrifice Christ offered on the cross. *Why* did I grow up believing in the (supposedly) same Jesus Christ as the Catholics do with all my heart and soul, sometimes, enduring side by side with them the reductionistic rationalist scorn of unbelievers, only to become a reductionistic rationalist myself on the topic of their holy eucharist? It is embarrassing, impolite, ungrateful, and I know I really should just keep my mouth shut about it, as it were. But.

There is, of course, no one answer, and, perhaps, if someday I finally take up the study of social science, I will find the combination of answers I need, but, on the basis of what I know now, Wittenberg between 1521 and 1525 was an O Little Town of Bethlehem for Protestant worship practices. In that little city during that little epoch were gathered the hopes and fears of many years. Everything in Western Christendom was truly up for grabs on a level of totality that had not been touched for a very long time, since, say, the Council of Nicaea, and, for me, has not been touched since. Wittenberg at that time was a hot-house of spiritual re-thinking and re-feeling. What Luther was thinking and feeling there at that time is obviously of great interest to all Christians. And what was going on in the incandescent spirit of Thomas Müntzer is a story unto itself. In Müntzer we see a socially and liturgically prophetic presence of great intelligence and, yes, creativity, a person who envisioned a very different Christianity from any we have yet found, unless some of the Liberation communities may be something like what he had in mind. But it seems to me that for regular bourgeois American Protestantism, in which you go to church to worship God, to sing and praise and pray and be with other people, but not to put Jesus Christ physically into your mouth, Karlstadt is indeed our spiritual forebear. For it was Karlstadt who spear-headed the Wittenberg revolt against the physical eucharistic presence of Christ.

Like Müntzer, Karlstadt supported the peasants in their rebellion, though he, unlike Müntzer, did not, either explicitly or implicitly, endorse the use of violence, and we like that approach. We bourgeois don't think the peasants should use violence to get justice, and we don't appreciate it either when Martin Luther stands up and says, in effect: if they take up the sword in the name of Christ (which is always illegitimate, since there should be no "holy wars" in Christianity), then the government has the authority and indeed the obligation to wage a just war against the insurgents. We might actually *believe* that, but we don't think a man of God should know about such worldly ways of thinking as that. Let the man of God talk peace and heaven. Let the people who use the sword take care of themselves. This holy peacefulness of ours, this shyness about the world as it is, in its relentless physicality, is, Luther is saying in *Against the Heavenly Prophets*, exactly what makes us bourgeois non-violent, idealistic Karlstadtians so disgusting and dangerous, so heavenly, so pretentiously pious, and self-deluded. Luther is speaking up on behalf of the relentless physicality of our world and of God's way in our world. God is not scared of the physical, Luther is saying. Do not pretend that you can fly to heaven to commune with God when you are in reality supposed to get in touch with a God who has come down here to earth to commune with you and who is so at home with relentless physicality that he will offend your tender, heavenly, spiritual sensibilities by entering, yes, even your ungrateful and most unworthy little mouth (and, we know Luther would add, in his physical way, digestive tract). Well!

We Karlstadtians have never been so insulted in our lives. We shall retreat in holy quietude to meditate and to commune with our spiritually present Jesus. Karlstadt is the first post-Luther hero of all of us who cannot imagine putting Jesus into our mouths because it was he who developed the first post-Luther theology of what I can only call eucharistic absence. To be sure, Karlstadt thought Christ is spiritually present to the believer in Christian worship. And, to be sure, he also thought that Christ was what I will call (faithfully to him I hope, though he did not put it exactly this way) figurally present, but as far as the relentlessly physical presence of Jesus Christ is concerned, it is not to be found on earth, said Karlstadt, until the day Christ visibly returns. And when that happens, there will be no mistaking it. For now, Christ is physically present only in heaven. For Luther, that approach meant the end of the whole idea of a gracious incarnation, of a mystical church, of the union betwen spirit and body which Luther had so laboriously rescued from the Bible by rejecting Greek mind-body dualism and discovering biblical personalism. So when Luther, in 1529, met Ulrich Zwingli at Marburg to discuss the physical eucharistic presence of Christ, Luther's mind was already largely made up, because, although he said that he, too, had once been tempted to take a non-physical approach to the eucharist, he had had to reject it because it ran completely counter to everything in Scripture. Hence Luther and Zwingli allowed what became Lutheran and Reformed Christendoms to go their separate ways because of this one eucharistic issue more than anything else. We, of course, are sure sociology, politics, and psychology must have had more to do with it, but they did not think so. I suppose we cannot reasonably claim to know whether Luther, Karlstadt, and Zwingli were right about what was really important to them or whether we are. We live, after all, in the age of unmasking and demystification, and we can hardly expect sixteenth-century people (having lived when they did) to have understood much about themselves. Fifteen topics were up for debate between Luther and Zwingli at Marburg in 1529. They agreed on fourteen and a half of them. The last half-article was on the nature of the eucharistic presence. But perhaps they did not really understand what is important.

And even if we do decide, for the sake of Victorian fantasizing, let us say, to take the unpopular approach of assuming that Karlstadt's eucharistic theology may be interesting even after all these years, it is more than a little embarrassing to try to explain that theology after Luther lampooned it so hilariously and famously in *Heavenly Prophets*. Karlstadt said that when Christ said, "This is my body," Christ was pointing, not to the bread at all but to himself. Then, when he said, "This is my blood," he must have had a nose-bleed, retorted the witty Dr. Martinus. Where can we Karlstadtians go for ammunition after a blast like that? If you don't get no respect even in your own Wittenberg, where can you find any?

You will certainly not get any respect from Paul Tillich, who follows Augustine and Luther into a near-deification, if not an actual apotheosis, of being. Since we found the Kyoto School Buddhism of Gadjin Nagao so interesting, however, in thinking about the relation between salvation and enlightenment, I suggest that we take another quick flight to Kyoto to see whether we can get any enlightenment there on our Karlstadtian self-esteem problem. Perhaps the Kyotans will be so kind as to help us think about the possibility that non-being is not evil, that it is, simply, the other side of the being-non-being duality, that it is a happy monster, not a Near Eastern Behemoth or Leviathan. If that can happen, perhaps we will have a way of becoming more sensitive to Karlstadt's spirituality of absence, and maybe we will even be able to make some suggestions to Luther for the inclusion of a little more non-being in his very solid and fortress-like being.

I would like to begin this inquiry by suggesting that Tillich's deification of being (inherited straight from Papa Luther and Gramps Augustine) goes hand in hand with his deification of reason and that he will feel much better if he can stop deifying both being and reason and leave deity to God. There is a statement on page 79 of Volume I of the *Systematic Theology* which I think neither Karlstadt nor a Kyotan Buddhist would have made (nor, incidentally, do I think Jesus Christ on either Good Friday or Easter Sunday morning would have made it): "Neither nature nor history can create anything that contradicts reason." The only thing a Karlstadtian or Kyotan can say to that is what Hamlet said to innocent Horatio: "There are more things in heaven and earth, Horatio, Than are dreamt of in your philosophy" (I, v, 166-7).

But what is so bad about deifying reason if the Gospel of John itself says that in the begining was the Logos and the Logos was with God and the Logos was God? The problem is exactly what Zwingli said Luther's problem was: the man could not admit sometimes that a metaphor is a metaphor. For Luther, when Christ said "This is my body," Christ was not speaking metaphorically. For Zwingli, Christ was consummately the poet when he called a loaf of bread his body. (For Karlstadt, of course, Christ was even more poetic at that moment: he was an absence-poet, like Emily Dickinson or Wallace Stevens. But more of that later.) Back to the presence-folk: Tillich and Luther. Tillich does not seem to remember that John was a poet. John uses such metaphors as bread, blood, water, wine, way, and many others without literalizing them. Why not include Logos in that list, too?

But why do I say Tillich has deified reason when he himself calls reason a human existential question which cries out for revelation as its answer? I argue that reason would need to have a super-human, truly divine power if it were to grasp and shape reality so thoroughly that nothing in nature or history could create anything that could contradict it. And this is exactly the kind of idolatrous power Paul Tillich gives to reason. I should point out that I know Tillich does not necessarily mean that nothing can contradict "technical reason." Technical reason is passive and snailish (although real snails, incidentally, are not so passive as they look to the casual human observer). Still, technical reason is always oafishly bumping into things that it cannot understand. Technical reason can easily be contradicted and often is but has such narrow horizons that it often does not know it has been contradicted. It misses the joke. But "ontological reason," "the structure of the mind which enables it to grasp and to shape reality" (I, 75), is active, creative reason. It always gets the joke. It is that reason which transcends the difference between subjective reason and objective reason (I, 77-78). This large, transcendent, ontological reason necessarily, for Tillich, transcends all that appears to contradict it. It must, by including it, transcend all that appears to contradict it, or subjective-objective reason would not be reason. If there were any point at which creative, dynamic, shaping, grasping reason failed in its task of comprehending everything, then at that point reality would cease to be rational, and if there is any point at which reality fails to be rational, then (I think Tillich would say) reality would not ultimately have a rational structure, and objective reason would really be just a kind of inter-subjective reason, a projection of rationality which we would collectively put onto reality rather than the rationality which reality already has before we come onto the scene to project anything. If Tillich thought reason were ultimately only a projection of our minds, he would be a sheer idealist. But Tillich obviously does not want to be an idealist because then he would be a Hegelian essentialist, and "it was in protest to Hegel's perfect essentialism that the existentialism of the nineteenth and twentieth centuries arose," Tillich said (II, 24). He said that, for Hegel, "Nonbeing has been conquered in the totality of the system; history has come to its end; freedom has become actual; and the paradox of the Christ has lost its paradoxical character. Existence is the logically necesary actuality of essence. There is no gap, no leap, between them" (II, 24). Tillich, like the existentialists, wanted to re-introduce the leap or gap, the non-being, into existence by saying that the move from essence to existence is irrational: "The common point in all existentialist attacks is that man's existential situation is a state of estrangement form his essential nature" (II, 25).

Tillich does not completely agree with the existentialists in the enormity of the gap they leave in existence, but he does a famously good job of telling what they did and why they did it:

> The world is not reconciled, either in the individual—as Kierkegaard shows—or in society—as Marx shows—or in life as such—as Schopenhauer and Nietzsche show. Existence is estrangement and not reconciliation; it is dehumanization and not the expression of essential humanity. It is the process in which man becomes a thing and ceases to be a person. History is not the divine self-manifestation but a series of unreconciled conflicts, threatening man with self-destruction. The existence of the individual is filled with anxiety and threatened by meaninglessness (II, 25).

I say Tillich does not necessarily want to go this far with the existentialists in stretching the gap between essence and existence because Tillich is insistent on the point that existential analysis requires (and actually presupposes) some revelation of the healing of this human illness. Revelation, which is always inseparable from salvation (I, 147), shows the essence from which we are estranged, and revelation shows us that essence not in a distant Platonic or Christian heaven but under the conditions of existence, thoroughly enmeshed in our world and our brokenness, as the ultimate revelation, one whose life ended on a cross, is so enmeshed.

Still, it is quite a discussion he gives us of human estrangement (as sin, unbelief, hubris, and concupiscence), of existential self-destruction (as self-loss and world-loss, death, finitude, guilt, suffering, loneliness, doubt, meaninglessness, suicide, and rejection by God), and the hopelessnes of all schemes for self-salvation (whether religious, legalistic, ascetic, mystical, sacramental, doctrinal, or emotional). That discussion would tend to suggest that Tillich meant to be very serious about the leap, the gap, the non-being, between essence and existence. Then, if Tillich does not shrink from being so metaphorical as to describe existence as being standing out of non-being, why can he not also use the metaphor of existence as reason standing out of non-reason? You say he does. I say, "Show me where." Let us say, for the sake of argument, that you do produce a passage in which Tillich says that existence is reason standing out of non-reason. Then I say that either he does not mean it or he does not mean what he says on page 79 of Volume I, surely some of the most astounding words ever written by someone who lived during the Holocaust: "Neither nature nor history can create anything that contradicts reason." "Why the either/or?" you say. Can Tillich not pull that transcending-the-duality rabbit out of his hat again to tell us that existence transcends the distinction between reason and non-reason? Of course he may try, but it will not work for reason the way it supposedly works for being because, although Tillich often says that non-being (both as relative—*me on*—and as absolute—*ouk on*—) contradicts being, he is saying on page 79 of Volume I that reason, as grasping, shaping, ontological reason, *cannot be contradicted* by anything in nature or in history.

What does this claim for reason say about the leap from essence into existence for Tillich? It says that the leap is only provisionally irrational, not so ultimately irrational as it is for Marx, Nietzsche, Schopenhauer, Sartre, for whom there are no essences from which to leap in the first place. I think these four famous atheists are closer to the Christian concept of creation than Tillich is, because the Christian doctrine is that God created out of *nothing*, not out of essences. By depreciating the nothing, Tillich ironically deifies being and deifies reason, creating pre-existing rational essences which turn out to be the mental "things" by which Tillich's God is Greekishly imprisoned. Tillich is asking us to worship being and reason, not the God of Abraham, Isaac, and Jacob. And so, the suffering, estrangement, concupiscence, despair, and death which we experience in existence are only provisionally real, for Tillich, since the presence of "faith" (the courage to be, which really means, as I see it, the courage to deify being) already relativizes suffering, estrangement, concupiscence, despair, and death, already undergirds them in the same way as being (in this Greekish depreciation of nothing) undergirds the self and the world. Here I must see Tillich as still on the Hegel side of the terrible Hegel-Kierkegaard Great Divide. Tillich is still an essentialist. Existence has not leaped from essence. Existence, in Tillich, is only one of those little rubber balls attached to a little wooden paddle by a little elastic rubber band, always rebounding to Mama-Essence, not a baseball smacked unreturnably out of nothing by The Celestial Babe.

I confess to feeling tackily anti-intellectual when I criticize Paul Tillich for being too rational. What do I recommend instead? A primal scream? How seventies. Well, a little primal screaming never hurt anyone. Besides, life was more fun in many ways back then when we primally screamed a little now and then. It is simply not O.K. (to hurl the deadliest possible seventies insult: "You're not O.K., buddy!") to say that everything in nature and history fits in fine with reason. No matter how ontologically or creatively or dynamically you define reason, it is not O.K. to say that the world as we know it is ultimately reasonable. It is not reasonable to be that reasonable about a world which in so many ways has gone mad—the disease and famine side by side with the wealth; the systematic large-scale cruelty; the vast de-humanization and oppression; the rapid and systematic destruction of the environment. By no definition of reason is it acceptable to say in the face of these realities that "neither nature nor history can create anything that contradicts reason." That is the talk of Gertrude and Claudius; it is the sweet sleep of Professor Horatio. But Hamlet (who also knew a thing or two about being versus non-being), told it as it is: "There are more things,...Horatio." But does not religion, or at least Christianity, *need* to assume that reality is ultimately rational? No. Not rational, I say, but savable if God is a Savior. And such a Savior God will undoubtedly use methods that are as irrational in our sight as was the madness Hamlet used. (But how mad was Hamlet? Ah, the answer must be that we do not know. So also with God!) The point is that God, like Hamlet, has no fear of what we call madness, the irrational. Indeed, it is perhaps part of his method.

I would like to suggest briefly two alternatives to Tillich's Gertrudian rationalism: one from Kyoto Buddhist Keiji Nishitani and the other from Tillich's own theological grandfather, Saint Augustine. I think Tillich's thought will be stronger, not weaker, if we pry his system open enough to include more non-reason and non-being in it. We must rescue Tillich for true religion. We must not let him slip into the abyss of being.

In his *Religion and Nothingness*, Nishitani includes a little exposition of the Diamond Sutra's dictum that "this is not fire, therefore it is fire." Nishitani sums up his point: that (as Tillich also knew in his heart of hearts) too much reason can mess you up bad:

> If all this sounds strange, it is only because we are used to positioning ourselves on the standpoint of reason. We may look upon things and make judgments about things one way in daily life, another way in science, and still another way in philosophy. And yet in each case, we position ourselves, in the broad sense of the term, on a standpoint of reason where we cannot come in touch with the reality of things. We are able to touch that reality only at a point cut off from the judgment and contemplation proper to reason, only on a field absolutely different from and absolutely surpassing such judgment and contemplation. We speak here of the field of the selfness of things, the self-identity of things where they appear *pro se ipsis* and not *pro nobis*. And since this field is absolutely other than the standpoint of everyday life, of science, or of philosophical thinking, the self-identity of a thing on this field—for instance, the fact that this is fire—can be truly expresed in the paradox: "This is not fire, threfore it is fire."[10]

Nishitani begins this disquisition by thinking about the statements "Fire does not burn fire," "Water does not wash water," "The eye does not see the eye." When we think about the fact that fire not only burns but does not burn (in the sense that it does not burn itself), we are thinking about "the self-identity of fire as fire in itself, on its own home-ground: the self-identity of fire to fire itself" (116). For us, fire burns, but, for fire, fire both burns and does not burn.

> The true mode of being of a thing as it is in itself, its selfness for itself, cannot...be a self-identity....Indeed, this true mode must include

a complete negation of such self-identity and with it a conversion of the standpoint of reason and all its logical thinking....Combustion has its ground in non-combustion. Because of non-combustion, combustion is combustion" (117).

To put it even more paradoxically, "Put in more concrete terms, genuine self-identity consists in the self-identity of the self-identity of self-nature (as being) on the one hand, and its absolute negation on the other" (118). This way of thinking resembles Tillich's view that everything that is, is through its participation in elements that appear to be negations of each other: individualization and participation, dynamics and form, freedom and destiny. And like Nishitani, Tillich stresses (in Part IV of the *Systematic Theology*), not the ontological gap between humanity and non-humanity, but the ontological continuity. "Things" have many of the attributes of self-dividedness and struggle which we associate with selves. But what Nishitani cheerfully admits and affirms is that this way of thinking bloweth the mind. For Nishitani, the rift between what Tillich calls essence and existence is so irrational and enormous that there can be no such reality as an essence. The "essence" of fire is to not be fire when it is most fire. Otherwise, it would burn itself and there would be no more fire. The "essence" of the eye is to not see when it is most seeing because, as something that sees, it cannot see itself or it would not see. Burning means not burning the burning. Seeing means not seeing your own seeing. For Christians, then, being God means not being God (which is what the incarnation of the unincarnatable God means). This is the Logos that is Logos by not being Logos. Therefore Logos is not as such divine. What is divine is Christ's unique way of both being and not being Logos.

Paul Tillich keeps a most un-Zenlike straight face in his ultimizing, thereby either denying or (more likely) misunderstanding the ludicrousness of all theological enterprises, including his own. Unlike Tillich, the Christian Zen comedian can say that ultimacy is not about being versus not being but about finding love and happiness, breakng through the serious God beyond God to the friendly God this side of God, named Jesus. What a friend we have in Jesus, says the comedic Christian. Tillich's Jesus disappears as the medium which must deny itself for the sake of that to which it must point by becoming transparent to it. But the comedic Jesus of Scripture disappears in a very different way. Jesus as comic hero appears to show us what his presence means and then, in his ascension into heaven, disappears to show us what his absence means. Both are sacred. Both are salvific: his presence (when he was physically present) and his absence (now that he is physically absent). In other words, the comedic Christ is salvific both in his being and in his not being, both in his fullness and in his emptiness. For the comedic Christian, Christ's present physical absence is a promise of his future physical presence. Jesus Christ is God as the God who, precisely in this way, is God by not being God. The friendly Jesus of Scripture does not break his own will but fulfils his own will in the Father's will, and the comedic Jesus of Scripture does not disappear in order to point to the God beyond himself but re-appears in order to affirm the undefeatability of the God who is God precisely in his way of not being God.

As you can see, I think religion is a matter of choosing the clown outfit that amuses you most. (Of course the joke may be on you, and what Tillich calls destiny and Gadamer calls tradition will have a lot to do with the outfit you choose, but that only makes the whole thing all the more hilarious.) Not that religion is not serious, but the important point is that it cannot be only serious. Religion must be more than serious. Religion is religion by not being religion. It concerns ultimacy by not concerning ultimacy. Christianity seeks, not being versus non-being, but love and happiness. Christianity does not idolize Hamlet's dilemma. It accompanies Hamlet into his solution, but that is a path of the loss of rationality, the path of a holy *froda* of madness. Otherwise we are Systematic Theologically stuck in tragic *forza* with Tillich, in the too, too solid, sullied, and sallied (all of the above) flesh.

When I say Christianity is the clown suit for me, I do so on the basis of Augustinian Pascal's wager, slightly modified. Pascal said that if Christianity turns out to be wrong, you have nothing to lose for having chosen it, while, if it turns out to be right, you have everything to gain. In this, Pascal is very different from grim Kant and the grim post-Kantians like Tillich: Kant and his Kantians see the essence of Christianity in self-sacrifice (no pain no gain; if it feels good, don't do it). Pascal sees the essence of Christianity in joy, in the peace that passes all understanding, in the reasons which the heart has of which the reason knows nothing, and in the eager expectation which Sara, Rebekah, and Rachel and their husbands had: the confidence that God is working his purpose out and that it will be a glorious conclusion, when all is said and done, because only a glorious conclusion can make sense of the hell that has stalked through all our human-made heavens. I want to live in whatever faith gives the most glorious possible culmination to human striving. I want to live in the sanctuary that has the most beautiful stained glass windows, not so that the glass can separate me from the world but so that, when the world is inside the sanctuary (in my imagination, for in this life the whole world can enter the sanctuary only in imagination), the world will look as beautiful as it looked in Eden. Why not? I think I can be somewhat rational, within the limits of my own experience, in picking and choosing among the avilable irrationalities, but only irrationalities are available. Religions, philosophies, mythologies, literatures, musics, and visions are those irrationalities (the arts and sciences). I am not looking for the most rational or the most irrational irrationality. I am looking as rationally as I can for the most beautiful irrationalities (plural).

This route to faith, which uses reason as a guide, is not based on reason but on what William James called the will to believe. In the *Varieties*, James argues that finally we choose what we choose in religious matters because of our will, not our reason. Our reason interacts kind of bunglingly, sometimes graciously, sometimes not, with whatever our unconscious tosses up to it, but finally it is our will that makes sense of all this stuff (or does not make sense of it) through its own vision of the true, the good, and the beautiful. And the will figures out what that vision is only by going through the process of using its reason-servant in trying to make sense of what the unconscious tosses up to it amidst the buzzing confusion of daily life. A positive-negative duality (is it not?), this Jamesian creative interaction between the will and the unconscious amid the buzz. It all adds up to a much more beautiful and realistic psychology than Freud's.

And in all this focus on the will, James was being thoroughly Augustinian (as he knew). But Tillich saw himself as an Augustinian, too. Tillich's emphasis on God as being itself, his constant insistence that we can seek God only because we already have God, his affirmation of a reason that is not just technical but ontological, not just mechanical, but ethical and aesthetic too— in all these things Tillich was thoroughly and self-consciously Augustinian. How does James's Augustinianism differ from Tilich's? What Augustine and his Augustinians, including James, have that Tillich lacks is exactly this awareness that we are much more the product of our wills than of our reasons. Aquinas, like Plato and Aristotle, put reason above will in the human hierarchy, but Augustine and James turned the order upside down, or rightside up, as I think: for Augustine and James, we human beings simply are not fundamentlaly reasoners. We are willers, desirers, yearners, strivers, runners, pushers. Our reason is a reason in motion, torn forward by time and our equine wills, torn backward by our home-sickness. If reason has any influence on our wills at all, it is only because will allows reason to do so. The challenge is what T. S. Eliot said it was, ripping off Dame Julian of Norwich: "You must make perfect your will." Of course that leaves only the little problem of *how* to make one's will perfect. That has to do with what one wills to choose and what one chooses to will. And that decision can be made only through a decision, itself destined, about the destiny (what Gadamer calls the tradition) within which one wills to choose and chooses to will. So the question is not: how shall I use my will? but, in which submission of my will is the most perfect guidance of my will possible? In obedience to which master is there the greatest freedom? In which discipline is there the greatest scope to become ourselves? In which tradition(s) do we find the most far-reaching graciousness, one that not only treats us graciously but also makes it possible for us to participate in graciousness in such a way as to be less ungracious to others than we now are? Which means: in what way of sharing love and happiness can we best find love and happiness? For the comic discovery is always that we can have only what we can give, since the important thing is not what we have but who we are.

The Augustinians have always been "willing" to blow their rational minds in the face of the proposition that God is both being itself (in whom we live and move and have our being) and a personal center of willing in his own right (distinct from us): in other words, that God not only *is* but also is alive, loving, and joyful. But I fear that Tillich too often feels that he must choose betwen God as being and God as personal willer. It is a fatal either/or. To choose the latter alone (dualism) is to eliminate ontology and ontological reason. To choose the former alone (non-dualism), as I think Tillich finally does, is to effectively eliminate the personhood of God and thereby finally the deity of God, because we can imagine nothing higher than personhood. Whenever we try to imagine something higher than personhood (say, the Trinity, or the ground of personhood), we still cannot imagine anything worthy of worship that does not culminate in the personal faculty, not only of reasoning (which, after all, could be done by a machine), but of willing, choosing, loving, and being joyful. Anything lower that this personal center of conscious willing (say, an impersonal ground and abyss) is lower than we are, and therefore (in Tillich's own terms) we would demonize it if we worshipped it. We cannot worship anything less than a person. If that means that God is not being itself but just one more being, then so be it. If that means God, like us, takes a risk called existence, a risk he could have (as far as we can tell, apart from Christ) lost, then so be it. That is what it means for contingency to be included in necessity, history in being, emptiness in fullness, apparent madness in rationality, love in suffering, joy in tragedy.

Tillich tries to include a personal, willing center in his God by including that center (the Logos) in the second person of the Trinity, but Tillich's reluctance to let the gap over which the Christ travelled, from being to existence, be a truly infinite, *irrational* gap, blocks Tillich's Christ from winning a truly significant battle in history. For Tillich's Christ only dies in history. He does not live in it. Tillich's Christ manifests God's presence on earth, for Tillich, and Tillich claims (I, 175) that this manifestation is an actualization, but, if so, it is actualization not in victory but only in kenosis (emptying, annhilating himself). Tillich gives us a Christ whose reason triumphs over existence but whose will must be broken so that God's will can be done. I prefer the equally irrational (but, to me, more beautiful) picture of a Christ whose life actualizes God's triumph, not over the conditions of existence (which do not need any triumph over them), but over sin. I prefer a Christ whose will is not broken but made perfect in his decision to bind himself in mutuality to the will of his gracious Father. That act of Christ's will went beyond reason. It went across the Hamlet-gap of utter irrationality (as does our faith in it) because God's grace is beyond our rational calculation. That was the statement Christ made by choosing to go to his cross.

The problems of our human situation are as dire as Tillich so wonderfully says they are (sin, unbelief, hubris, concupiscence, self-loss, world-loss, death, finitude, guilt, suffering, loneliness, doubt, meaninglessness, suicide, schemes for self-salvation, whether religious, legalistic, ascetic, mystical, sacramental, doctrinal, or emotional—these are troubles everyone has seen), but God's solution of those problems is infinitely (and I mean infinitely) more complete and effective than Tillich says it is.

To make this more radical vision work, however, we must imagine a God who is both being itself *and* non-being itself, both ground/abyss *and* a personal will, both at peace with himself *and* in active combat, not against non-being (which needs no combat), but against only sin, which this God is an expert at removing. My God works only if he is both tragic and comic, both non-dualist and dualist, both monistic and ethical. But, beyond the fallible and errant, God-breathed record of the life of Jesus Christ which we possess in Scripture, we have no third stage of reconciliation for these dualities. In Christ as we see him in Scripture the dualities are reconciled, but not beyond him, not philosophically or theologically. For sin fires its machine gun straight through all our monisms, no matter how ethical they may be. Sin introduces a surd into the human story which is so irrational that we cannot say that neither nature nor history can create anything that contradicts reason. They do exactly that thousands of times per hour. This is so not only because history is shot through with the bullets of cruelty and oppression but also because *our* reason, unlike

God's, is—even in its glorious Tillichian ontological mode—so sickened and distorted by the corruption of our sin-polluted will that it is only the shadow of its true self, only what we must call "fallen" in comparison with God's, which we see in Jesus Christ. If God can have perfect reason, Mr. Tillich, then why, in the name of Augustine, can God not have perfect will? And if God has both perfect will and perfect reason, is not God a person, a being among beings, taking the risk, side by side with us, of existence? Why shield God from that risk? Why shield God from the cross of Christ when God did not choose to shield himself from it?

The great contribution which ideas like Nishitani's make to Christians is that they can allow us to see that non-being is not Satanic, as it effectively became in the static ontology of the West. That insight allows us to recover a much more serious Satan than Augustine envisioned, one who is not simply the privation of being but is a willer and reasoner in his own right and desperately determined to distort, not just being, but the good, the true, and the beautiful, and all God's other creations, as well. More importantly, de-Satanizing non-being allows us to see that non-being, absence, can be a positive negative, that Andreas Rudolf Bodenstein von Karlstadt (though he may indeed have committed the sin of political radicalism) was perhaps not such a fool as Luther deeply needed to believe that he was. Karlstadt may have been making a very useful contribution to our spirituality—and *could* have to Luther's also—when he insisted that Christ is as real in his absence as he is in his presence and indeed that the comedy of Christ's absence intensifies the tragedy of his presence. But more of that later.

Appendix

The Khomeini-Rushdie Dispute

When the good Ayatollah Khomeini issued his death sentence to Salman Rushdie, some friends of mine at California State University, Northridge asked me to speak about the situation at a faculty luncheon meeting . I had hoped to present a brief review of *The Satanic Verses*, but by March 8, 1989, the day on which I was supposed to speak, I had still not been able to obtain a copy of the book! Yet I wanted to stand up and say something public and awful about the situation. The following effort was the result. I include it here because it illustrates my belief that we should, even in the eighteenth-century Enlightened ethos of the secular university, treat one another across the boundaries of faith as mature sparring partners rather than as children. Trying to tell the truth is more important than trying to be courteous, if one must make the melancholy decision to go one way rather than the other. Finally, the piece illustrates my conviction that we are always talking to ourselves in interfaith dialogue, whether or not we are talking to anyone else. It will be obvious in the following open letter to the Ayatollah that I am really speaking about the fundamentalist-modernist controversy in my own Christianity rather than anything the Ayatollah would have had the slightest interest in. I ripped off the Khomeini-Rushdie incident in order to give a sermon to myself. This non-dialogue is a statement about the *absence* of real-world interfaith dialogue between Muslim and Christian in our time (as opposed to the also very important enlightened interchange that occurs in universities). My non-dialogue is (without denying the importance of *forza*) a cry of *froda* for more *froda* across religious boundaries as soon as possible.

Dear Mr. Khomeini,

There are so many questions I would like to ask you: do you have any hobbies or things you do in your spare time to relax? do you ever read novels or watch TV? and so on. But I feel I should begin my letter by apologizing for calling you Mr. Khomeini when I know your title is Ayatollah.

You see, I am a Christian. My understanding is that Muhammad had no objections to Christianity as long as Christians simply obeyed the prescriptions of their religion, except that they may not obey the prescription of Jesus that they should go into all the world and teach all nations, baptizing them in the name of the Father and of the Son and of the Holy Ghost, teaching them to observe all things whatsoever Christ has commanded us. That's fine. It's not as if we haven't tried that one! I for one would be willing to vote to put that one prescription on hold for a few centuries if we could have some serious interfaith dialogue instead. The way I read the gospels, dialogue was Jesus' preferred method of discourse anyway.

In the meantime, Jews and Christians are grateful that Muhammad called us "people of the Book," thereby allowing us to keep our religions as long as we keep them to ourselves. Since some of us have long considered interfaith dialogue central to the act of keeping our religions, however, we will proceed with that kind of dialogue even when it may involve reading and discussing books you do not approve of. Now the way this relates to my calling you Mister is as follows: Jesus said (Matthew 23:8, 9 KJV) that we should not be called rabbi and should call no one on earth father, for one is our Father, which is in heaven. So if Jesus said I should not call anyone rabbi or father, I do not think he would cotton to my calling anyone ayatollah. If obedience to this prescription of my religion gets me into hot water, it will not be the first time.

I remember the year and two weeks I spent in a fine prep school. It was seventh grade and the first two weeks of eighth grade. The prep school was sponsored by that pre-Christian religion called Episcopalianism that you may have heard of. Not only were we all required to go to the Episcopal chapel every day, but we were also required to take a (you will pardon the expression) God-awful course called Sacred Studies, which was taught by an Episcopal priest, the school chaplain, who insisted that we call him Father. In later years I have sometimes wondered whether I would have been wiser to knuckle under. Perhaps conforming and staying at the school for the full six years would have mellowed me a bit, but, as we Calvinists say, it was not to be.

My departure happened on this wise. Not only did the priest insist that we call him Father; all the other teachers insisted that we call them Master: Master Jones, Master Smith, and so on. I said conscience would not permit me to call the priest Father, but I would be happy to compromise and call him Master. The only problem was that his last name turned out to be Bate. I blush now to confess that at that time I could not understand for the life of me why it made the priest so furious and the other students so uncontrollable every time I spoke up to call the good man Master Bate. At least transferring to the local public school gave me a chance to find out.

So, believe me, Mr. Khomeini, I know that following the presciptions of your religion can get you into hot water. You believe Salman Rushdie is implying in *The Satanic Verses* that Muhammad was receiving some of his revelation from Satan, even that, as Mahound, he is represented as being Satanic himself. Therefore, you feel the presciptions of your religion require you to invoke the death penalty against Salman Rushdie for the crime of blasphemy. In a moment I shall attempt to suggest a different way of thinking about such concepts as revelation and blasphemy, but first I would like to be so bold as simply to suggest that you lighten up a little. This time last year my brethren and sistern and I were a little out of joint about a movie based on a novel, *The Last Temptation of Christ*, that says some false things about our Lord and Master. (The temptation to say "Nyeh, nyeh, ne nyeh, nyeh" this year is almost overwhelming, but since we are supposed to be on our good behavior during interfaith dialogue, I shall restrain myself just this once. Besides, it is a very difficult expression to spell, and who knows what it might mean in translation?)

But, with the wisdom that a year of religious pouting can bring, I think I can say, Mr. Khomeini, that we have a certain duty to let a sense of humor seep into our religious seriousness sometimes. If our seriousness loses touch with the zany and the fantastic, are we not claiming to be something higher than our frail and always potentially risible humanity allows us to be? Are we not, by removing humor from our humanity, exceeding the limits assigned to us by our Creator, distorting our status as creatures, which means children, of God? Surely the God who created dolphins, baby elephants, and Harpo Marx has a sense of humor. If God is God, will he not share our amusement at the kind of lampooning that brightens overly serious countenances? Do the Psalms not assure us that if we become too blasphemous, God will laugh us to scorn? Surely God knows about laughter and satire. The real blasphemy is that you think a novel can make God scowl the way you scowl.

Faith in a good God requires us to look for good lessons in bad events, even in the worst of them. But it is very hard to find any good lessons in your treatment of Mr. Rushdie. On one level, we can draw the familiar moral that we consider our hard-won freedom of artistic expression absolutely non-negotiable. Free expression is not the solution to the world's problems, not is it a substitute for a solution, but it is the necessary accompaniment of any and all solutions. On another level, you remind us that the fundamentalism which is currently so attractive to some people in many different faiths is indeed a scourge that must not be allowed to spread without serious public challenge from people who believe in open inquiry and the obligation to dissent publicly. Also, you unwittingly show us once again how important are the semiotics, poststructuralisms, postmodernisms, and deconstructionisms of our time because these studies are reminding us that the arts do not exist in an air-tight compartment, walled off from the rough and tumble of politics and religion.

Your screeching, obscene death sentence reminds us of the power of a word, both your word as a fanatic and Mr. Rushdie's as an artist. We have become so accustomed to freedom of expression in the West that, in our own way, we have lost touch with it, because, by allowing everyone to say everything, we have forgotten how to listen. We hear a din but very few words. When your word is that this novelist's word must cost him his flesh, you remind us that all words are in fact flesh. Every word is an incarnate word. That is why literature always involves politics. Our word is our act.

When we hear your call for assassination and, even more shockingly, we hear other fanatics saying they will obey it, we feel like patients waking up from anesthesia after surgery. "What? What?" we say, "Did someone just say that our word is our flesh? that in this world you must be prepared to pay with your life for what you say? No one said *that*, did they?" No one except our own religions for centuries and centuries. That is why literature always involves religion. Our word is our life.

Your call for assassination of an artist has an effect which the best interfaith dialogue often has: the result is not that we go away feeling more like our dialogue-partner. Very often we go away having discovered once again what we were really supposed to be about in the first place. The terrorism of your death sentence reminds us of the conditions under which religious people have always had to work: as the Buddhist parable puts it, we live in a house that is on fire. If we allow any stupidity or insensitivity to drug us into thinking that the house is not on fire, that we are not choking on the smoke of our injustice and burning with the flames of our greed and insecurity, all over the world, then we are fools and worse than fools: we are the fire fighters who failed to get up and bring water. We failed to tell it as it is. We said "Peace, peace" when there was no peace. When, on one side of the house, millions of people are desperate to defend the dignity of Muhammad and, on the other side of the house, millions of people are desperate to defend the freedom of the arts, our desperation, our screaming, is because the whole damn house is indeed on fire. The din of our words is a ghetto-blaster pounding to high heaven its cry of pain.

If some of us in the West are sitting around reading novels and telling jokes, listening to rock music or looking at Rembrandt, it may be partly because of stupidity and insensitivity (which we possess in arrogant abundance), but it is also partly because the only excuse for free art and free discussion is that they are essential equipment for the fire fighters. Art, disagreement, and even satirical blasphemy are all part of the the incarnating of the word of liberation. You remind us that art does speak flesh. The bread and wine in the painting are real body and blood. Metaphors cost, as T. S. Eliot said, not less than everything.

By using (or, I should say, misusing) the Qur'an to kill a novelist, you have reminded us of the religiousness of art. As children of the eighteenth century, we Americans tend to shrink from any linkage between art and religion. To defend the arts from authoritarian religious attacks like yours, we tend to seal them off in a sanitized museum, each art-work in its own place, untouched, unjudged, but often unappropriated, statically distant. But we know better. The very frenzy with which, as soon as your death sentence was delivered, we all tried to get a copy of Rushdie's supposedly wicked blasphemy is a symbol of the longing we have for real revelation. We hunger for a revelation that is so human and solid, so dense with imagery, dream-sequence, exotic characters, and fatally potent allegory that it touches us exactly where we live, in our faithless, but ironically faithful souls. We hunger for a revelation that touches us in our politics, so alienated and disappointed and always daring to hope. We hunger for a revelation that touches us in our sexuality, so merchandized by Hollywood, so violated by the government. We hunger for a revelation that touches us in our religiousness, that private religiousness which is so unlike any religion we have ever heard or dreamed of, our own undiscovered inward country of transcendence, into which we have sometimes glimpsed in wonder, especially during childhood, and which, even now, is just waiting to be unlocked by exactly the right art-work, a truly steamy, giant, awful hell of a blasphemously revealing art-work.

O, Mr. Khomeini, what hopes you arouse in us for Mr. Rushdie's book! Until someday the book will be available everywhere, and it will become just another interesting paperback; then our hunger for a revelation full of blasphemy will go back into abeyance again until the next scream of terror reminds us once again that the house is on fire and we are desperate for a revelation that redeems. I think, Mr. Khomeini, that you should consider looking more often for revelation in the apparently profane, in the arts. You have the Qur'an; the Jews have the covenant; I have Jesus; I assume we all respect the presence of the sacred in Socrates, the Buddha, Confucius, the Bhagavad Gita, and thousands of other explicitly religious locations, but, Mr. Khomeini, many of us in the West have gone so far in linking art with religion as to hear the agony of God in the quartets of Beethoven, as they carry us through the deep waters of turmoil and doubt. We ask why anyone should think that God knows everything in the universe but does not know about music. Or why say God knows about music but he doesn't like it? Or why say God likes music, but he doesn't feel he can express himself very well in that medium? And if you will grant me that the ground and abyss of being (as Paul Tillich called God) can become manifest in music, why can it not also breathe through the novel? Do we really want to say that novels are the one thing God chooses not to know about or is threatened by? Is God too dull to understand human irony, to feel the reasons for novelists' cries of blasphemous rebellion?

Islam recognizes the value of the Hebrew Pslams. What shall we say about such words as these? "How long, O Lord, how long? Be not far from me; for trouble is near; for there is none to help. O my God, I cry in the daytime, but thou hearest not; and in the night season, and am not silent....My God, my God, why hast thou forsaken me?" Blasphemy? Yes. Feelings beyond the comprehension of the God who created you and me? I say No. Who put up with Jonah? Who went on loving Job? God met Job's cries of rebellion with one of the most massive and gracious self-revelations of the Bible.

The revelation on which Islam is based is what God told Muhammad, not what Muhammad told you and not what God told you. The Qur'an written in Arabic is, you remember, just a copy of the real Qur'an, the Qur'an written in heaven. That is a luminous, symbolic way of saying that Muhammad saw some stuff you and I have not seen. Muhammad's revelation was uniquely his. The Qur'an is our guide to the interpretation of Muhammad's experience, but it is not Muhammad's experience. Centuries of Islamic Sufi tradition are based on this distinction between religious experience and the written Qur'an. Why impoverish the Islamic tradition by reducing revelation to the written book? Why not turn, as generations of Sufis have, to riddles, jokes, dances, poems, songs, and brilliant blasphemies in fictional form in order to let the always shocking Word from God cut through to us in such a way as to knock us out of our spiritual habits and make us *new* as well as making us wise?

There is a real danger of blasphemy if we say that the Qur'an is the sum total of God's revelation to humanity. The Qur'an itself affirms that God has spoken to human beings in many different ways, on countless different occasions. If we say that only the Qur'an is revelation, we go against the Qur'an itself. Furthermore, we run the risk of making ourselves, as interpreters of the Qur'an, into new prophets, and at the heart of Islam is the conviction that Muhammad is the last prophet. If Muhammad is the last prophet, this means that you are not a prophet and neither am I. We must leave to Muhmmmad, just as we leave to Abraham and Jesus, what God left to them, their own unique revelation. We do not have access to that revelation, only to records about it. And when we interpret those records, whether the Qur'an or the Bible, we are not prophets. We are only fallible interpreters, doing the best we can with what we have at the moment. The record of the revelation remains. We do not. There will be new interpreters of the revelation and new appropriators of it as long as human civilization endures.

Think of the sacred black rock in the Kaabah in Mecca, Mr. Khomeini. When God sent that rock (according to Islamic traditon) hurtling from heaven to earth, the rock was on fire. So it was with the revelation God gave Muhammad. Now, however, the rock is not on fire. The rock is utterly sacred, but it is only the residue of the rock that was once on fire. So it is with the Qur'an and the Bible, with the Bhagavad Gita and the symphonies of Mozart: these are the residue of revelation. They become revelation for us—they burn in our souls—only when they are re-enacted, translated into our own framework of discourse, performed, and this is the work of the artist, even the blaspheming artist. It is the work of the artist to enact what strikes him or her as revelation, in as shocking a way as possible, so that in the art-work we can hear the voice of the same God who speaks to us normatively in the Scriptures of our religion. If truth is truth and truth is one, then the same truth will eventually appear in the arts as in the Scriptures if the Scriptures are true. If we feel compelled to use violence to coerce the arts into telling what we think is the truth of our Scriptures, we show how unsure we are about the truth of our Scriptures. Shakespeare's Paulina in *The Winter's Tale* said it best: "It is a heretic that makes the fire, Not she which burns in't."

The Jewish philosopher of religion Martin Buber has had a profound influence on both Jews and Christians in their efforts to think in fresh ways about revelation, so great an influence on Christianity that Buber is often called one of the greatest Protestant thologians of the twentieth century. Well, I doubt if you are too interested in becoming a Protestant Muslim, a liberal Protestant Muslim at that, but, for the sake of dialogue, please allow me to summarize a few of Buber's ideas about revelation. Buber saw revelation as the gift of personhood. There can be no impersonal personhood, no personhood that is not indebted to the persons who are giving their lives to us right now to make us possible. We do not exist apart from their self-giving. This is revelation. Torah, for Buber, was the guide to this broad kind of revelation. It was not the sum total of revelation. Jesus, for me, is such a guide. The Qur'an, I suggest, could be seen as such a guide for Muslims. Revelation is much broader than a book. Revelation in Buber's sense is what happens when we keep our word. Revelation is our baby crying in the night when we need our sleep, or someone else's baby, or an adult, a teenager, or ourselves, or an animal crying. Revelation invades the uniquely private, translating our privacy into something which, while still private and still uniquely our own, also has a public meaning. Revelation, like deciding to get married, is a private experience that demands a public action. Revelation always seems to happen in spite of us, not because of us. Revelation pulls us out of ourselves, and pulls ourselves out of us. It makes you you, me me, and us us. Revelation is what is descending upon us when our covenant obligation dawns on us and we realize with gratitude, and with the kind of shock that only truth can bring, that we are not the first person on whom a covenant obligation ever dawned. To sum up, revelation is not, to coin a stupid word, inter-bookal: revelation is inter-personal. The Qur'an, the Bible, all our Scriptures, Mr. Khomeini, are residues of revelation, guides to the interpretation of revelatory experience: none of them is the totality of what God can say or has said to his universe.

In the meantime, the house is on fire. You and I and millions of other people see themselves as fire fighters for God. As the Buddhists insist, it is not our job to speak authoritatively about how the fire got started or why: it is our job to get busy putting the fire out and helping those who are screaming and waking up those who are asleep so that they can scream too. Blasphemous novels and obscene assassination orders have a part to play in that waking-up process, if only we can wake up enough to learn from them. While working in our own way to rescue and to awaken, however, we must remember that we too are being judged by One who is infinitely more righteous and insightful than we are. How shall we keep our accountability in our mind's eye?

I would like to be so bold as to suggest, Mr. Khomeini, that you consider a little parable that I find edifying. Just in case your dish can pull in our Channel 9, I urge you to watch People's Court at 3:30 every week-day (or, like me, have your VCR record it for you, so you can watch it at night when you get home from the office). You'll find it at that magic moment when early afternoon hard soaps have pretty well melted into late afternoon soft soap, just after Divorce Court and just before Geraldo. People's Court is true religion, in my opinion the best religion on TV. It is the story of a righteous judge. If there is anything more sacred as a symbol of God than the righteous judge, I do not know what it would be. Now, the hero, Judge Wapner, would be horrified that I compare him to God because he would insist that, unlike God, Judge Wapner is a less than perfect judge. Still, Judge Wapner is like God in this respect: that he listens so carefully it could make your skin crawl. Just when you want to say, "O poor judge! The plaintiff and defendant really have him over the barrel this time. Judge Wapner, what *will* you do? What *will* you do?" and you have given up all hope and perhaps even uttered a blasphemy, the judge says he will be right back; he departs. We get the commercials. And a few false alarms that he is about to return: here come de judge, here come de judge. Then, Mr. Khomeini, the judge does return, and when he does, he shows you how well he has been listening. It is very shocking to discover how quietly and consistently he had been delivering his judgment all along, even before he had left for the commercials, if only you could have heard it then. The judge calls good good; he calls evil evil, and he kicks ass when ass needs kicking.

Then, when it's all over, Doug Llewellan lets them that are weeping and gnashing their teeth have their say, and he lets them that are happy have theirs. Then Doug Llewellan says, "And so next time someone does something wrong to you and you feel your rights have been violated, don't take the law into your own hands. You take'em to court." Well, Mr. Khomeini, with all due respect, I say to you, next time someone writes a novel you don't like and you feel your rights have been violated, don't take the law into your own hands; don't even take'em to court. You write'em a letter. Remember that there is a righteous Judge who sees into your heart and into Mr. Rushdie's. Consider the possibility that you could benefit from a reconsideration of your views of art, revelation, and blasphemy. The damn house is on fire, Mr. Khomeini. Don't make things worse than they already are.

Meanwhile, though the earth be removed and though the mountains be carried into the midst of the sea, though the waters thereof roar and be troubled, though the mountains shake with the swelling thereof, we will go on reading whatever we want to read and discussing whatever we want to discuss.

Faithfully,
Mr. Crerar Douglas

Tragedy and Comedy in the Luther-Calvin Dialectic

No one knows exactly why Erich Auerbach wrote the *Mimesis*.[1] Working away in Turkey to preserve everything Hitler was destroying, Auerbach was too busy to say, but I cannot help thinking that the book's main point is that the Bible made all the difference in Western literature. For here the tragic wrath of the Iliad and the comic reunion of the Odyssey came together in the Messiah, who, to everyone's surprise, became a servant and died in our stead. Tragedy and comedy were no longer separate lines but changed sides on the cross. The high became the low; the victor became the victim; the end became the beginning, and then the victim became the victor again so that the killers who did not know they were dead could be brought to life by the dead man now alive, who, though still man and though dead for three days, had now been shown to have been the living God all along.

What would a Greek tragedian like Agathon or a comedian like Aristophanes have done with such a tale? They would have had to collaborate to write it, but if they had, the Greeks would have given them the hemlock, for good citizens had always known that if you ever did away with the distinction between high tragedy and low comedy, there would be a revolution: slaves, madmen, prostitutes, and thieves would think they could rub elbows with the king. The Christian Bible sets forth such an irrepressible revolution, and Christian worship is supposed to advance it. The question for classical humanism, however, is whether a mixing of tragedy and comedy can occur apart from revelation. Could Agathon and Aristophanes have collaborated? In the last paragraph of the *Symposium* Socrates expresses his hope that a tragedian will someday be a comedian also, but his disciples have had the most important supper of their lives. After the bread and wine they are ready for nothing but sleep. The Dionysian peace in the midst of tumult, the shared goblet, the words too full to be comprehended by disciples too sleepy to follow the argument, the eerie incompleteness of the scene, and the crowing of the cocks bring this famous paragraph as close to Maundy Thursday as reason alone can go. This is the outer limit of classical humanism: the vision that tragedy and comedy will at last be one. After this, there is nothing to do but sleep and hope, pass the day as usual, and return to the theater.

Although the Christian Middle Ages had its share of disaster stories and comedies, the focus of the tragi-comic dialectic shifted to the sacramental life of the church. As long as the mass was advancing the irrepressible revolution, comedy was slaying tragedy every time the Host was broken. But, with that rupture known as the Reformation, the eucharistic mystery was pushed more and more to the edge of Protestant worship, to the consternation of the reformers themselves. Sacred victims and mystic victors were transferred from the altar back to the stage, and in Shakespeare the humanist parallel to the mass reached its fulfillment. Shakespeare like a magician kept showing that just as *Romeo and Juliet* is but *Pyramis and Thisbe* from the other side of *A Midsummer Night's Dream,* so all tragedy is but comedy inside out, until in the last plays he put the tragic fall and the comic regeneration within the scope of a single five-act arch.

The Puritans, of course, wanted the English to go to church instead of the theater, but the English wanted to go to the theater to find the sacred drama which the Puritans did not want them to have in church. For the Puritans, the sacred drama was supposed to shift from something external (whether on stage or altar) to something internal, in your heart of hearts and mind of minds. But Shakespeare resisted this shift. Whether Shakespeare was Catholic, Puritan, Anglican, Jewish, agnostic, or Zen Buddhist is beside the point, but his magical translation from altar to stage of the sacred union of comedy and tragedy was Shakespeare's contribution to the history of religion. In this, Shakespeare fulfilled at last the hope of Socrates and, for England at least, brought classical humanism to its consummation. The fertile soil of the Renaissance was ready for Milton's invasion and Calvinism's frantic search for an Eden on earth.

The romance form of Shakespeare's last plays and Spenser's *Faerie Queene* is the strange boundary land between Shakespeare's tragi-comic world of drama and Milton's apocalyptic world of epic. Northrop Frye was the twentieth century's great elucidator of this never-never land of romance, which he called the Green World. The importance of this boundary land is not only that it allows us to explore the differences between drama and epic but that romance uses its variegation, its wandering, its refusal to let the eye rest on anything too long, as a way of showing us comedy emerging from tragedy inside an apocalypse emerging from epic. No wonder romance novels are so popular at news-stands and in super markets. Romance reveals motion in stasis. It meditates on structure for hurried people who are always losing their structure in their busyness. Romance reveals that an apocalypse is in fact an epic compressed beyond the limits of human endurance. In apocalypse the action speeds up almost to infinity while the scope of the narrative expands to include the war in heaven, the primal generation of the world, and the final battle of the cosmos, and all of this within the shortest possible time. Thus Daniel compresses the whole Old Testament almost to the point of explosion, and Revelation of course does the same for the entire canon. Romance has the difficult job of slowing that speed-up down in the imagination's eye without destroying the speed-up, because it is beyond the power of romance, indeed of imagination, to slow the apocalypse down once it starts speeding toward us. The most we can do is to try to maintain our sanity in the face of it. Luther suggested going out to plant a tree.

Romance reveals the structure of apocalypse by studying violent (Mannerist and Baroque) motion in delicate (Late Baroque) repose, coming as close as possible to Rococo irreverence without ever quite completely dynamiting the *mysterion* it is charged with revealing. Romance always operates in a half-comedic distance from The Serious so that we are always wondering whether this whole thing is about to tumble down a hillside of tom-foolery into destruction. We always know how silly romance is at every second of our enjoyment of it so that we can at best only half forget reality while entering playfully into romance conventions. And it is this half-forgetting, half-remembering of reality that we need in order to find in good romance a sacramental newness of vision. The healthy thing about romance is that its silliness (unlike drugs) does not allow us to fully escape reality but only to escape from our need to escape from it. Romance makes reality bearable, not heroic, but bearable.

Frye showed us the apocalyptic dash toward canonicity in the history of the English language. By specializing in the elucidation of romance Frye showed us the meaning of the weird, haunted waterway that joins Shakespeare's forest and Milton's garden. In religious terms, we might say that in guiding us from Arden to Eden Frye showed us the pre-Calvinism of Shakespeare and the sheer Calvinism of Milton. As a Canadian, Frye had the necessary proximity and distance to see the whole thing unfold: the transition from England's pre-Calvinist humanism to America's post-Calvinist apocalypticism. Once the sacred had shifted from altar to stage, life was bound to become more and more an imitation of art, and as the end of classical humanism in England was Shakespeare holding the mirror up to nature, the end of post-Calvinism in America was Disney holding nature up to the mirror.

Odysseus' task, since we insist on being cutesie about the whole thing, was to find a way for Homer to end the Odyssey (otherwise there was absolutely no end in sight). It should be a happy ending, in which justice is rendered: the impostors expelled, husband and wife, father and son, the community and her warrior restored. Odysseus had to help his community recover from tragedy. He had to make them believe that the Iliad contained only half of the truth about life. Frye devoted much attention to the contrast between Iliadic and Odyssean themes: *forza* on the one hand and *froda* on the other; wrath, alienation, and tragedy on the one hand and wandering, home-coming, and comedy on the other. With Coleridge, Frye believed that there are Iliad critics and Odyssey critics. He placed himself among the Odysseans.[2] To meditate on this point for a moment, we might note some differences between Frye and a great critic from the Iliad's side of the fence: Paul Tillich.

Tillich prophesied against barbarism from World War I until the eve of Viet Nam. Violent conflict was the context in which he worked, and he was something of an Achilles. Tillich maintained his personal integrity by leaving the fold. He left Germany. In a sense he left the church. Although Tillich would not have agreed with them, orthodox Lutherans could certainly claim that anyone who denied a literal resurrection was a former Christian, not a Christian. In a sense, Tillich, like Scotus Eriugena, whom he so much resembled, hellenized his way out of the new Israel. Yet he was serving the church even as he was slamming her door behind him. Good foundations can always use a little shaking. To leave Germany in the name of a better Germany, Lutheranism in the name of Luther, and perhaps even Christianity in the name of (the) Christ is to follow the Achillean path of heroic solitary protest.

In comparison, Frye must look more like Odysseus. Even his context was different: Frye prophesied against barbarism from World War II until the eve of Orwellian totalitarianism. Like the Calvinists, Frye was more concerned with the reformation of the community than with the justification of the individual. Rather than leaving the community, Frye's task was to stay within it to keep its imagination sane. Frye's environment was not war for the most part but a period of dangerous Cold War wandering among our nuclear weapons arsenals and toxic waste dumps. Tillich had to devote much attention to showing people what was demonic, indeed to reminding us that there is such a thing as the demonic, while Frye had to remind us that there is such a thing as the natural. Tillich's enemies were crazed followers of the madman Hitler, while Frye's were drugged worshippers of illusion, spaced-out devotees of the unnatural. In all of Frye's criticism there runs the theme that Ithaca is a true and natural human environment, a safe and peaceful city, even if we are temporarily alienated from it and impostors are struggling to make it their own. Frye's criticism is a Zen-like analogue to theology.

With regard to theology, Frye was as sly as the Sphinx, and, within the canons of his own critical theory, he had every right to be. The best parallel to Frye is not a theologain like Scotus Eriugena but, if one may dare say so without falling into criticolatry (or even if one does fall into it), sly Shakespeare himself. For Frye self-consciously planted his criticism outside the church door, magically duplicating in his churchyard the actions of the priests on their altar. Frye's work, like the Bard's, points explicitly neither toward Christian theology nor away from it but mystically imitates it. The *Anatomy of Criticism* is filled with tacit theological presuppositions and implications which are notoriously difficult to describe.[3] Here again it seems to me that an analogy with Tillich may be useful. With every passing year Tillich's *Systematic Theology* and Frye's *Anatomy of Criticism* (my two most treasured keys to dreamland when I was young) come to look more like period pieces with much in common. Both were dedicated to the search for a unified structure of discourse adequate to include all of religion and culture. Logocentric with a vengeance, both books were oblations laid at the altar of higher education in an era which perhaps had too much confidence in education. But their differences are equally important. The *Anatomy* is Anglo-American, the *Systematic Theology*, German-American. The *Anatomy*, which claims to be no more than "four essays," assiduously avoids making ontological statements, keeping its philosophical lineaments as concealed as possible. The *Systematic Theology* was of course exactly the opposite in this respect. It seems to me to be useful to note that if the *Systematic Theology* was a great vision of religion and culture which might best be called post-theological, the *Anatomy of Criticism* was an equally dazzling vision which was pre-theological. That is, the *Anatomy* is on the road to theology (*Unterwegs zur Theologie*, as we Heideggerians put it).

Frye said that the *Anatomy* would need to be followed by studies in practical criticism, and indeed the ensuing decades brought a harvest of practical studies from Frye's pen, but why did his whole corpus culminate in those massive efforts to recover the Bible? Whether or not they provide a Great Code to the Bible and to all of art and culture, Frye's Bible books provide a great code to Frye, and that in itself is a monumental achievement. The Bible books reveal that Frye's whole corpus, including its *Anatomy*, was a body of implicit theology, or, since he did not choose to elucidate the theology explicitly, a body of pre-theology, churchyard, outdoor theology. Frye's corpus is the confession of a vision in which the man who died and rose again (and builds his cities out of the Milky Way) is dreaming all of literature, including you and me (who are the conversation, as we Hölderlinians put it). The apocalypse, as Frye used to love saying, is God seeing nature through our eyes. Thanks be to God that Frye kept the theology humanist, kept it pregnant with intimations of divinity, and did not theologize it. Sometimes pre-theology, like post-theology, is the best theology, especially when the (reportedly still dead) word "God" is, though not necessarily dead, stolen from its tomb by the drugged worshippers of illusion. God's corpus has been stolen by the international power brokers, and Frye is suggesting that if we keep working with faith, hope, and charity in our secular gardens *zwischen den Zeiten*(as we Barthians put it), someone who looks like the Gardener will some morning appear in the twinkling of an eye and speak to us. That gardening in the outdoor church without a roof is what Frye called us to (because theology was not here yet) and Tillich called us to (because, for him, theology had already departed).

More precisely, the *Anatomy*, I would say, was not only pre-theological but specifically pre-Calvinist, while the *Systematic Theology* was not only post-theological but specifically post-Lutheran. Lutheranism and Calvinism are each other's positive negative. They are exact complements which (Taoistically) make each other possible. When Lutheranism dries up to undergo a metamorphosis into some new life, that new life-form is often a humanism of some sort (Goethe, Hegel, Tillich), but when Calvinism dries up and rises again, it is frequently a secularized apocalypticism of some sort (Blake, Thoreau, Disney). The general principle is: *Lutheranism in decay becomes humanism: humanism in fertility beccmes Calvinism: Calvinism in decay becomes secular apocalypticism.* Lutheranism begins with a Catholic monk and ends with humanists, while Calvinism begins with a Senecan humanist and ends with apocalypticists. Lutheranism ends in an effort to accept the world as it is but on the largest possible scale. What else would you call Hegel? Calvinism ends in an effort to change the hell out of the world, apocalypticize it, re-establish Eden once and for all, even if Eden turns out to be no damn bigger than Thoreau's pond or Emily Dickinson's bedroom (or, on the tinsel level, Disney's happy-face movie screen). The point remains the same: that Calvinism is a search for paradise regained. Calvin's Geneva is More's *Utopia* read by a literalist. Calvinism is an effort to bring diamonds out of coal by compressing the social order until it is miniaturized enough (just one perfect city: that ought to be possible!) to be a metaphor of heaven (as Emily Dickinson's life was), and thus has no choice but to be orderly. In such people as Thoreau and Dickinson we see the order hovering between transcendence and immanence on a horizon that can only be called lived poetry. It is not that Calvinism is so poetic but that poetry is the only way to survive it because it is so all-encompassing and totally demanding (having harnessed for its own purposes, as it has, even Luther's proclamation of forgiveness).

The man in the middle, nervous Melanchthon, became the father of Protestant humanistic education precisely because he found himself in the funny situation of being the first post-Lutheran pre-Calvinist in history. But of course, though Melanchthon was finally the most influential post-Lutheran pre-Calvinist, there were oodles of others equally interesting or maybe (for me at least, since I hate success stories) more interesting. Between Luther and Calvin, Protestantism was born. Luther justified us; Calvin sanctified us. Luther freed us from the law; Calvin put us back under it. Luther gave us the mystical, autonomous side of theonomy; Calvin, like the later al-Ghazali and the later Augustine, gave us the post-mystical heteronomous side of theonomy, or rather he both gave it to us and purified it for us. All appearances to the contrary, Calvin never forgot Luther's mystical break-throughs, just as al-Ghazali and Augustine never forgot theirs. But Luther feared the apocalypse he (Luther) had unleashed. Calvin re-leashed Luther's impending apocalypse for him. Calvin rescued the Wittenberg movement from the fanaticism of the Münster movement by creating the Geneva movement, which blended the radical aspirations of the Anabaptists with the Christian realism of the Lutherans. Conservative Luther flapped Christianity's non-dualist wing, and radical Cavin flapped its dualist wing, but, by the grace of God and the kind intelligence of Luther and Calvin, it is one bird, not two, all appearances of schism to the contrary notwithstanding.

Out of understandably anxious Melanchthon's plight has come whatever has been of value in the Protestant humanistic tradition, including the typically Protestant doubt about whether any of it has been valuable. Melanchthon had to mediate between the Greek-influenced Eastern Europe of Luther and the Latin-influenced Western Europe of Calvin. Frye stood in the western wing of Melanchthon's heritage: philological, optimistic, funny, donnish, orderly, but always switching the order around, defending the freedom of the will but keeping the astrology charts handy, always inventing formulas with which to crack the latest code the Germans have just invented a machine to keep secret (also known as the German language). It is the humanism of the Western educational establishment: dedicated to the university as a tidier thing than the creaky old church but never quite able to shake off the memory of the older devotion.

But if pre-Calvinist humanism began with Melanchthon, it culminated in Shakespeare. The tradition of pre-Calvinist humanism was in essence a Westward Movement. If it had been allowed to flourish, as it began to do, in the France of Calvin, Rabelais, and Montaigne, this Westward Moving Calvinism would have influenced a very different modern Europe. Having misfired in France, however, pre-Calvinism reached its height, with all the pent-up intensity of a lost cause, at the northwest edge of European civilization: in Britain and more especially Shakespeare, poet of self-limitation. Shakespeare was the secular fulfillment of the classical Roman vates ideal as Milton was to become its sacred fulfillment: Shakespeare, poet as seer, the man of perfect vision and drama; Milton, seer as poet, the blind man, poet of the epic; Shakespeare, externalizer of the inward; Milton, internalizer of cosmic vison, indeed of the outermost canyons of heaven and hell. Shaskespeare, then, was that perfect Renaissance soil out of which apocalyptic Calvinism like Milton's could grow. Without a Shakespeare, poet of earth and limits, Milton would not have had the spiritual structure from which to ascend to the war in heaven and our first parents and justify the ways of God to man. Shakespeare staked the claim: Milton made it cosmic. Milton went to work digging up the gold and paving heavenly streets with it. Shakespeare and Milton are (you guessed it) each other's positive negative.

Milton could only succeed in the realm of epic, beyond drama, because Shakespeare had already pushed the dialectic of drama, that is, the dichotomy of tragic and comic, to that infinity in which opposites merge. None of France's Miltons succeeded in the realm of epic because France's pre-Calvinist humanism had been prematurely thwarted and no Shakespeare had been allowed to develop. Frye's prolonged wandering along the hugely fertile boundary between Shakespeare and Milton is in fact a meditation on the end of classical humanism and the beginning of apocalypticism in modern (and of course—that funny word—postmodern) culture. But Frye knew that garden-worlds of romance are meaningless and disgusting, even demonic, if they have no relation to the tragic. If romance is to be a Geneva and not a Disneyland, the tragic must precede the garden world of romance and found it. Tragedy and romance must be each other's positive-negative, as William Empson suggested that pastoral poetry makes possible radical critique of disastrous social structures. It is when we lose touch with radical critique that our romance world slips from Walden to Anaheim. The garden in which Mary Magdalene found The Risen One was the garden in which the tomb was, not far from Golgotha. The churchyard in which Frye leaped and played with such lambish glee was as prophetic as Walden: a reminder of nature, I say again, in a world of nuclear weapons, toxic dumps, and a sky full of CFC's. Milton's Eden and his regained Paradise were protests against the Philistine bastards who did Samson in, the toxic dumpers of their day. Romance, then, has dignity and meaning only when, like Shakespeare's romances, it is relentlessly serious commentary on tragedy. Aristotle, our peripatetic biololgy professor, was himself able to name every plant and animal in the garden only because he also (perhaps unlike his student, Alexander the Little, and there is the difference between the Classical and Hellenistic eras) was able to name the tragic. If we cannot understand the tragic, we cannot understand the garden. If we cannot see our ignorance, we cannot start our education. We crash in premature, self-started, ungodly apocalypse.

Full humanity, the goal of education, depends on a naive, romance, perhaps finally fraudulent, confidence in the coherence of human symbols. This confidence is continually threatened by radical irruptions of evil, both moral and natural. The demonically irrational character of evil seems at first to shatter any hope of coherence in life, but the agents of civilization, the poets, priests, law-givers, healers, and builders, respond to the demonically incoherent by ritually surrounding it. They temporarily capture evil, isolate it, and then encase it in a re-organization of the ancient symbols of human culture: these symbols, pictures of a humanity annihilated but made more alive than ever, are used by human communities to provide modes for the renewed envisionment of the tragic, that is, a coherent approach to the demonically incoherent. The *Anatomy of Criticism* is a labyrinthine temple diagramming the coherence of human symbols in the face of our apocalyptic vision of possible annihilation. It is Ariadne's guide to the out-smarting of Theseus. Frye knew that the coherence of our symbols can never be empirically demonstrated. Indeed, our loss of confidence in the coherence of our own imagination was one of Frye's main concerns. But the attempt to work through imaginative destruction and come out alive is the task which might be summed up, for Frye, in the word education.

Education is, like the Odyssey, a continuing recovery of home. Education is possible only when we dare to envision our existence in a framework in which we are at home in the human community and the human community is at home with us, even when the most demonic arrows of annihilation are falling around us. We are educated when we are ready to harrow hell usefully, and that requires a continuing vision of the Ithaca which will be restored on the other side of our perdition. The beginning of education, in this vision, is, then, the perception of tragedy. Tragedy organizes disaster. Tragedy provides the first step in the conquest of the demons by naming and isolating the demons and then casting them out by name. Tragedy is the first step in love's triumph over evil, but, in true romance, tragedy must be supplemented by the larger, more inclusive category of comedy, just as the autonomous realm of mystical self-discovery must, if theonomy is to be complete, be supplemented by the heteronomous realm of post-mystical re-self-submission to those demanding moral norms by which the community can move from its *is* to its *ought*. Forward to Geneva! The non-dual autonomizing enlightenment of tragedy must be supplemented by the freely chosen heteronomizing dualism of life under civilization's law. Humanistic education originates in the envisionment of tragedy and culminates in the community's decision to commit itself to a restored Ithaca. Only if we are able to include in our psyches both the non-dualism of tragedy and the dualism of comedy, both the myth of freedom and the myth of concern, can we keep the two wings of the monotheism bird in proper harmony with each other.

It seems to me that H. Richard Niebuhr's influential Christ-and-Culture pentad can help us do exactly that if we translate it into a positive-negative structure based on the dialectic between tragedy and comedy.[4] To accomplish this little sleight-of-hand, we need only clump Niebuhr's first four models of Christ and culture (**Christ Against Culture, the Christ of Culture, Christ Above Culture,** and **Christ and Culture in Paradox**) into one big box called **Christ and Culture in Paradox.** The four separate boxes can remain four separate boxes, but they are only sub-headings beneath the main heading: **CHRIST AND CULTURE IN PARADOX.** The reason for this reduction is that the first three categories were always intended as paradoxes anyway. No one ever wanted Christ and culture to be simply stuck in antagonism to each other or simply reducible to each other or simply in a relationship of subordination: the point for the defenders of each model was that the model represented a problem. The point was to solve the problem so that Christ can visibly rule both our individual lives and the human race. The point, therefore, for all four of the non-transformationists was to become transformationist. It was not so static as Niebuhr's pentad suggests. The particular problem Christ needed to solve for denizens of the first model was the antagonism between Christ and culture. The problem that needed solution for denizens of the second model was the invisibility of Christ in the culture. The problem that needed to be solved for denizens of the third model was the gap between Christ and the culture. And the problem that needed to be solved for denizens of the fourth model was the invisibility and apparent incompleteness of Christ's rule over culture. But in all four cases the Christ-and-culture situation was a paradox. And in all four cases the point of the paradox was to solve it, so that Christ can transform us in actuality as he has already transformed us in principle.

I argue, then, that the first four categories are still magnificent and need to be retained, but they need to be included together in a larger category called CHRIST AND CULTURE IN PARADOX. This large category is in positive-negative dialectical relationship with the final category, CHRIST THE TRANSFORMER OF CULTURE. The former corresponds to *forza*, non-dualism, the myth of freedom. The latter corresponds to *froda*, dualism, the myth of concern. In one sense, then, the former corresponds to tragedy and the latter to comedy, but I would like to refine our dialectic a bit by saying that the problem of transforming culture into the image of Christ is always a tragic problem. Yes, it issues in the *divina commedia*, but there is no way around the tragedy of it, the journey into absurdity, pain, destruction, and utter repentance. There is in reality no easy Chrstianity that leaps over the cross (though, of course, the vast majority of production lines that stamp, package, and market entities called Christian are efforts to manufacture exactly that: Christianity without tears). So, yes, we are talking about a move through tragedy to comedy, but first and foremost we are dealing with two complementary kinds of tragedy, one that emphasizes the paradoxical side of tragedy and the other that emphasizes the comedic, transformative, *froda* side of it.

Luther is of course the great exponent of paradox for Niebuhr, and Augustine, Calvin, and Frederick Dennison Maurice illustrate transformation. To make my point, however, that paradox and transformation are always inseparable (since Christ's transformation of culture is always, this side of the parousia, paradoxical and the paradox of Christ's relation to the world is always transformational), I put Saint Thomas Aquinas, the master of those who believe, also in this transformation category while simultaneously letting him stay also in the (now paradoxical) Christ Above Culture category in which Niebuhr placed him and where he seems to have been relatively happy. But only relatively, because Thomas clearly intended his vision of Christ above culture as a paradox. And he clearly saw the paradox as transformative. So Thomas must, if anyone must, be on both sides of our paradox.[5]

The tragedy of paradox (Luther) is closer to what Northrop Frye called irony, a world of endless pain and anxiety, relieved only by the hero's consciousness of the pain and anxiety. Paradoxical tragedy is consciousness-tragedy. Transformational tragedy (Calvin) is action-tragedy. It is closer to the comic world of romance (in Frye's categories), tragedies that put more emphasis on the hero's action and the hero's post-tragic regeneration than does paradoxical tragedy. Hence I am associating paradoxical tragedy with Frye's humanistic, fatalistic, and horrific tragedies and transformational tragedy with his genetic, edenic, and normal tragedies. Thus has our double-winged positive-negative schema melted down both Niebuhr's pentad and Frye's oxagon. Our dialectical machine is now lean and mean, ready for some fancy *forza* and *froda*. So watch out!

The tragedy of paradox is represented by Antigone as expounded by Hegel and the tragedy of transformation by Oedipus as expounded by Aristotle.

The tragedy of paradox shows us a hero (a term I will use for both males and females, since heroine, like poetess, authoress, or aviatrix, sounds patronizing and furthermore implies such images as "shivering virgin" and damsel-in-distress-soon-to-be-rescued-by-dragon-slaying-hero, by which we tirivialize not only female heroes but also the very idea of the Antigonean tragedy of paradox) who is trapped by *being*, while the tragedy of transformation shows us a hero who is trapped by *action*. In many tragedies, of course, both kinds of trap are present. That is the power of the dialectic of tragedy. The more paradox and transformation can press against each other, the more powerful (in the sense of pregnant) the tragedy is. Still, tragedies often tend to emphasize either the paradoxical or the transformational side of the duality.

Antigone shows us the paradox (says Hegel) of someone who is trapped, not between good and evil, but between good and good, between the good of family and the good of the state, between private good and public good. The question is: which is the greater good? Better yet, how can both goods be affirmed simultaneously (as in Luther's *simul*)? Antigone's tragedy is that she does not have the option of taking a heroic action that would reconcile the two goods (the positive and negative that should be complementary but are tragically caught in the trap of opposition). Instead, Antigone's heroism is in the nobility with which she affirms both goods even though both cannot be affirmed. Antigone becomes guilty, not because she has done anything wrong, but because the situation in which she has been placed through no fault of her own is a guilty situation (as Christianity would say, a situation itself trapped by original sin, illustrating the extent to which sin is not only an act but a state of being that is ultimately social in its dimensions). Oedipus, on the contrary, as expounded by Aristotle, tries to avoid taking the action which he is fated to take and thereby takes the action which only appears to avoid the fate which he is fated not to avoid. But although Oedipus was fated to take the action to attempt to avoid his fate, his action of trying to avoid his fate was the freely chosen action which made his fate not only fate but also freely chosen and therefore led to a justly deserved catastrophe, which is exactly the catastrophe he was fated to freely choose. Oedipus's tragedy, then, is paradoxical indeed, but more specifically his tragedy is the tragedy of transformation. He has the apparent option of taking an action that will make a difference, that will *transform* his situation.

Oedipus's (male) tragedy is that he mistakenly thinks he can take transformative heroic action. Antigone's (female) tragedy is that she knows she cannot (because of the unjust laws of unjust rulers). Oedipus can apparently choose between good and evil. And apparently he does choose. Apparently he does choose good. But the tragedy is that good and evil (which should be in opposition to each other) are actually complementary in Oedipus's world of fated freedom. The good Oedipus tries to do becomes the evil he tries to avoid, and yet he is the one who takes the action and is thereby responsible for committing the very evil he had tried to take action not to commit. It is a story of an effort to transform reality by means of an action which is in turn transformed *by* reality. Both Antigone and Oedipus are emblems of the paradox of fate and freedom and of the transformation of consciousness which comes when the tragic depth of the paradox is recognized and accepted for what it is. But the story of Antigone emphasizes the paradoxical side of the paradox of transformation, and the story of Oedipus emphasizes the transformational side of it.

When we translate this Greek emblem of fate and freedom into Christianity, we have the emblem of predestination and freedom. The story of Jesus Christ as Luther and the other paradoxicalists tell it emphasizes the salvific bondage of the human will to God's will. Christ paradoxically uses his divine freedom as Lord of all to become the human servant of all, thereby freely emptying himself of his human freedom in the service of his divine freedom for the sake of the very human lords and potentates who destroy his power and deny his lordship because they think they do not want the freedom he knows they need. Luther's Christ paradoxically reverses the fallen situation which Hegel's Antigone confronted by using the cross as an Archimedean lever with which to elevate our situation from its fallenness to his graciousness. Because Christ, as divine, has the option in his integrity of succeeding exactly where Antigone, as human, had no choice in her integrity but to fail, we can defy the state and bury our brother; we can affirm in Christ both public good and private good in the knowledge that Christ reconciles the two claims. In Christ's obedience is our freedom. Our good deeds can do nothing to save us. The paradox of our justification is that it rests on nothing but Christ's free act. It is not our action that saves us but, paradoxically, our faith in Christ's action. And our faith in Christ's action on our behalf is so crucial that we do not even have the power (freedom) to choose for or against that faith. Not only the act but the faith in the act is sheer gift. Hence all that matters is Christ's act and Christ's gracious transfer of the power of that act to us, an action which will finally show us that, as Luther put it at the end of his life, God is a fiery furnace full of love.

That is Luther's gospel of paradox. It is still tragedy, of course, but it is Christian tragedy, the paradoxical Christian tragedy of predestination and freedom, not the Greek tragedy of fate and freedom. Since ours is the tragedy of predestination to salvation, it is a most ironic tragedy. It is salvific tragedy. And Luther's Christ reflects the paradoxical side of Christian salvific tragedy. He allows us to be Chrstian Antigones, lords of the *Simul*, the simultaneity of public good and private good, of state and family, of servanthood and lordship, of chosenness and freedom. Luther's Christ does not remove Antigone (us) from her dilemma of conscience, hanging like Christ and Prometheus between the dual goods of heaven and earth, but instead says it is necessary to hang there like that. It is where God calls the Christian to live, *On the Boundary, Simul* in heaven and on earth, between public good and private good. Luther's Christ does not rescue Antigone from her plight, then. Christ identifies Antigone's plight as heroic. He lets the efficaciousness of her suffering shine through by showing that it is his suffering, too, for Luther's Christ is, like Antigone, The Tragedian of Paradox, filling all of nature with ubiquitous salvific presence but being available for you, at the altar, only when his plight has been properly proclaimed. Luther's Christ (his Antigone) does not need to be transubstantiated from female to male, from Antigone to Oedipus, from Paradox to Transformation, in order to be efficiacious. She is already here and now fully present and fully efficacious. Luther's Christ is a non-dualist, vindicated Antigone.

The Christ of Niebuhr's transformationists reflects the transformational side of Christian salvific tragedy by ironically reversing Oedipus's tragedy. This Christ is not so much one who empties himself as one who retains his Lordship. Luther emphasizes the paradox of the incarnation, but the transformationists emphasize the transformation of human history by the entry of the eternal Logos into its logic, reversing its flow from regress to progress. The transformationist Christ solves the problem of fate and freedom not by submitting to the Father's will so much as enacting the Father's will. Luther's theology of the cross is opposed to a theology of glory. It rules out all Christology *von unten nach oben*. The transformationists' theology of triumph establishes for all to see the Christology *von oben nach unten*. The difference is a matter of emphasis. But the difference in emphasis is real, and its consequences are far-reaching. For Luther, the state is a place where the devil is loose; for the transformationists (who do not deny that the devil is loose in the state) the state is also a means of grace. For Luther, the paradox of Christ's divine humanity makes possible the ubiquitous presence of the body of Christ on earth. For the transformationists, Christ's Lordship over the earth leads to an emphasis that Christ's body is in heaven. From this difference, flows a very different view of reality.

The Christ of the transformationists chooses effectively, acts effectively, both in heaven and on earth, and rules all the world as sovereign Lord, making everything bend to his will. In this, Christ does exactly what Oedipus would have needed to do in order to break the power of his fate, but this is exactly what Oedipus could not do because the (nasty dualistic Greek) cards were stacked against him. And, besides, Oedipus was not Christ. As the one who knew the answer to the Sphinx's riddle, Oedipus was the man who knew the answer was man, but, since he was not predestined to know Israel's question, Oedipus could hardly have been expected to know Israel's answer. Oedipus was the man-man, but Christ was the God-man. In Christian predestination the cards are stacked in favor of the free and Lordly Christ, who does the Father's will completely, thereby transforming human history so that history, too, in spite of itself does the Father's will, delivering to the Father those whom he has known from before the foundation of the world. The demonic net in which Oedipus tripped himself becomes in Christian salvific tragedy the gracious net which Christ's fishermen cast into the sea to lift us out of our perdition, the baptismal net of transformation.

Thomas F. Torrance has expounded this transformation image in an especially interesting way.[6] He has argued that a false metaphysic caused the church after the time of Athanasius to forget the extent to which Athanasius and others in the early church had succeeded in transforming the static categories of Greek thought into the kind of dynamic, Hebraic categories which the Gospel demands. In particular, Athanasius had tried to replace the notion that space is a container with the much more adequate (and, since Einstein, obviously more accurate) notion that space is inseparable from time; that time and space exist in a dynamic continuum with each other, not in a static opposition to each other.

The container-concept of space leads us to underestimate the extent of Christ's transformation of history because, by placing time and space in separate compartments, it separates who Christ is from what Christ does. The container concept of space locates the miracle of the incarnation too exclusively in the paradox of Christ's person, hence reducing the incarnation to a temporal vanishing point, a timeless sacramental instant, or non-instant. Luther rightly recognized that if this happened (if *hoc est corpus meum* became *hoc significat corpus meum*), the incarnation would become meaningless, and he tried to compensate for the inadequacy of his space and time concepts by setting forth a paradox which located the miracle of Christ's continuing presence on earth in a concept of his infinite extension in space. The danger of this approach (according to Torrance and his Calvinists) was both that it led to an emptying of the power and personhood of Christ and that it led to a deifying of humanity. Since the finite could contain the infinite, the finite was increasingly conceived (in Goethe, Hegel, and, though less obviously, in Tillich) as inherently but hiddenly infinite. The human was seen as inherently but hiddenly divine. All that was needed to make humanity obviously and effectively divine was a titanic act of will (also known as German Romanticism and finally Nietzsche's Will to Power and so many other *post-Lutheran*—NOT Lutheran—tragic efforts to bring Antigone out of her *Simul*, Prometheus off his rock and out of his chains, by means of sheer paradoxical, and sometimes demonically irrational, WILL).

Torrance argues that, over against Leo the Great, the Cappadocians, Augustine, Aquinas, Luther, Newton, Kant, Hegel, and Bultmann (the bad guys), there was a rival strain of thinkers who fought to free Christendom from its bondage to the container-concept of space, and this list includes Athanasius,

Cyril of Alexandria, John Philoponus of Alexandria, Hilary of Poitiers, Richard of St. Victor, Robert Grosseteste and Pseudo-Grosseteste, Calvin, James Clerk Maxwell, Michael Faraday, Einstein, and Michael Polanyi (the good guys). The former list (the bad guys) consists of dualists, people who (in my categories) posit an opposition between space and time and therefore also body and mind, humanity and divinity, where there should actually be not an opposition but a complementary duality, a (in Torrance's terms) dynamic continuum.

For those space-time continuum people who also happen to be Christian, Christ is seen as the dynamic Logos of God, not just touching humanity at a timeless vanishing point made permanent only by the miracles of the church and its sacraments, but as the living logic of the evolution of the universe, which is conceived of not as timeless but as created by the Logos in time, upheld and transformed by the Logos in time, and to be received again by the Logos in glory at the end of time. This Logos is the God-man Jesus Christ, who is now, not physically ubiquitous as for Luther and Strong, but physically in heaven and spiritually, logically (as it were), ubiquitous as the very logic of the universe. By this way of thinking, the incarnation, atonement, and resurrection of Jesus Christ are all real events in the physical world of time and space on our earth. Although this was true also for most of the container-model Christians, Torrance argues that the logic of their position drives them toward Bultmann's sad position, in which the cross, the vanishing point of the incarnation, is the normative locus of the incarnation, while, for the continuum-model Christians, the cross is but one locus of the incarnation. The normative locus of the incarnation, for the transformationists, is the incarnation's trajectory through the space-time continuum, the whole passage from creation to incarnation to cross to resurrection to final consummation.

Torrance thinks the space-time continuum concept leads to critical realism, while the space-container model must lead eventually to an idealism of some sort. The continuum people see the models with which physics describes the universe as disclosure models. These models disclose the universe as it is in a way that Torrance describes as open at the top. Disclosure models, both in theology and in physics, show us reality from the bottom up, from our perspective, that is, but they really do show us reality. The models are open on the top because they can be fully comprehended only by the more inclusive models above them, models which become more and more inclusive until they (at the point of a theoretical infinity) would open onto God's own models. Jesus Christ is such a disclosure of reality. He shows us as much reality as we are able to see. In Christ we really do see God's will for us and God's gracious action on our behalf. Christ is infinitely more than the occasion for a desperate (finally idealist) leap of faith, whether Kierkegaardian or Bultmannian. Christ is more than a symbol, just as the models with which physics describes reality are more than human constructs. Torrance's often repeated claim is that God has created reality in such a way as to make reality revelatory. By the grace of God, the miracle of comprehension does happen. Reality does disclose itself to us, both in natural science and in theological science. Science, both natural and theological, is the orderly study of reality's disclosure of itself to us. It is not just a set of guesses that provisionally work either by fluke or by some reason unknown to us. Reality and our human reasoning powers (even in their present fallenness) really do match up with each other because God has created both reality and human reason for the purpose of matching up. They are both disclosures of the one divine Logos made known to us normatively in and by Jesus Christ.

Just as Einstein placed geometry in a category subordinate to physics, so Torrance places natural science as a natural theology in a category subordinate to revelation. In this model, geometry and natural theology are not preparatory to some other task but the result of another task. For natural theology to be preparatory to a theology of the revealed Word of God, there would need to be an analogy of being between earth and heaven. But there is none. So natural theology is carried out in the light of, and as a sub-divison of, theology of the revealed Word, just as Einstein's geometry is carried out in the light of, and as a sub-division of, physics. In this way, Torrance believes he can, even as a Barthian, have a natural theology, a Barthian natural theology. Indeed, only in this Barthian way can there be any natural theology at all, as Torrance sees it. I would place the study of the arts and of comparative religions in a similar position.

Notice that I say I think *the study* of the arts and of comparative religions can become a post-Christic natural theology for the Torrantian. I have no idea whether Torrance would agree, but it seems to me that the scientific study of these phenomena is as compatible with natural theology as is the scientific study of physical nature. And this introduces the vexed issue of the possibility of a scientific study of religion and the arts. In his *Anatomy* of 1957, Frye notoriously made the case for a scientific literary criticism. Controversy aplenty resulted from the fact that, instead of stressing only the orderliness of a scientific knowledge of the arts and the fact that this orderliness presupposes an ultimate coherence which may or may not be already visible in whole or in part (difficult enough claims in themselves), Frye seemed to be saying that (in such books as his own of course) the ultimate coherence was already visible. When he combined that impression (and I am convinced that it was an impression he did not intend to convey) with his claim that literary critics, as literary critics, have no reason to (or solid basis on which to) make *value judgments* in the empirical science of literary criticism, Frye brought down the very evaluative heaven and hell of an angry literary critical community on his head. What, no value judgments? What, are we to become another block-head social science?

Frye's *Critical Path*, with which we began Chapter Three, can be interpreted as a major effort to respond to that wrath by means of his distinction between the myth of freedom (which is not concerned with value judgments) and the myth of concern (which is). This dualism between the two myths will simply remain so much Kantian fact-value bifurcation, however, unless we link the myths of freedom and concern up with an explicit theology, as I have tried to do in this book and as Frye would not do. I think that Frye's work is science in the same sense in which other great humanists of recent times have been so preternaturally obsessed with calling their work scientific (Darwin, Wellhausen, Marx, Mill, Weber, Freud, Jung, de Chardin), even when their stuff is most obviously half sheer vision (at best). But the work of these geniuses is scientific, not in some pseudo-empirical, narrow correspondence-of-statement-to-fact but in these visionaries' concern to be utterly holistic in their visions, to connect absolutely everything they are interested in with absolutely everything else and to insist (like Hegel) that the truth of the part is only in the truth of the whole. In this sense they all do, in spite of themselves, presuppose theologies because theologies are verbalizations of one's ultimate vision which are able to take account of the fact that the vision ain't here yet, only the ultimacy with which it is loved and longed for and (in mystic vison) "known" to be real.

In that sense, the study of the arts and of comparative religion is (in both its *forza* aspects and its *froda* aspects) part of an enormous *Geisteswissenschaft*, and, precisely as such, is also natural theology, but the paradox is exactly where Torrance puts it: that our ultimate vision of coherence (our revelation) must come before the science (otherwise we have no hunches about what to look for or how to look for it, no basis on which to develop disclosure models), and the revelation comes only as what Torrance, following Michael Polanyi, calls tacit knowledge, personal knowledge, which is qualitatively more than a hunch. Our apprehension of a unified field theory in religion and the arts is not just a paradigm-projection. It is more realist than that, more organic. But it can never, this side of the parousia, be in our grasp. In that respect it is always natural theology based not on an *analogy of being* between ultimacy and ourselves but only on the *analogy of faith* between ultimacy and ourselves. Most ironically, there can be a natural science (whether physical or spiritual) only to the extent that it based on a theological science. Thank goodness, that is as true now as it was in the Middle Ages and always has been. The difference is only that in the Middle Ages it seemed as obviously true as today it seems obviously false. But I vote with the Middle Ages on this one.

I think that, when Strong says poetry constitutes a natural religion, he means that it does so only after we start with Christ, not with natural religion itself. *In the light of Christ* we can look back at Homer and see the "natural religion" in him, not the other way around. Natural religion is, for Strong, something that we can see only as a result of a natural theology, which Strong practices, like Torrance, not pre-Christically but *sub specie Christi*. This is why I think Strong's theological approach to the poets is the redemption of Frye's natural theology *manqué*. Strong's theology of poetry makes Frye's "literary science" a continuing possibility, but not as an untheological science, not as some supposedly value-free empirical science, but as a theologically based natural science linked with an empricism, not of literature alone, but first of all of Christian mystical experience. That business about mystical experience is not Barthian, Torrantian, or Fryeean, of course. It is Strongian, though I think that, from a Strongian perspective, we can see a great deal of personal Christian mysticism operating in both Barth and Torrance, as much as in Frye (to the probable consternation of all three of them, though perhaps not Torrance or the later Frye). I think that if Barth, Torrance, and Frye would, like Strong, haul off and call their visions mysticism, while at the same time calling them science, we would get at the spiritual substance of what they are talking about much more directly.

This comment on Christian mysticism leads me back very briefly to my claim in Chapter Two that Tillich was actually deifying reason. I argued at that time that the Gospel According to John uses Logos only as a metaphor for Christ. John's point is no more that human reason is divine than that human bread, water, and flesh are divine. Yet, I argued, Tillich works on the assumption that human reason is a divine element in humanity. How does that differ from Torrance's talk of the divine Logos made manifest to human reason in all of nature? Although I do not think they would agree, I would be happy to call both Tillich's and Torrance's theologies mystical, but they are very different mysticisms. Tillich is presupposing the Lutheran image of a glorified body of Christ filling all of nature, while Torrance, Strong, and Barth are all presupposing Calvin's image of the divine Logos as essentially heavenly from the ascension until the second coming. For Torrance, Strong, and Barth, we human beings, even in our fallenness, can indeed apprehend the divine Logos and even experience a mystical union with Christ as the Logos, but our fallenness separates us infinitely from that very Logos with which we experience mystical union. Otherwise, there would be that ugly analogy of being between heaven and earth which we saw in Chapter One to be so dangerous. The paradox for Torrance, Strong, and Barth is not that there is anything divine about human reason but exactly the opposite: that the divine Logos links itself to us in spite of our inability to contain it. For Tillich, in traditional terminology, the *finitum* is *capax infiniti*, while, for Torrance, Strong, and Barth, the *finitum* is most definitely *non capax infiniti*. This is why there can, for Tillich, be an analogy of being between God and us, while, for Torrance, Strong, Barth (and Frye), there is only the analogy of faith. The importance of this difference was clear, I hope, in our discussion of male and female symbolism in Chapter One.

Before concluding this chapter, I want to add an important qualification: while embracing Torrance's exposition of the continuuum vision, I want to stress at the same time, as Torrance does also, the continuing importance of Luther's side of the paradox. The tragedy of paradox epitomizes the position of the space-container people. Martin Luther is at stage center. With his, often very un-Lutheran, followers Hegel, Kierkegaard, Tillich, and Bultmann, Luther has the important task of reminding eager transformationists that what they call a space-time-continuum may actually be nothing but one more illusory ladder by which heavenly prophets claim that they can ascend to heaven. There is still a paradox, say Luther and his Lutherans. God is still in heaven, and you are still on earth. The miracle is precisely that God has descended to our earth to be with us, and because God wills to let this little manger of an earth contain him, it can contain him. Therefore the earth is filled with grace. Christ is everywhere. In Christian worship the meaning of his presence *for you* is proclaimed, and in the eucharist you have him, already today (and before you were able to prepare for him) both physically and spiritually, just as you have him both intellectually and spiritually in the Word.

Torrance rightly criticizes the dualism of the container model. But this dualism is the very stuff of Luther's paradox. In Christ the dualism becomes non-dualism, but it is through paradox, *through (as usual in non-dualism) a new (tragic) consciousness*, a spiritual insight into the depth of what is right in front of us. There is a solidity, a Here-I-Stand character, to this Lutheran paradox that Christendom will always need as a mighty fortress against the heavenly prophets, the apocalyptic fanatics (like me) of every stripe. Most important, however (and this is Douglas, not Torrance), is the Antigonean tragedy of paradox in Luther's vision. That rootage in creative and morally earnest, unlegalistic *Angst* must be a permanent presence in all of Christendom. Legalists like me need it especially. When it drops out of the Gospel, both life and the Gospel are impoverished and ultimately trivialized.

But Torrance's Calvin is also needed. The acute awareness of the moral demand that good must transform the world today and conquer evil immediately, in short, the tragedy of transformation as transformed paradoxically by the Gospel, has its proper place as well if the monotheism bird is to keep flying.

4

On Not Swallowing a Metaphor: Karlstadt's Eucharistic Radicalism in 1523-24

In *Karlstadt's Battle with Luther: Documents in a Liberal-Radical Debate*, Ronald J. Sider has made an excellent selection of materials that shed light on the controversy between Luther and Karlstadt when Wittenberg was what I called in Chapter Two an O Little Town of Bethlehem for Protestant worship practices, before the divisions among Roman Catholicism, Lutheranism, Calvinism, and Anabaptism had solidified. In Sider's anthology we have, for example, selections from Karlstadt's "Sermon for the First Evangelical Eucharist" from Christmas, 1521, selections from Luther's attack on such innovations from the spring of 1522, an account of the personal meeting between Luther and Karlstadt in 1524, selections from one of Karlstadt's 1524 defenses of reformatory radicalism and from one of his 1524 eucharistic tracts, and finally selections from Luther's famous response of 1525: *Against the Heavenly Prophets*, along with selections from Karlstadt's *Review of Some of the Chief Articles of Christian Doctrine*, written in 1525 in response to Luther's charge in *Heavenly Prophets* that Karlstadt is so obsessed with eccentric details that he neglects the main points of Christian doctrine. Sider appends to this invaluable collection a discussion of "Karlstadt, Luther, and the Perennial Debate," which argues that, in the perennial debate between liberals and radicals, Luther plays the role of liberal, while Karlstadt is the radical, risking too much action for the sake of taking *some* action in the face of socio-political injustice.[1]

In this chapter I propose to supplement Sider's collection by giving some account of the spirituality of Karlstadt's eucharistic meditations during 1523 and 1524, when he developed and announced his shocking idea that Christ is not physically present during the eucharistic celebration. If The Real Absence still has a place in Christian spirituality today, what shape (or what emptiness?) did it take when Karlstadt risked his life by enunciating it in opposition to vigorous Dr. Luther's emerging spirituality of eucharistic fullness? How did it *feel*, spiritually, to meditate on a eucharistic Christ who was not on the altar or in the bread and wine (as one had been taught since infancy) but in heaven? I stress, as I did in Chapter Two, that I have no wish to dispute the modern and postmodern wisdom of our time that spirituality must have had very little to do with the Reformers' spirituality. They were doubtless more interested than they consciously realized in political, sociological, and psychological tactics and were, much more than (as pre-Marxo, pre-Nietzscheo, pre-Freudo naifs) they could possibly have known, using spiritual talk as a cover for this kind of real-world strategizing. As I say, I have no quarrel with such sophisticated hermeneutics. I only say that it is also fun to study what these Reformers said they thought they were most interested in: spiritual stuff. Hence this chapter's effort to sort through some of the spiritual themes that appear most often in Karlstadt's eucharistic writings of 1523–24. But although the task is interesting and important, the sledding is not always easy. I call to witness Gordon Rupp, who said:

> There is badly needed a full consideration of the eucharistic controversy of the Reformation in the English tongue. We also need a careful monograph on Karlstadt's specific contribution to that great debate. For his writings are obscure and contradictory, while the theme itself abounds in difficulties.[2]

Rupp goes on to remind us that the eucharistic presence had been debated for centuries "and that all manner of spiritualizing alternatives had been put forward by theologians, while among the common people plain, commonsense blasphemies were current in a score of catch-words."[3] Listing "the spiritualism of the Platonist revival, discernible, say, in Erasmus" as a possible background for the eucharistic radicalism of the writings of Wessel Gansfort and the letter of Cornelius Hoen, which was making its way around the cities of the Reformation in the 1520s, Rupp registers his agreement with Hermann Barge when he concludes: "It does not seem likely that Karlstadt was either aware of this teaching or influenced by it."[4] But, for the purposes of this chapter, we may leave aside the important topics of influences on Karlstadt and influences of Karlstadt to ask simply what the man was saying about the eucharist when he first set forth his theology of eucharistic absence.

Karlstadt's first actual statement of that position came in a series of tracts which he published in October–November, 1524, but in December of 1523 Karlstadt published a tract, *Of the Priesthood and Sacrifice of Christ*, which comes so close to asserting eucharistic absence that the assiduous Hermann Barge concluded in 1905 that it actually did make that assertion. Rupp said he found no evidence of eucharistic absence in the tract, however, and I agree with Rupp. What we can say, however, is that this tract of 1523 sets forth the soteriological basis of Karlstadt's 1524 eucharistic radicalism. What does *Von dem Priesterthum* really say?[5]

There are two very different kinds of priest: the priests of the law (who are outward and outwardly anointed) and the priests over the law (who are inward and inwardly anointed) (Aiib-Aiiib). Karlstadt clearly defines "priest" at the outset: "the priest is one who inwardly or outwardly is established by God and men to give offerings and gifts for the sins of the people or also for his own sins to the Lord and God in heaven above" (Aiib). It is important to note the exclusive emphasis on the giving of offerings as the priest's task. Karlstadt uses this definition throughout the treatise to establish the point that no priest since Christ is necessary and in fact that every priest since Christ has given offense to God since he has attempted to give an offering which was already given once and for all by Christ. An "offering" is defined as concisely as a priest: "An offering is a gift which a man brings to the priest so that he might offer it to God for his sins and propitiate him. Or an offering is that which a priest himself takes and brings to God's city and offers to God for his own sins" (Aiib).

Just as there are two kinds of priest, so there are also two kinds of offering. Those of the Old Testament are for the most part unintelligent animals which, since they are guiltless, are offered by the priests to God as a propitiation for the sins of the people (Aiiii). The offerings of the New Testament, however, are intelligent (Aiiiib). Those of the Old Testament were fleshly and although they could be used on a fleshly level, they could not purify the conscience. They could only point in their incompleteness to the complete offering of Christ in the New Testament (Aiiiib).

Christ's offering was complete because, like the animals of the Old Testament, he was without sin but also, unlike the animals of the Old

Testament, he was intelligent. In his intelligence Christ chose to be perfectly obedient to his Father. Karlstadt does not say that Christ was more susceptible to pain in making his offering than were the animals; the difference is that Christ knew the reasons for what he was doing; he knew the meaning of his obedience. Another characteristic trait of Karlstadt's soteriology is evident here in that Christ's offering was alone sufficient for our salvation; all our efforts to save ourselves are useless, and yet we must imitate the obedience of Christ. Since he has already made acceptable "our life, our soul, our spirit, our flesh, our blood, our good will to God" (Bb), we must also be obedient to God and give "our life, our soul, our spirit, our flesh, our blood, and our good will to God" over to Christ the High Priest as our offering. Christ did God's will more fully than any other being: "Therefore is Christ a prince and a head, not alone of priests, but a justification of all offerings in heaven and earth which the angels in heaven or the holy men on earth offer to God" (Bii). Karlstadt refers, in speaking of Christ's offering, to the words of consecration in the Lord's Supper. This is a foreshadowing of his 1524 exegesis of the words of consecration, for Christ in this passage is using the words of consecration in reference to his own crucificxion, not in reference to the elements on the table:

> For Christ has as a highest priest offered to God his Father the best of all and highest offering for our sins and has earned for us forgiveness of all sins and has richly gained it and has sufficiently reconciled us to his Father from whom we were far on account of our sins which cut us off from God. As Christ said, "This is my body which is given for you. This is my blood which is poured out for you for the forgiveness of sins" (Cb).

The association of the forgiveness of sins with the words of institution is familiar from Karlstadt's tracts of 1521, but the application of the words of institution to the crucifixion rather than the supper is new. There is no need to claim that Karlstadt has already developed his famous exegesis of the words of institution as referring exclusively to Christ's own body and not to the elements. But it is striking that he is at least beginning to think in this direction at the end of 1523.

The offerings of Moses, even if they were incomplete, did point by *figura* to the complete offerings of the New Testament in the person of Christ (Cii). "So wonderfully Moses wrote about Christ" (Cii). The food offerings of the Old Testament were a particularly apt *figura* of Christ's offering, Karlstadt says

(Bb). This may be an indication that he is attempting here to work out an understanding of the meaning of Christ's body as a food, the central problem of the move from his 1521 to his 1524 understanding of the eucharist.

In his discussion of the question "whether Christ can often be an offfering" (Ciii-Ciiib), Karlstadt moves a step nearer to an explicit consideration of eucharistic theology as the culmination of his soteriological treatise. This section begins with the curt argument that "The figurative offerings of the Old Testament could not often be offered" (Ciii). The reason was that the offerings were living animals: they could only die once. Karlstadt concludes that the same must be true of Christ: it is "already said of Christ through the figurative offerings of Moses" (Ciii). Hence Karlstadt is using the Old Testament as a figural revelation of Christian verities. Karlstadt works on the principle that the Old Testament is incomplete in itself, but that which fulfills it can only be understood when the fulfilling testament is understood in its figural linkage to the testament which it fulfills.

Karlstadt refers again in this vein to the serpent in the wilderness, a figure of Christ. Since all who looked upon the serpent with faith that they would be healed, were healed, so all who look upon Christ on the cross with faith will be healed (Ciii). Christ, like the living animals of the Old Testament, can only die once, and since he is more complete as an offering to God than they were, he can through his one death redeem all people in past, present, and future times. As Karlstadt puts it elsewhere in the treatise, "For Christ's *Gelassenheit* was higher and purer than all the world's *Ungelassenheit* was, now is, or ever will be" (Cii). In the light of these conclusions, Karlstadt is ready to ask "whether Christ is an offering in daily priestly masses." Karlstadt, like Luther, was able to answer with a resounding No, but Karlstadt's line of defense for his argument is characteristically not the most common. Here also Karlstadt is moving closer to his 1524 understanding of the eucharistic elements as unable to contain the body of Christ.

Karlstadt says, "Neither bread nor wine can take to themselves the powers or gifts of Christ" (D). He argues that the priests have no other sacrifice to make to God than the body and blood of Christ, so they offer that daily, as they believe, in their mass (Civ). In saying that Christ's sacrifice must be daily repeated for daily sins, they contradict all the figures of the Old Testament as well as the words of God and Christ (Civb). Even though it is obvious that Christ did not come as dead bread but as a living being and even though he is not now dead bread but alive in heaven, the priests still try to sacrifice him as a dead creature, namely the bread or the wine (D). If these dead creatures could take the powers or gifts of Christ to themselves, they would be better creatures than the angels (D). These are strong words to use in a battle which had already been carried on in Wittenberg three years previously with much weaker accusations. The question of whether the mass was a sacrifice was not the burning issue in Wittenberg or Orlamünde in 1523. It was certainly not the issue that separated Karlstadt from his erstwhile colleagues: all the Wittenberg reformers had long before agreed to reject the sacrifice-character of the mass.

We must ask whom Karlstadt is attacking. It is undeniable that he could have been far more explicit if he had wanted to announce in this tract that he no longer believed in the phsyical presence of Christ in the eucharist. It is possible, however, that, not untypically, Karlstadt was mapping out his theoretical justification in advance of taking a public stand on a controversial practical issue. For, without going so far as to deny the physical presence, Karlstadt is claiming to be assaulting Catholic doctrine in the spirit of the Wittenberg reform, while actually attacking Luther and by implication setting forth a very different vision of what the Wittenberg reform should be. It is interesting to note the use to which Karlstadt is now putting his observation that the offerings of the New Testament are intelligent. The bread and wine not only are not alive but cannot *know* what is happening to them. This is at present used as an attack on the sacrifical character of the mass, but it is easily convertible (and within a year he would so convert it) into a barrage on the very possibility that Christ would choose to be present in unintelligent creatures like bread and wine (D-Db).

We noted above Karlstadt's interest in the Old Testament food offering as a particualrly good *figura* of Christ's offering. Karlstadt is now able to use that observation also: if the priests are right, Karlstadt argues, in claiming that Christ can be a daily offering in the food of the bread and wine, then the priests are contradicting Moses, the Bible, and the Holy Spirit, for the priests would then be treating food offerings as complete offerings. Actually, though, the food offerings were only powerful *figurae* of Christ's offering, in themselves utterly incomplete. The priests cannot help themselves by citing the Scripture that Christ is a living bread of which we are to partake, because Christ's bread came down from heaven to earth while theirs goes up from earth to heaven (Db). This is another argument of which Karlstadt will make frequent use in the eucharistic tracts of 1524. Its affinity to his distinction in *Von abtuhung der Bylder* between heavenly and earthly signs should also be noted.[6] The distinction between Christ's heavenly body, which is also heavenly bread of which Christians may partake, and the earthly signs of his body, the bread and the wine, which Christians should not mistake for his body, is fundamental to his 1524 understanding of the eucharist. The categories for that distinction are already present in *Von dem priesterthum* even though they are not explicitly used for the purpose of denying the physical presence.

If the priests think they are sacrificing Christ in four hundred devils' houses every day, says our unecumenical Karlstadt, then they must admit that they would also be sacrificing Christ in his heavenly and invisible tabernacle as many times (Diib). (Here is another argument which could soon do double duty as an attack on the sacrifical character of the mass *and* on the physcial presence of Christ in the elements.) The priests make Christ's ascension into nothing (Diii). Attempting to sacrifice Christ day after day for new sins is such an attack on the once-and-for-all justification won by Christ that Kartlstadt considers it as evil as trying to win justification through our own obedience to the law (Diiib). Karlstadt can still use the words "the Lord's bread and blood" to refer to the eucharistic elements, but he stresses that they should be partaken of with an ardent (*herzfreuntliche*) memory of the suffering, death, and offering of Christ, as one might remember a dear brother who redeemed him from death by dying in his place (Diiii). Karlstadt is also familiar with the argument that the church fathers thought of Christ as a sacrifice in the mass. He says that he cannot believe St. Augusstine and St. Ambrose believed the mass to be a sacrifice (Divb). Besides, he says, even if they did, the fathers are not Scripture. Even Peter was able to err and had to be corrected by Paul. Anyone who calls Christ a sacrifice in the mass is, Karlstadt avers, guilty of the death and blood of Christ because he speaks evil of Christ. He thereby is worse than the Corinthians (Eb).

In fact, those who now think they sacrifice Christ must be murderers of Christ, just as Annas, Caiaphas, Judas, and the others were. Just as the devil was a murderer before Christ died, so the priests are Christ's murderers after he died (Eiib). Yet the priests are not the only guilty parties. They would not have performed the masses as sacrifices if the lay people had not offered them money to do so. Every lay person wants to have a priest offer a sacrifice for him. The very word "mass," Karlstadt (incorrrectly) says, means "sacrifice" in Hebrew. Laity and priesthood are both responsible for its reprehensible presence in Christendom (Fb). The continuance of the mass violates the *figurae* given to both Abraham and Moses (Fiib-Fiii). It is an offense to God, a devilish confession that the sacrifce made by Christ was insufficient (Fiv). A broken and a contrite spirit is the offering God has found well pleasing (Fii).

In our lives, not in masses, we are to attempt to hear Christ (Fiiib). No love and obedience can be greater for us than his (Fiiib).

Von dem Priesterthum und opffer Christi ties together Karlstadt's 1521–early 1522 concern with the practical reform of the mass and his 1523 concern with Gelassenheit. It blends the practical and the contemplative. And, as was Karlstadt's custom, it does so by means of an extended reflection on the meaning of Christ's life for the Christian's life. Hermann Barge was incorrect to conclude that Karlstadt had already announced his new, 1524-type understanding of the eucharist in *Von dem Priesterthum*, but, perhaps more importantly, Barge was almost right, for Karlstadt did develop in this treatise the soteriological basis for that later radicalism. In this respect Barge was closer to the mark than interpreters such as Gordon Rupp who have seen the October–November 1524 eucharistic tracts as sudden developments. Since Luther first accused Karlstadt of rashness, it has been common to say that Karlstadt took action more seriously than theory. But the fact that Karlstadt could have laid the logical foundation of his new doctrine of the eucharist in print by late 1523 and yet could resist a public announcement of its practical application (that Christ is not physically present in the eucharist) until October of 1524 (only after Luther publicly attacked him) does not argue for rashness. At the very least it would oblige us to admit that in eucharistic thology in 1523-24 Karlstadt's thought preceded his acts. The development of his eucharistic ideas at this time was slow and quiet, but it was a major development.

After accepting Luther's challenge to attack him in print, Karlstadt published a series of eucharistic treatises in October–November, 1524, that sound very violent indeed in the ecumenical world of 1990s American Christendom. Yet, in basing his arguments for the eucharistic absence on a figural typological argument, Karlstadt is a pioneer of that very Puritanism which, acccording to Sacvan Bercovitch, lies at the origin of "the American self." Bercovitch himself does not trace Puritan figural typology to Karlstadt, but Karlstadt's eucharistic tracts of 1524 suggest that Karlstadt is in fact proceeding along the lines that Bercovitch has associated with, not only American Puritanism (that would hardly be surprising), but, more importantly, Puritan Americanism.[7]

Following the order in which Barge placed the tracts, *Ob man mit heyliger schrifft erweysen müge* comes first in the series. Its method is distinctive in that it introduces each of its seven major portions with an argument *against* the view Karlstadt is defending. As usual, Karlstadt does not name the individuals who defend each argument he seeks to refute.

The first argument against himself, says Karlstadt, is the citation of I Corinthians 10:16 to mean that the cup of blessing is a consecrated cup containing Christ's blood and the bread a consecrated bread containing Christ's body (Aii). They say that Christ's word is powerful: God brought heaven and earth into being simply by speaking his word. Christ's word is surely powerful enough to make the cup which he calls the communion of his blood into his blood, and so also with the bread and his body (Aiib).

Karlstadt cites in response I Corinthians 11:29: that he is guilty of the death of the Lord who does not properly *discern* the Lord's body (Aiii). One must properly remember the death of the Lord: his love, his sinlessness, his great understanding, his power, the will of his father, and his obedience to that will even to the point of pouring out his own blood (Aiii-Aiiib). Characteristically, Karlstadt places much emphasis on the "understanding" Christ possessed and on his obedience. Immediately afterward, he puts a parallel emphasis on the need that one *understand* Christ's death properly. The right recognition or knowledge (*erkänntnuss*) of the Lord's body and blood is as important in Karlstadt's new doctrine of 1524 as it was in 1521. This proper understanding naturally brings a giving over of our soul, a washing away of our sins (Aiiib). Words of blessing are not the same as words of consecration, Karlstadt continues (B). The priests are unable to make anything holy because their heart is far from what they are doing (Bb). Nothing in the prophets, Moses, or the gospels or apostles supports their understanding of what it means to make something holy (Bb). Christ's word, to be sure, is powerful, as Paul teaches, but where does it give priests the power to bring Christ back down from heaven? (Bb-Bii). Even though the lists of their powers include baptizing, preaching, healing, forgiving sins which were committed against them, driving out devils, and teaching, nowhere in the Bible are priests given the power to change bread and wine into Christ's body and blood (Bii-Biib).

Nor does it help them to claim that Christ changed himself into bread and wine the night he was betrayed and thereby passed the same power to his apostles: for they cannot prove that he performed that change (Biib). Even if he had, the apostles did not receive all of Christ's powers. They were unable, for instance, to drive out the most obstinate devils (Biib). Furthermore, the priests have less faith than the apostles did. Far from receiving more powers than the apostles received, the priests did not even receive so many. It is not known, Karlstadt says curtly, that our priests have used Christ's words to heal a deaf or blind person (Biiib). Another argument which becomes highly important for Karlstadt is that God's and Christ's miracles were performed openly, but the priests' "miracle" is performed secretly. Hence its authenticity must be held suspect (Biii). God's use of his word to create heaven and earth and Christ's use of his word to raise Lazarus were profoundly different miracles from any the priests have performed lately (Biv). When they give up on their argument about the blessing as a powerful word of consecration, the priests claim the words "communion of the Lord's blood" in their favor (Biv). They neglect, however, that cup and wine are two different things. By their argument it is the cup itself which should become Christ's blood, not the wine, a clearly absurd idea. Karlstadt acknowledges that he is aware of the figure of speech by which the container can stand for the thing contained ("*continens capitur pro contento*"), but if the priests will grant that Paul is using a figure of speech in speaking of the cup, Karlstadt will tell them what the figure of speech really means (Biv-Bivb): when Paul refers to our communion with the cup of blessing, he means our "society" with Christ. We cannot have society with such soulless creatures as a piece of bread and a cup, and therefore it would have served no purpose for Christ to change himself into them (Bivb). Having community requires intelligent creatures with whom to have the community. Paul is using bread and cup in a figurative sense in order to stress that we are all members one of another in Christ and that we must understand our communion with him properly (C).

No one should think of Christ's cup as blood without remembering the blood poured out on the cross. The apostles preached Christ crucified; none of them spoke of the bread and cup except as bread and cup of remembrance. To be participants in Christ's "bread" we must be mindful not of something that happens in a sacrament but of his body on the cross (I Corinthians 10:21) (Cb). Anything less is something other than Christ's body. Paul said that you cannot drink both out of the Lord's and the devils' cup and participate at both tables (Cii).

The second argument Karlstadt thinks could be raised against himself would cite Christ's words "This cup is the new testament in my blood which is poured out for you." Christ's words are clear and need no interpretation: he has said that the cup contains his blood (Cii). Karlstadt begins his response to this objection by discussing the word "testament." A testament is a last will. This will is an inward thing: therefore, it cannot be an outward thing such as a cup (Civb). Both Matthew and Mark speak of the blood of Christ and the New Testament, but these two are not identical, any more than the robe of Christ and Christ could be identical. Matthew and Mark are distinguishing between what is *of* Christ and what *is* Christ. The New Testament is of Christ, and hence of Christ's blood, but it is not identical with Christ or his blood (D).

Furthermore, Christ had his disciples drink of the cup *before* his supposed transformation of the wine into blood: according to Mark's account the disciples would already have drunk the wine before Christ made the transformation. What then would the transformation have to do with the cup? (Ciii-Ciiib). Christ's testament was his inner will. His blood had not yet been shed on the night of the last supper, and therefore he had not yet fulfilled his last will and testament. Therefore, he could not have delivered the will or the blood to the disciples at the supper. When Christ referred at the supper to the blood of his last will, which would be poured out for the forgiveness of sins, he was referring not at all to the cup out of which they were drinking wine but to the very blood which had been promised figuratively by Moses and the prophets when they carried out their incomplete Old Testament offerings and said that someday the incomplete offerings would be completed perfectly (Ciiib; Db).

The fact that Christ had not yet poured out his blood in death when he met with the disciples at the supper explains why Paul said to proclaim the Lord's *death* whenever you partake of this meal. It was only through Christ's death *the next day* that the will of Christ was fulfilled. Any other interpreteation runs directly counter to the figures of Moses and the prophets (Dii). If, on the basis of figural arguments, an objector were to say that Moses sprinkled *real blood* on the animals and the people in the Old Testament, and hence Christ must have used real blood in announcing his last will to the apostles, Karlstadt would respond, he says, that, to keep all things parallel in the *figurae*, Christ's blood would need to be visibly blood in the cup rather than only blood under the appearance of wine, for the blood Moses sprinkled was visibly blood (Diib).

Karlstadt sums up his argument in three points. (1) The believer should remember first the inner will of Christ, his will to suffer all that his Father demanded for a sufficient sacrifice (Diib-Diii). (2) Out of this inner will flows the outward blood of Christ. Christ was an honest man: he outwardly fulfilled what he inwardly willed. So, as a testator, he died only once, on the cross, and there he perfectly fulfilled his inner will to be obedient to his Father for man's sake (Diii-Diiib). (3) Christ often said that we must eat his flesh and drink his blood, but there is a vast difference between his real body and the cup and bread at the supper. It is the former of which we are to partake. Christ nowhere says that we are required to partake of his sacrament (Div).

Many have been saved without partaking of the fleshly sacrament (e.g. the angels) (Divb). In fact, the outward cup could pass away, and another outward remembrance would come in its place, equally adequate for Christ's purpose (Divb). Nor can the priests help themselves by denying that they believe Christ's body and blood *are* the elements of consecrated blood and wine. Claiming that they only believe the body and blood to be present "under" or "in" or "under the form of" the elements will do them no good since by such a device they change the clear words of Scripture, which do not say Christ was "under" or "in" or "under the form of" his bread and cup. Scripture makes an identification between the body and the bread. The only possible way to understand this identification correctly is to reach the proper interpretation of what Christ means by his body and his bread (E).

The third argument Karlstadt raises against himself is that the word *eucharistia* suggests a transformation of the substance of bread and wine into the substance of Christ's body and blood. Christ took the bread and "blessed" it and through this blessing made it into his body (Eb). Since Karlstadt has already discussed the concept of "blessing" in his discussion of I Corinthians 10:16, he can handle this argument with relative ease. He repeats his point that, if a blessing automatically effects a transubstantiation, Christ must have entered the pieces of bread he blessed before giving them to the crowd, when he fed the five thousand and the four thousand (Eiii). This time he adds that Christ must have changed himself into the dead Lazarus when he raised him from the dead after saying a blessing (Eiii). He also adds that when Paul says in I Timothy 4 that we should give thanks for all our food, Paul must mean that all food is Christ's body and blood as soon as it is blessed (Eiib).

The fourth possible argument is to cite Paul's words: "I have received of the Lord what I give to you" (Eiii). The entire passage introduced by these words (I Corinthians 11:23ff.) stresses the power and seriousness of Christ's institution of the supper. The Corinthians treated the meal disrespectfully, and Paul had to cite the power and seriousness of it because it was the sacrament of Christ's body and blood. Christ said to do this in his memory, and Karlstadt notes Christ's promise (John 14:12) that those who believe in him will be able to do yet greater things than he does. Hence they will be able to do what he did and commanded them to do in his memory: bring his body and blood into the elements (Eiiib-Eiiii).

Karlstadt grants at the outset that Paul was indeed urging the Corinthians to be more serious about the supper. He was telling them above all, however, not anything about the transformation of the elements but to partake of the meal with good Christian morals (Eiiii). When Christ in this passage refers to the breaking of the bread and the giving of it, however, he is referring to his own suffering and death. It would have been meaningless for him to speak of the suffering and death of an outward piece of bread (Eiiii). Christ is referring to *what is going to happen the next day*, when he will be crucified. Christ also refers during the supper to his betrayal, but he had not yet been betrayed when he referred to it: he was referring, again, to what was *going* to happen (Eiiiib). When Christ said "this" is my body, the word "this" referred to his body, which would be crucified, and Paul cited this passage especially to make it clear that no host, no outward bread, or other object should be confused with Christ's one wholly sufficient body which went to the cross (Eiiiib). Here it is very imporant to note that it is not until nearly the end of his treatise that Karlstadt uses this notorious exegesis of the word "this." It is also important to observe that Karlstadt has moved into this exegesis from many laboriously developed theological starting points. It is by no means the sole support for his new understanding of the Lord's Supper.

Karlstadt frequently cites John the Baptist soon after using his "this" exegesis: when Jesus pointed at his own body at the Lord's supper, he was performing an act of prophecy as John had done when he had said (John 1:29), "Behold the lamb of God." Karlstadt frequently cites this passage in connection with Christ's words at the supper to show that both are prophecies of the perfect sacrifice of Jesus Christ. Yet since Christ had not yet been crucified when John the Baptist called him the lamb of God, Christ was not yet, strictly speaking, the lamb of God. He would become that sacrifical lamb only on the cross. Christ's figural prophecy at the supper is the same kind of statement as John the Baptist's, a specification of the meaning of a future event.

Karlstadt says that the priests generally understand that Christ was making a prophecy and a promise in the words of institution, but they forget that this was the *last* such prophecy and promise, for it was in fact fulfilled the next day when Christ was crucified. Hence it is no longer available to us to repeat as a prophecy (and therefore to use in order to bring Christ into the creaturely elements of the mass). It was a prophecy, a *figura*, which like those of Moses, Isaiah, and John the Baptist, *had* to be fulfilled once and for all. It had to be fulfilled because God would be a liar if it were not. Once it was fulfilled perfectly by Christ, the prophecy could never be repeated as an unfulfilled prophecy but only as a fulfilled prophecy. That was exactly why, Karlstadt believed, Paul placed so much emphasis on the proper "discernment" of the Lord's body. He wanted us to discern the difference between the fleshly elements which, like Old Testament offerings, came from the earth up and Christ's true body, which alone came from heaven down.

The fifth argument rests on the text John 6:51. The priests could argue that Christ is referring here to the bread of the mass (Fii). In response, Karlstadt distinguishes between the outward flesh and Christ's heavenly, Lordly flesh. If the priests really think Christ is referring to his outward, earthly flesh when he says that he is the living bread which came down form heaven, then they would have to hold that the outward, earthly elements of bread and wine *are* the essence of Christ in the mass, and they do not hold this view: they only say that the outward, earthly elements *contain* Christ's flesh. Hence Christ could not have been speaking of his outward, earthly flesh when he said that he was the living bread which came down from heaven. Therefore, the papists cannot use this passage in support of their thesis about outward, earthly flesh (Fiib).

Christ's flesh suffered for us when Christ suffered for us, but where does Scripture say that the outer, visible bread suffered in the form of the sacrament? Just as the old fathers in the wilderness with Moses died when they ate of the heavenly bread, so they die who eat of the sacramental bread, for they fail to discern the true body of Christ properly. If the eating of the sacramental bread were necessary, it would necessarily follow that even the angels need to eat it, that no one can be saved without it, that the sacramental bread has replaced Christ as our redeemer and savior, that a soulless creature (the sacramental bread) is better than all the angels and saints, and that the sacramental bread was received in Mary's womb (which even the papists deny) (Fiib-Fiii). Finally, if Christ's heavenly bread were in fact the sacramental bread, Christ himself would be of no use to us either in the sacrament or out of it (Fiii). Partaking of Christ's flesh is indeed necessary, but this is not an eating with teeth: for Christ himself says in the same chapter of John that the flesh is not needful. It is alone the partaking of Christ's heavenly flesh in communion with Christ which is needful (Fiii-Fiiib).

Citing with approval the Augustinian principle "Believe and you have partaken," Karlstadt confesses that he himself did not formerly understand this doctrine correctly and at that time wrote a bad book defending the adoration of the sacramental bread (Fiiii). Now he believes that the adoration of the sacramental bread is as senseless as trusting in the robe of Christ rather than in Christ himself. Furthermore, we should base our understanding not on Karlstadt, he explains, but only on the justification and truth of God (Fiiii).

The sixth argument is that Christ lived in two ways: one in poverty and misery, the other in Lordship, the former according to his mortal flesh, the latter according to his resurrection. His sacramental flesh, so the argument goes, is neither of these but a middle state, as purgatory is a middle state between heaven and hell (Fiiii). Karlstadt confidently says that this argument deserves a laugh. In response to it he returns to his argument that Christ always acted openly. Why should he at the supper alone have acted secretly? All the events of Christ's life were open, revealed. Why should Christ (and the prophets) not have revealed this important secret? No one is able to say that he saw Christ in the sacrament, but Christ was indeed seen on the cross. If Christ were secretly lodged in the sacrament, we could neither seek him out nor follow him. Christ was once on the cross and now is in heaven. The idea of a secret middle-level presence in the sacrament is contrary to the honor of Christ (Fiiiib).

The seventh argument permits Karlstadt to choose the conclusion which he can handle most easily. It is by no means an attack on the doctrine of *sola fide*, but Karlstadt's response to the seventh argument against him does permit him to attack the extraordinary claims which he thought were being made in some (Wittenberg?) quarters for faith alone. For the seventh argument against Karlstadt states that the words "This is my body which is given for you" are a promise, and faith in the promise can allow the body of Christ to enter the elements. Faith in the promise of Christ can make all things happen (Fiiiib).

Karlstadt's answer depends on a few of his familiar distinctions. The words of institution were indeed a promise when they were spoken, but now they are no longer a promise, for they have already been fulfilled. If for eternity we could continue to treat these words as a promise, we would never allow them to be fulfilled, hence never allowing the gospel to be proclaimed. Now that the words in which Christ's body was promised to his apostles have been fulfilled (on the cross), the words are no longer promise but proclamation of the Gospel (Fv). Furthermore, even if these words were not now a proclamation of the Gospel and were still a promise, faith in the promise would not be sufficient to bring about its fulfillment. For there is a difference between words that affirm and words that promise. The Gospel is a word that affirms. "This is my body" is now not a promise but an affirmation (Fv). Finally, we must recall that even Moses could not do all things through faith in a promise (Fvb). No one can do all things through faith in a promise. As a parting blast, Karlstadt reminds his readers that Christ in making the promise was not promising anything about what his apostles would do with his words but what he alone would do with them (Fvi). Karlstadt's closing statement, as in many of his other treatises, is an expression of the wish that anyone who could find further Scripture to raise against his views would tell him about it (Fvi).

The next eucharistic treatise in Barge's list, *Dialogus oder ein gesprechbüchlin*, is more clearly aimed at an audience of lay people than was the foregoing tract, but it too is exceedingly intricate. Karlstadt reveals at the beginning his sensitivity to the charge that he is developing such a new understanding of the Lord's Supper merely for novelty's sake (7). Among such accusers he names the "learned in Scripture" and their princes, who mislead the common people (7). A bold indictment of the authorities in Wittenberg, the entire tract makes no effort to hide a strain of anti-clericalism. Karlstadt holds, of course, that his new doctrine of the eucharist is being developed not for the sake of novelty but for the sake of truth and eternity (7).

Karlstadt feels that he must combat the misuse of all outward signs, no matter how well-intentioned their users may be. God has now cancelled out signs. Even the serpent in the wilderness, symbol of the Christ to be raised up, had to be destroyed by Hezekiah. The people become confused by signs: they think the sacrament contains the suffering of Christ or forgives sins or allows Christ to be always with them (8). Karlstadt warns that no one should imagine that he is any less serious in this tract just because he has chosen the dialogue form in which to write it (9). The dialogue is expanded after Peter the layman enters it part-way through, but the characters who open it are Victus, a confused but devout layman, and Gemser, a priest who reluctantly learns during the dialogue to have more respect for peasant theology.

When Gemser sees that Victus is downcast, he seeks to help the layman. Victus is worried about the sacraments. Gemser attempts to summarize the seven sacraments to Victus, but Victus protests that he knows nothing about this. Since Nehemiah said that God has well chosen his words, Victus wants to know whether such a word as sacrament appears in the Scripture. If so, he wants a good biblical definition of it (10). When Gemser admits that "sacrament" is not in the Bible, explaining that not all words need to be there, since God gave Adam the power to name every creature, Victus objects that the church should not be given Adam's power of naming (10). Furthermore, Victus does not seem convinced by Gemser's insistence that we have the same powers as Adam had (11). This point is allowed to drop, in favor of a discussion of the sacramental bread which, Gemser has discovered, is the true object of Victus's worry. Victus says that he does not see how Christ could be present according to his divinity in all creatures (11). Nor can he imagine how Christ could be as big in the host as he was on the cross (12). He has searched the Scriptures but can find no answer. When Gemser tells Victus that he should not take it upon himself to search the Scriptures in this way, Victus explains that he thought he was supposed to test false prophets.

It is no help to Victus when Gemser assures him that the bread itself does not become Christ: the bread is made into nothing by the priests, leaving only the form of the bread. Within it is the Lord's body. Victus says that this should not be called *sacramentum*, he has heard, but *fermentum phariseorum*(11). The conversation next moves to the words of institution and Victus's interest in Gemser's qualifications to interpret them. He gets Gemser to admit that he knows Greek, Hebrew, and Latin "in need," as Gemser puts it. Victus insists that this is a case of sufficient need, for Victus cannot see how "This is my body" can stand alone in the scriptural text (13). It seems to him that since the word "this" begins with a capital letter, it and the words following it constitute an independent sentence with an independent meaning. He admits that he may be wrong, since he does not know Greek, but when he asks Gemser to read the Greek to him and translate it, Gemser protests that the lay people standing around might overhear them (14).

Gemser's fears are justified, for the layman Peter now enters the discussion. He says he is not familiar with this word "*touto*" which Gemser is using (15). When Gemser finally explains a little about the demonstrative, Peter says that he thought the word "this" referred to Christ's own body rather than the bread, although, he admits, he does not know Greek (16-17). It is possible that Karlstadt is again illustrating the contention that there are not only grammatical but also theological reasons for his this-exegesis. In any case, when Gemser asks Peter who taught him this interpretation, Peter gives a notoriously cryptic answer: the spirit, whose voice he hears. When Gemser says he would like to have been taught by that spirit, Peter responds by asking Gemser whether he is not the poor man who gives creaturely form to God's living voice. Does he have a burning wish for justice as justice and does he not wish to understand what the Greek text means? Gemser is thus encouraged to continue the discussion, Peter proffering his demonstration for his own view of the "this": he says that if the sacrificial suffering had occurred in the bread, then the bread was a necesary place for it and it could not have occurred on the cross without first occurring in the bread, which is patently false (17).

If Christ had suffered in the bread, he would have had to suffer secretly there, which is contrary to Scripture. If he had suffered in the bread, then it was not on the cross that he gave himself for us, but it would be for the priests to accomplish his sacrifice in the bread. The baker's bread would have to be the body which Scripture says is given for us, another travesty of Scripture. Gemser does not see why Peter was so happy when he discovered the meaning of the Greek if he already knew all this. Peter's answer: that even though the outward witness is not needful to him who has the testimony of the spirit in his inwardness, he can use it in argument (17). Peter explains that the Spirit to which he is referring is the Comforter which the apostles received and went on to preach outwardly. When Gemser protests that this gift was received by the apostles, not necessarily by us (18), Peter answers that St. Peter had testified that Cornelius had received the same Spirit as he. The Spirit alone leads us into an understanding of the kingdom of God. They are not Christians who do not have the Spirit. When Gemser asks why Peter had not revealed this teaching of the Spirit earlier, Peter explains that the Spirit had not sufficiently driven him to do so. A fire has to grow up within one. Impressed by Peter's seriousness, Gemser confesses that the phrase in the words of institution is in fact set off by quotation marks, a further possible confirmation of Peter's exegesis (19).

After getting Gemser to admit that he cannot yet bring anything against Peter's exegesis, Peter goes on to discuss the proper "discernment" of the Lord's body. The priests, he says, eat the bread like pigs. They kill Christ. Gemser, offended, is not allowed to resist the charge. Peter says he cannot believe that Gemser considers himself "Paulinian" without knowing what Paul meant by the proper discernment of the Lord's body (20-21). Peter notes that when wise people eat the food of a great lord at his own table, they are not afraid of the food but of the lord. The Pope puts all emphasis on teeth and food, thereby stealing God's honor from him, because he places Christ's suffering under the *gestalt* of the bread, concluding from the bread (rather than from God and Christ) that God is merciful to him. The Pope makes us remember the bread but not the cross. At this, Gemser has to wonder whether or not Peter has in fact been taking the sacrament under the Pope's ordinance for very long. Peter says that he has not taken it for twenty years (22).

The Pope lifts the bread so high in the air that everyone gets worried about *it* instead of the cross. Gemser is willing to grant that it is the recollection that makes one worthy, but Peter asks what recollection. Recollection of the sacrament? of the *gestalt*? or of Christ? Gemser says that all his life he has heard that preparation to receive the sacrament and prepartion to receive the body of Christ are the same thing (23). Peter points out, however, that Christ always left one place when he went to another, and when he said that he must leave in order that the Comforter might come, Christ was making it clear that he was going to heaven. Gemser, however, cannot understand what Christ meant when he said (John 6) that we must eat his flesh if in fact his flesh could not be made available to us. Peter explains that Christ had one intention when he made this statement and another when he gave the bread at the last supper. Eating the flesh of Christ has nothing to do with eating sacramental bread: it is "an inward taste…of the suffering of Christ" (24). Karlstadt characteristically can have Peter cite Isaiah to prove his assertion: according to Isaiah 53 one cannot be justified apart from the action of Christ And the sacramental bread is very different from the activity of Christ (24).

Gemser says that the word *sacramentaliter* answers many questions. Peter, however, answers that the God-fearing speak *spiritualiter*. "Spiritually we must eat the flesh of the Lord. Sacramentally it is no more useful than the natural outward flesh of Christ" (25). When Gemser asks what we must do to receive Christ's body spiritually, Peter says that we must let go and do nothing. We must have only "a fervent memory of the given-over body of Jesus Christ" (25). There is no substitute for having the right memory of Christ's body. The sacrament provides the wrong memory. At Gemser's request for Scripture citations on this "memory," Peter states that although it is cited many times, the best reference is I Corinthians 11. We are to remember the Lord's death as often as we eat worthily of his bread (25).

Gemser still has reservations. What about the little word "broken"? How could spiritual bread be broken? Peter handles this problem quickly: citing first the Old Testament tradition that not a bone in the Lord's body should be broken, he goes on to say that one can have a "broken" heart and this does not refer to anything outward or physical. Finally, Christ could hardly have broken his own body when he broke the bread. Gemser insists that there were two different essences in Christ, one in the sacrament and the other not. Peter has an anti-clerical zinger for that one: then there must be two Christs, one for you priests and one for us laymen, ours on the cross! (26) But Peter has yet more demonstrations. Christ did not break himself without the use of anyone else's hands: he certainly could not have broken himself by himself in the bread and still have fulfilled the prophecies about the manner of his death. No apostle writes that Christ broke himself in the bread (27).

Gemser still has more problems, however. What is meant by this word "discern" in I Corinthians 11:29? The church's teaching is that forgiveness of sins can be found in the sacrament when one has properly confessed. If one eliminated confession, how could sins be forgiven? This is one of Karlstadt's favorite points to answer. Peter, not surprisingly, attacks it with similar gusto. Secret words and secret changes in a piece of bread cannot forgive sins (29) any more than the Pope's letters of indulgence could. They give a false peace and security to the people and nothing at all to God. At the mention of indulgences the name of Luther comes up. Peter has a curt opinion about that individual: his followers are more attached to him than to the truth. Luther broadly blocks them from the truth (29).

Gemser's weak protest has already been heavily battered by Peter even before Gemser makes it. Cannot the fact that Christ's body is in the bread forgive sins? Peter repeats that such a theory would detract from the suffering of Christ on the cross. Showing signs of retreat, Gemser says he thinks the priests are wrong to put the bread in monstrances, for what they ascribe to the sacrament they take from Christ (30). The battle is not yet over, however. When Gemser regrets that there has been so much talk about the sacrament, which is after all only an outward thing that cannot cure us or make us holy, pious, better, just, or free, Peter calls his wavering convert a Proteus. At this point, Gemser, referring to Haggai 2:12, admits that the priests try to call themselves holy by taking what is God's. They have not a letter of Scripture to support them: Christ says that we need to love him even more than father and mother, and yet the priests love a little creature like bread more than Christ (31). Gemser is remarkably close to seeing the light!

Peter summarizes his doctrine briefly. Gemser says it is frightening when Peter shows that the priests' unworthy eating makes them guilty of the body and blood of Christ (32). Gemser concludes that it would be better to hold back entirely from taking the sacrament than to eat of the bread of the Lord incorrectly. Gemser, giving a list of the topics on which he wants to learn more, a list so extensive that it covers almost every detail of Christology, now finds it hideous that the priests try to bring Christ into a little piece of grain when Paul said that the supper should be partaken of only according to an exact memory of Christ's own prescription for it (33).

It is an indication of the intensity of debate over the meaning of Christian worship at this time that even after he has reached this height of conviction Gemser (and dear reader) still stands still for fifteen pages' worth of further convincing, and that Peter is so ready to oblige him. Peter says he has an answer to the objection that Christ's word gives priests the power to bring him by magic into the bread: if it did, then Moses' word must have given us power to make heaven and earth, and, in fact, Moses must have made all creatures when he began to describe the creation of the heavenly and earthly kingdoms. No,

Christ pointed to his own body when he spoke the words "This is my body" in order to show us that no other body or creature would take our sins upon himself in suffering as he alone was about to do (34).

This idea raises another doubt in Gemser's mind: Gemser points out that Christ blessed the bread. When Peter explains that this merely means that Christ thanked God, Gemser persists in believing that Christ used a special power in the blessing in order to put his body into the sacramental bread. Peter, however, considers that he has already won this argument about the power of certain words. When Gemser explains that he has three grounds for his argument and can move from one if it falters to another, Peter calls him a born sophist and cheater. Nevertheless, Gemser enumerates his grounds: (1) Jesus took the bread and blessed it; (2) this is my body which is given for you; (3) this do in my memory. Peter fails to understand how these grounds support the priests (35).

With regard to the blessing, Peter asks what words were used in it. After all, Jesus gave a blessing, a thanksgiving, when he raised Lazarus. Such a thing was not unique to the supper. Peter believes Gemser should know exactly what words Christ used in the blessing if these words were powerful enough to put him into the bread (36). And, as one more argument for good measure, Peter points out that whenever Christ went to a mountain, he always left a valley: i.e., Christ always left one place when he went to another. How could he have gone into the bread without leaving the place where he was when he gave the blessing? (36-37). Furthermore, Christ said, referring to his ascent into heaven, "I go and will come again." He made it clear that when he leaves one place to go to another, he truly leaves, and when he returns, he truly returns, as he will on the last day. Gemser agrees that this is true "naturally," but "sacramentally" and "supernaturally" Christ can be in many places (37).

When Peter gets Gemser to admit that he can cite no Scripture for this contention, he says Gemser is a liar and the whole crowd is lying (a possibility for which Peter can inded cite Scripture, Leviticus 4 and Exodus 19). Peter does not see how these words of blessing or thanksgiving, words which the priests do not even know, can be used to force Christ into the sacrament. Besides, Paul in I Timothy 4 uses the word "blessing" as a common customary act for all sorts of foods. Hence, Peter concludes, Gemser's first ground is a shadowy one (37).

Gemser is eager to move on to his second ground. "This is my body," retorts Peter, is contrary to your view. For the priests do not say that Chirst *is* the sacramental bread but that he is "under" or "in" the bread, thus making an addition to Scripture. Gemser was not aware that it is a sin to make an addition to Scripture. Peter assures him that it is a great sin (37). Peter will even grant that the words about the cup as the new testament in Christ's blood (I Corinthians 11:25) would be a better ground for Gemser than would the words of institution. Peter says Gemser should perhaps try with faith to see the blood "in" the cup. Gemser, however, confesses that he sees the cup but not the blood. Gemser would rather return to thinking about the bread. Peter finds no scriptural warrant whatever for Gemser's understanding of the sacramental bread (as Gemser should have noticed by this time). The bread the baker bakes, Peter concludes, was not born of Mary's flesh, nor was it given over to death (38-9).

Gemser is now ready to try his third ground: This do in my memory (I Corinthians 11:24). It is perhaps understandable that Peter (not to mention the reader) should be somewhat exasperated when this ground is proffered. Peter has already had a good deal to say about the proper remembrance of the Lord's body. Peter's first response (like the reader's perhaps) is to break into a rage: he castigates the priests for their corruption, and the *doctores* are no better. Gemser calmly reasons that he knows his Christ has given this power. Peter says, "O, poor blindness..." (39).

Peter reiterates the Karlstadtian insistence that the remembrance refers to the Lord's death on the cross; it is this that is to be proclaimed as often as we eat the Lord's flesh and drink his cup. Nothing about sacramental bread is to be either remembered or proclaimed (39). Understandably, Gemser wants to move along. He has the nerve to bring up the thanksgiving again. Peter gives his familiar response: Gemser must in that case imagine then that Christ also changed into his own body the bread which the apostles gave him for feeding the crowd (39).

It is indicative of a certain eccentric strength of the controversy-method of theologial thought, however, that, for all its repetitiveness, it does sometimes bring new insights to a familiar argument when the old argument is re-introduced in a new polemical context. For instance, Karlstadt now for the first time in the *Dialogus* gives a strong theological reason for rejecting the idea of words of blessing as occasions for transubstantiation. Whereas he had, in his previous references to the blessing spoken over the pieces of bread at the feeding of the crowds, merely dismissed as absurd the idea that Christ then changed himself into bread, he now gives his theological reason for judging this possibility absurd: Christ would in this case have given his body over in sacrifice on many occasions previous to the crucifixion. Admittedly, this is no great systematic advance beyond the insights contained in the this-exegesis itself, but it is one small gathering together of diverse insights which previously might have been felt but were not stated. It comes from a different direction at the important Karlstadtian point that the real issue in the quarel over eucharistic presence is eucharistic sacrifice. Either the sacrifice occurred once and for all on the cross, or it did not. Karlstadt's controversy-method of thinking may not be an overtly systematic method, but it does have a snowball-like power to gather up a great diversity of corollaries in the service of its central theorem. The problem is that sometimes the snowall becomes a bit heavy.

Peter further batters Gemser's third ground by showing (again) that the priests do not have the same powers as Christ had and that whereas Christ did all things and spoke all things openly, the priests speak their words of consecration secretly. If Christ changed himself into the bread by speaking the words of blessing, then the priests must change themselves into the bread by speaking the words of blessing. Now the conversation has come back to Victus's level. Victus is still concerned about the same thing that had bothered him at the beginning of the dialogue: how can the flesh born of the mother and crucified on the cross, large as it was, fit into the little bread? Gemser's *opportet credere* does not satisfy Victus, who somehow has had occasion to master enough Latin to say "Maledictus qui credit verbis mendacij" (40).

When Victus asks to be shown the free and luminous words of God on this matter, Gemser says that since Victus is not a priest, he cannot know the powerful words of consecration. This clerical superiority is too much for Victus. He enumerates the three things he needs to ask about: (1) how Christ, who has one *gestalt* in heaven and had another on the cross, can be brought from heaven into the sacrament by priests and monks in such a way that he is as big in the sacrament as he was on the cross; (2) the meaning of "words of consecration;" and (3) the meaning of "host" (41). Gemser starts with the last. The host is a bread which the priests bless and which receives the body of Christ. Victus, predictably, does not understand. When Gemser explains that the priests have been given the power to do this, Peter gives an enumeration of the powers biblically conveyed to the apostles and finds no mention of the power to bring Christ down from heaven. He can only conclude that poor Gemser is a cheater (41). Gemser asks whether Christ, then, is supposed to stay up in heaven eternally. Peter retorts that when Christ will come down from heaven, sacraments and all outward things will pass away. Gemser has heard this argument before: it refers to the "open advent," the last coming, but Christ's coming in the sacrament is of a different nature: it is secret.

Here is another argument with which Peter is familiar. He replies that if Christ comes to the priests secretly in the sacrament, he must either be ashamed of his future coming or afraid of the priests. In fact, Peter judges, Christ must come so secretly to the priests that they are not sure whether he comes at all. Peter, like Victus in this instance, holds that no priest can claim that Christ exists in the sacrament in the same proportions as those with which he existed on the cross, another point which one might think had been adequately covered heretofore. Gemser admits that he has held many masses but never felt Christ come from heaven in a secret mode. He wants Scripture on that. Peter cites Acts 1:10ff. to show that Christ will come visibly just as he departed visibly. Peter is certain that the apostles did not hope for Christ in their bread. Peter also cites Matthew 16:22ff., where one is enjoined not to believe those who say that Christ is here or there: when Christ comes, he will come obviously and clearly. This argument is related to Karlstadt's emphasis on the obviousness, the luminosity, of Scripture, a theme he shared with Luther.

Gemser, however, cannot accept Matthew 16:22ff. as an attack on his concept of the sacramental coming of Christ, for he is certain that it applies to the other coming (42). Peter, somewhat gratuitously, warns Gemser not to start talking about three comings of Christ. Christ will stay in heaven until the day when all things end (cf. Acts 4:21) (43). Gemser does not see why Peter cannot believe that Christ has the power to be present in ten thousand places at once if he wants to. Peter says he does believe that Gemser and the priest would try to put him there if Christ forgot and came down from heaven for them. When Gemser persists, Peter says the priests have made up a god who is no God. Gemser curtly replies that his God is Christ. The pace quickens, Peter asserting again that Christ is in heaven, Gemser continuing to insist that the priests bring him down to earth. When Peter claims that this would be a greater power even than casting out devils or throwing mountains into the sea, Gemser protests that what the priests do is with a good intention and to honor Christ. Peter answers that it is like a cat honoring a captured mouse. St. Peter also was well intentioned when he did not want Christ to die, and Christ called him a Satan (43).

Gemser, on the other hand, likens the eucharistic coming of Christ to Moses' act in making a tabernacle for the Lord. So also Solomon made a house for the Lord. When Peter asks what basis Gemser has for calling the bread a house for Christ, Gemser says it is an *argumentum a simili*. Here Gemser has strayed into Peter's (and Karlstadt's!) territory: Peter protests that this *argumentum* runs counter to Scripture, for Scripture says that Christ inhabits a heavenly tabernacle not built with human hands (44). Now Gemser is desperate. Grasping for any straw, he again cites the cup of blessing argument. Peter tells him again that the blessing refers to a memorial and proclamation of Christ's death on the cross. The communion of Christ's blood refers to our communion with the heavenly Christ, not with something in the cup or bread. Gemser rushes back to the power of the words of consecration. Now Peter takes the opportunity to ask Gemser, in part presumably for the sake of Victus, what these words are and how many of them there are (44).

Gemser says that just as Christ received five wounds, so there are five words of consecration: whoever leaves one out cannot consecrate. Hence they are powerful words. Peter asks how many words of consecration there are in the Greek text. When Gemser admits that there are only four, Peter goes on to argue that other languages like Syrian and Hebrew would have had yet different numbers of words of consecration. What about them? Gemser is not convinced. Does Peter expect there to be other words somewhere? Peter's point is the same one it has been all along: that the words following "This is my body" are endowed with the same power as "This is my body." Those equally powerful words are: "which is given for you." Since it is not Christ's body as a piece of bread which is given for us, Christ must be referring to his body which was given the next day on the cross, and hence Christ was making no reference to the bread. The priests do not have the power to throw Christ back and forth. They stink with wine and beer. They are so corrupt that they play cards during mass. Gemser says he does not believe that Christ has communion with priests of that sort. Peter compares the problem of the sacramental bread to the problem of pictures: many lay people simply cannot understand what kind of reality a picture has and does not have (45-46).

God, however, wanted all done according to his own will. Gemser protests that we know pictures have no reality. Peter continues to believe that the priests' practice gives a different idea to the lay people. He asks Gemser whether the priests think they bring into the sacrament the mortal body of Christ or his Lordly and immortal body. (When Peter asks why, Gemser explains that Christ already died once and will not die again.) Peter again chides the Paulinian Gemser for not knowing Paul. Paul reports that Christ said "This is my body which is broken for you." If it could be broken, it was the mortal body. If it was mortal, it died and could not possibly be brought back into the sacrament. When Gemser protests that it is another form of the body that is brought in, namely, the Lordly body, Peter asks Gemser to repeat the words of consecration. Gemser, as is his wont, leaves out the part about "which is given for you." Peter, as is his wont, protests because this is the part that proves that Christ was talking about his mortal body, not his Lordly and immortal body. If he had given his Lordly and immortal body for us, then we would have received no justification from such an act. For our justification came only through the *death* of Christ's *mortal* body. Hence, if the priests are correct in imagining that Christ referred to his immortal body in their words of consecration, then Christ won no justification for us, and their sacrament certainly wins nothing (46-48).

It is of course Karlstadt's characteristic figural argument that Peter cites: Christ must fulfill the *figura* of the Old Testament sacrificial animals, hence winning our justification through his death (48). When Peter needs to answer Gemser's claim that it is not so much through Christ's death that we receive justification as through his resurrection, we see how deeply Karlstadt has based his soteriology on a *theologia cruicis* of his own. Perhaps it is not so much that Karlstadt clumsily borrowed a *theologia crucis* from Luther as that he developed one of his own, one consistent with his own understanding of *figura*.

This argument for a shift of emphasis from the resurrection to the cross finally, to the relief of all, provides Karlstadt with an opportunity to end his dialogue. Peter, asking Gemser to change his ways and confess the truth, proclaims that our task is to preach the Lord's *death* until he comes, for when he comes, he will drink a new cup that the priests could never have anticipated. When Christ comes, our death with him will be at an end, but not until then. We are to find in Christ our death. Our justification also is to be found, not in ourselves, but in Christ. Gemser's response is to praise God. Peter says, in words which could serve as an epitome of Karlstadt's eucharistic doctrine: "God help us in the ardent knowledge of the death of Christ" (49). At the end, Karlstadt invites instruction from Scripture, and he offers instruction in the form of a list of a few of his other books.

The next eucharistic tract in Barge's list, *Auszlegung dieser wort Christi...*, centers on Luke 22:19 and is directed against what Karlstadt calls the once-and-twice-over papists who use these words as a breach of the cross of Christ. Although it is not so clearly aimed at a lay audience as the *Dialogus*, this tract, too, could be read by lay people with edification and occasional glee, for, lacking none of the vituperation which spices the pages of *Dialogus, Auszlegung* is, if anything, even more direct in its attacks on Karlstadt's enemies.

At the outset, Karlstadt attacks the papists' exegesis of the words "This is my body." Since they say that Christ's body is "in" the bread or "under" it or "in the *gestalt* of it," they do not mean that his body *is* the bread. Hence they add words to Scripture, a practice which is in clear violation of God's commandments (Deuteronomy 4, Revelation 22). Furthermore, what Christ put into the nominative they put into the ablative (Aib). When Christ refers to the bread of which we are to partake (John 6), he is not speaking of the papists' bread but of his heavenly flesh (Aii). The claim that faith can make such an anti-Scriptural miracle happen is worthless (Aiib). The papists omit the words which immediately follow "This is my body" because "which is given for you" contradicts their narrow interpretation. Not only the Greek language but all of prophecy teaches that Christ is referring to his body, which will in the future be given for the apostles, i.e. on the cross. So Christ, who was more than a prophet, spoke also as a prophet when he proclaimed his *future* task, the event in which he would give over his body on the cross the next day. This is the same event and the same body of which John the Baptist prophesied (Aiii-Aiiib).

John the Baptist's prophecy was greater than that of all previous prophets because he was pointing directly and physically to one who was *there*, locally present, in his midst. Now Christ's prophecy at the supper was yet greater, for now Christ himself was pointing to his own body when he said that it would be given over to take away the sins of the world. This passage has the same role as John 6, where Christ spoke of his flesh, which would be given for the life of the world. Christ often spoke of what he was going to do in his sacrifice; yet we are guilty if we imagine that he performed the sacrifice the instant he spoke it. At the supper, Christ said "This is my body" precisely in order to call attention to the words which followed and which the papists ignore: "which is given for you" (Aiiib).

Yet just as the apostles refer to Christ's work as a fulfilled promise (Acts 13), so we must not stop with the observation that Christ was making a promise of a future event at the supper. For it was a promise which he completely fulfilled when he went to the cross. That fulfillment was so complete that it will never be repeated. We can no longer hang on Christ's words at the supper as a promise but must now see them as Gospel, a fulfilled promise (Aiv). It is contrary to all prophecy to think that the body of our salvation and Messiah is still being given for us and now is given as a piece of baked bread. When the prophets speak of Christ's great suffering, they do not say that he was baked bread! Why did Christ say, "My soul is afflicted to death" if he was all the while a piece of bread (Aivb)?

Did Christ ever say that his natural body would not suffer but a piece of bread would be given to suffer? The body of Christ which suffered was the naturally born one, born of Mary, and it truly suffered. It is heretical to say that

Christ's body is still being given for us. Christ was not nailed onto the cross in the bread or sacramentally or secretly, but on the cross Christ openly and publicly died for us (B). The papists often tell us to take the Lord's body. In saying that Christ gives his body for you, they as much as say that Christ gives his body *to* you. But this is against John 6, where it is said that he gave his body for the life of the world. Christ could not have given his body to his apostles at the supper and then again at all later sacramental meals because then Christ would have been crucified and have died in the bread at the supper. When Christ poured out his blood for the forgiveness of sins, as both Peter and Paul say, this was with the understanding that he would never die again (Bb).

We are not expected to believe that the cup contained Christ's blood. It goes against the whole text about the meal the night before his crucifixion to say that he was giving his body at that time (Bii). At that time Christ was speaking in the future tense. Scripture has a customary way of speaking of future things through words which refer to present things, and sometimes even past things (Biib-Biii). If Christ had given his body for the life of the world during the supper, his death on the cross would have been superfluous. Christ needed actually to die in order to win our redemption. If he had not fallen to the earth, he would not have risen to bear fruit. Christ said, "If I am raised up, I will bring all to me" (John 12[:32]). If he had not been raised up, he would have brought no one to himself. On the cross in his obedience, and there only, Christ is a full prince and king. God raised Christ above all things and gave him a name higher than all other names. This did not happen at the supper but on the cross (Biiib).

We have yet further scriptural support by which we can know that Christ's intention at the supper was to give a promise, to preach and speak of future things, not past or present things. Paul, for example, says that we are to proclaim the Lord's death as often as we eat the bread and drink the cup. Paul gives us to believe that Christ was proclaiming or preaching at the supper. When I Peter 2 says that "Christ took our sins to the cross," it can hardly mean that he atoned for our sins the night before the crucifixion. Perhaps Christ's reason for using the present tense at the supper was that he knew the time was near, and he was ready, about to suffer (Biv).

When Christ spoke of his betrayal at the supper, he was referring to the future, for he had not yet been betrayed (Bivb). John the Baptist, when he said "Behold the lamb of God who takes away the sin of the world" was also using the present tense to refer to the future. And, when Christ tells the sons of Zebedee that they are to be baptized with his baptism, he uses the present to refer to the future. Mark has Christ say "Can you drink the cup I drink?" while Matthew says "the cup I *will* drink." It is clear that Mark is using the present to refer to the future.

The papists' interpretation simply runs contrary to Scripture. John 3, 6, and 12 all say that Christ made his body a food *on the cross*. The sacramental bread is an earthly bread, rising from the earth up, but Christ's bread is from heaven down, a living bread (Ciib). "Since now the body of Christ is to be a flesh or food of life and the blood of Christ a drink of life, so must his flesh be raised up and his blood poured out in the height of the cross" (Ciii). Whoever seeks to live in the flesh and blood of Christ must seek to live in the spirit and the raised-up Christ on the cross. It is here that Christ is a food and a drink, not in the sacrament. Whoever seeks these in the sacrament punishes Christ, since he says, "The Son of Man must be raised up." This is also grounded in a prophecy of David. God gave as a remembrance a *teraph* for those who feared him. The *teraph* was a living creature which was bitten and slaughtered by wild beasts. Christ according to his humanity became the same living creature, for he is bitten and slaughtered by the insensate princes and tyrannical priests. They are wolves and other beasts which bite and nail Christ (Ciii). But God gave Christ not to them but to those who feared him. One other important point is that the law said (Leviticus 3:17) that no one was allowed to eat the *teraph* flesh and whoever did so was impure, and so the papists who eat of Christ's human flesh become impure. The food, however, which is referred to in John 6, is a wonderful and new food. Christ became common flesh, impure with our sins, and accursed, since whoever hung on a tree was accursed, and, by cursing Christ, God blessed us (Deuteronomy 27; Galatians 3) (Ciiib). Christ, through his obedience (Romans 5), hanging between two murderers as one whom God had thrown out (Isaiah 53), overcame our disobedience. The *teraph* was a common and impure food which only the God-fearing could eat. On the cross, Christ became that food. Faith is the necessary recognition or understanding. When Christ says that whoever eats of his flesh has eternal life, he refers to the appropriation of the justice wrought for us on the cross. He who eats and drinks of that flesh and cup has an "inward and spiritual life"(Civ).

Thomas Aquinas writes that both the good and the bad partake of Christ's flesh, but that is against the prophet David (Pslam 100) and against Christ (John 6). The evil can only take the Lord's bread to their own judgment (I Corinthians 11). The evil can indeed get hold of Christ's body: Annas, Caiaphas, Herod, Pilate, and such murderers took his body, to their own judgment. But they do not eat the flesh which David calls a *teraph* and Christ calls his food. The God-fearing alone take Christ's food inwardly. The sacramental bread lets one die. Therefore, we must *discern* between it and the heavenly bread. It is impossible that the text John 6 refers to the sacramental bread (Civb).

The sacramental bread is from below upward and is made by men's hands. So these words of Christ, "This is my body which is given for you," stand against the papists old and new (Db-Dii). No one, therefore, may say that the Lord's bread is nothing but mere bread; why did Paul speak against the misuse of such a piece of bread? With many Old Testament references Karlstadt says that God is a Lord and wishes to be feared in all his ordinances. Paul stresses even more than the Old Testament that we are not in either baptism or the bread to act otherwise than God ordained. We are to do what pleases God well, as Moses says three times in one book. Therefore, all those who seek the Lord's body at the sacrament, some knowingly, some out of blindness, do it against the will of the Lord (Dv-Dii).

If Paul had said nothing more than that we are to proclaim the Lord's death, we should have been satisfied and should have discerned the over-flowing love of the Lord on the cross. But Paul went further, giving to the Corinthians and to us to understand more. Thus he began by saying, "In the night that Christ was betrayed...." For the Corinthians had come together to enjoy the meal without seriously remembering Christ. This proves that in the time of the apostles the bread was thought to be mere bread. Paul, however, had to remind them that the supper had to do with something as serious as the betrayal of Christ. We must *properly remember* the Lord's death when we partake of the supper: the meaning of the supper is that the body of the Lord was going to be betrayed and killed (Diii).

Hence, one must rightly discern the body of the Lord. Karlstadt says that this in itself is so great a subject that he could write a book on it alone, citing Scripture. Briefly, however, Paul thinks of the Lord's body *figuratively* as a sign of our body. Christ is a head, he says, and are we not all one bread? In this way Paul is saying that those who come together to eat the Lord's bread must rightly discern and judge themselves as Christians, as the body of Christ, and must discern the powerful love, oneness, peace, and heart-felt society among them as members of one body. Therefore, the communicants should have a just, brotherly, and Godly love among one another as members of one body; without such love among one another, they will not rightly judge the Lord's body and will eat unworthily. In their love Christians answer the figure of the outward bread. This love of the figurative body comes from the love of Christ for his church, a love which was poured out on the cross (Diiib).

Karlstadt's summarizes by telling his brothers and sisters that they have three arguments: (1) when Christ points to the bread and says "This is my body," it follows clearly that it is impossible that the body of Christ is the bread; (2) if Christ had said of the bread, "This is my body which is broken for you," then all prophecies, gospels, and apostles' books which have been written on the open suffering of the natural body of the Messiah are false; (3) Christ was speaking in future terms, meaning that his body was to be given afterward. These words, "This is my body which is given for you," standing fast against papists old and new, are like the sling-shot David used against Goliath (Dvi). After further summary Karlstadt says at the end of the tract that he had hoped the truth would come to light without trouble and that he would not have disputed with him, referring obviously to Luther, but not by name. "He," however, attacked Karlstadt and in fact drove him out of the lands of Saxony "to my insurmounable harm." Karlstadt says, though, that he will not fear even death (Dvi).

The next tract in Barge's catalogue, *WIder die alte un newe Papistische Messen*, is by far the shortest of the October-November blasts. Karlstadt's stated purpose in writing it is to answer questions about the German mass and related issues. That one in our German lands, Karlstadt says, should read and preach in German is not only right but necessary. I Corinthians 14 exhorts us to discover whether one's word is of God or not. Paul bases this on Deuteronomy 27, where it is stated that the people are to say Amen at certain times. This cannot be done unless the people can understand the language in which they are being addressed. Some, Karlstadt says in clear reference to Luther (un-named), give the reading to the poor lay people in German, but in words, works, and deeds they call the mass a sacrifice and thus confuse the poor lay people in their misunderstanding (i). It is good that they read the epistle and Gospel in German, but it is wrong for them immediately afterward to say by their actions [i.e., elevation of the host in Wittenberg] that Christ is a sacrifice in the mass (ii). Karlstadt says that in his little book *Von dem priesterthum und opfer Christi* he shows that it is a sin to call the mass a sacrifice of Christ.

Some preach and write that Christ is not a sacrifice, but they continue to use the word mass, which is not a German or Latin word, but Hebrew, meaning a free-will offering. Karlstadt cites Hebrews (Chapters 4, 5, 7, 9, and 10) to show that Christ, the highest and purest priest, is the only one who can offer Christ as a sacrifice. Yet the stinking, impure priests think they can do it.

Indeed, it is worse to say that Christ is a sacrifice when a priest holds a mass than to say that Christ's suffering was insufficient (ii). Dr. Martinus and the poor bishop of Zwicaku (Bishop Hausmann) err particularly in this. In this case the poor bishop has a papist holiness. For Dr. Martinus and Bishop Hausmann raise the host. Karlstadt cites Leviticus (chapters 8, 9, 10, 14, 23) and Numbers 6 to show that this was the method in the Old Law of making a sacrifice. In Hebrew, *thruma* was the raising up and down (which makes the papists old and new into murderers of Christ), and the *thnupha* was the right and left movement of the sacrifices (iii).

Thus they say that the stinking, faithless priests can make a sacrifical offering of Christ and hence that the newly offered Christ forgives sins. In the first raising, all of Wittenberg errs. But they say they do not understand it as a sacrificial offering, and they are so freed from the law that they think they can give a meaning to what God has established which is different from the meaning God himself gave it. How Christian that is, Karlstadt says, his readers can decide for themselves. Christ never broke the law but fulfilled it. Their protestation that they do not call their mass a sacrifice counts as nothing against the substance of the act (*substantia actus*). Their elevation agrees perfectly with the Old Testament method of sacrifice. So it is a sacrifice (iv). Christ's ordering of the supper was best. Scripture is luminous in explaining that order (v). Anyone who seeks to improve on Christ's own ordering is seeking to use the wisdom of his own flesh to improve on God's ordering, an activity which Paul warns against (Romans 8). The wisdom of the flesh is enmity against God and is the death of man (vi). When Christ called Peter a Satan, it was because Peter had been trying to be wise in his own flesh and blood. God's ways are beyond our dark ways and must not be violated by us (vii).

Von dem wider christlichen missbrauch, the last of the October-November eucharistic tracts in Barge's list, begins dramatically. Karlstadt confesses that he can no longer be silent about the misuse of the Lord's bread and cup, a misuse by which Christians become guilty of the death of the Lord. He must confess that his earlier writings on this subject were mistaken. He must say these things whether it results in his life or his death (Aii). First of all, says Karlstadt, it is a very common and terrible harm that people think the sacrament forgives their sins. He who thinks that must have a magical and unintelligent doctrine of Christ. (It is not difficult to remember how vigorously Karlstadt had, in his 1521 Christmas sermon, defended the forgiveness of sins as a fruit of the eucharist. But much has happened since then!) An indication that this tract may be among the later of the October-November eucharistic series is that

Karlstadt notes that he has already written far and wide on this matter in a *gesprechbüchlein* and other books (Aiii). Here he chooses to study I Corinthians 11. In this chapter Paul explains why, how, and when we are to partake of the Lord's bread and cup worthily and usefully. Paul presents the same argument here as the prophets and apostles did. Whoever presents a different argument must also bring the Gospel to prove it (Aiii).

In I Corinthians 11:26, Paul has given us a rule when he said that we are to proclaim the Lord's death until he comes. This proclamation is the fruit of a certain tree: the memory. For the proclamation must come from the heart, from one's inwardness. God judges the heart and the inner person. This is where the memory is. Isaiah 29 and Christ himself (Matthew 25) say that the people praise God with their mouths, but their hearts are far away (Aiii-Aiiib). In Romans 10, Paul says that he who believes from the heart is justified. It is impossible that anything be justified if the heart is not first justified. He who is without faith has no justified soul. To the unbelieving, all things are unclean (Habakkuk 2, Titus 1, Jeremiah 5), while to believers all is pure. It is the memory that is the ground of this purity (Aiiib). He who would outwardly preach the death of Christ must have gone into his inner heart, to the *grund* of his soul, as a branch goes into the tree. "Memory...is a fervent and loving knowledge or recognition of the body and blood of Christ. No one can remember that body and blood who has not known it (Aiv).

Rightly to know Christ's body and blood, one must look for what Moses and the prophets spoke of: a new testament-maker, forgiveness of sins, poured out blood, and so on. As Paul says, those who have the right knowledge, or recogniton, of Christ have righteousness in their *grund*. Romans 10 says that faith is the righteousness of the heart. So also Isaiah promises the Messiah. The form in which the Messiah will be recognized is the form of a lamb offered for sacrifice, and so as the crucified one (Aivb). In brief, knowledge of Christ means knowledge that the words "This is my body which will be given for you" were fulfilled on the cross (B). We should have a memory of Christ's death that is not cold but fresh, warm, and powerful, one that brings joy. For example, suppose the judgment had been given that you had to die but someone else took your place, and he gave you something you should do in his memory.

"The memory of Christ has two parts. One is of the body which was given, the other of the blood which was poured out" (Bb). A proper partaking of the Lord's Supper depends on a proper knowledge of the causes of the Lord's death. Christ himself is, as Paul said (Hebrews 6:19), a priesthood and sacrifice. Therefore, it is not the sacrament that forgives our sins. If the priests

put the power of forgivenss of sins in the sacrament, they deny the importance
of the cross (Bb-Bii). For the blood was not poured out in the sacrament but
on the cross (Biib). Karlstadt again refers us to his *Dialogus* for further
discussion of this matter (Biib). The proper knowledge and memory of Christ
are vitally important because of I Corinthians 11:29: we are guilty of the body
and blood of the Lord if we eat unworthily of his bread and drink unworthily
of his cup. The reason is that in unworthy eating and drinking we do not
properly *discern* the Lord's body. Karlstadt asks to be shown one word where
Paul says that the proper disccernment is in the sacramental eating. We are
supposed to discern and recognize the body on the cross. Worthiness and
unworthiness come from our knowledge of the body and not from eating of the
meat (Biii).

Whoever remembers the crucified body of the Lord must understand
what Christ means by "This is my body which is given for you." Whoever does
not understand these words correctly either does not remember the Lord or
does not remember him the way the Lord said to. Hence he becomes guilty
because he does not highly value the body of the Lord (Biiib). We cannot
discern the body in the sacrament because Christ did not die in the sacrament.
The sacrament is hardly big enough that Christ and his cross and the whole
crowd of people around the cross could get into it. The Jews and the pagans
must also have gotten into the little sacrament(!) (Biv). Discerning, judging,
testing means to know with a certainty what happened. This is what we are
called upon to do in the case of the body of the Lord (Bivb). We are supposed
to be "*Christformig*" and thankful. We are to go into our spirit, into our
inwardness, to make an inner testing of our knowledge of Christ (C). Some
incorrectly conclude from this that through the bread and cup one can know
with a certainty that Christ's death has brought one's redemption. This is
wrong because it would make the prior self-examination unnecessary and thus
would go against Christ's statement that we should discern his body properly.
It is an extremely serious matter: we need only remember the improper
wedding guest who was cast into outer darkness. Paul says that one should
examine oneself and then eat the bread afterward. One must find out whether
one remembers Christ's death in the manner Christ ordained and whether one
can proclaim the death of the Lord:

> If he has that in his *grund*, then he also has the spirit of Christ, who
> shows him his salvation, Christ hanging on the cross and the same
> Christ in full obedience, in utmost rightoeusness and joyful love and

innocence, dying, and he assures his heart that he has redemption through Christ (Cb).

If one has this certainty, then one may eat of the Lord's bread. But one does so with the assurance that Christ has already paid for the world's sins before one takes the sacrament. Christ points all of us to the cross. Christ is the way, truth, life, and peace. We have all of that through Christ (cii). He is a thief and murderer who does not enter the Kingdom through Christ. The sacrament does not make us cry to God "Father, Father!" "For it is much too coarse to touch the ground of the soul." No one but the Spirit can give the certainty of forgiven sins. Such creaturely things as the bread and wine cannot do Christ's work (Cb).

In my categories, Karlstadt was trying to liberate duality from dualism by refusing to literalize the metaphor of Christ's physical presence on the altar. By not swallowing the metaphor of Christ's physical eucharistic presence, Karlstadt was (in Torrance's categories) rejecting a container-concept of sacred place and replacing it with a space-time continuum-concept. The riddle of Christ's presence cannot be discussed in spatial metaphors alone. The spatial metaphors must be temporalized. Christ was here physically. He will be here physically again. But such sacred presence is always time-bound. To remove the time-bound character of sacred presence is to lose the duality (mutuality) of dualism and non-dualism by reducing the space-time continuum of incarnation-ascension-second coming to a fictive eternal now. Literalizing the fictive physical presence, however, forces us into a lie. It places the burden of all eternity on the now at the altar, and the now cannot bear that burden, even at the altar. The linearity of salvation (by which the then of the past and the then of the future are qualitatively different from the now of the present) is a gracious deliverance for us creatures of the now. That linearity is a liberation of duality from dualism, of the dynamic from the static, of the continuous from the discontinuous, of the monotheism bird from its cage. For the monotheism bird cannot be monotheism only in the now but only by flying both backward and forward to the thens that are qualitatively different from this now. The now is not eternal, and Christ is not physically on our altar.

The Real Absence
in the Soteriologies of Richard Hooker and *The Winter's Tale*

What made Luther pull back when he looked into the abyss of unsacramentality in 1525? We have seen that one thing was religious fanaticism and its accompanying political violence and chaos. The end of physical sacraments would mean the end of the fortress-character of the church, and that would mean the end of even the pretense of a separation between church and state, and that would mean the collapse of the Word into the Sword, the triumph of sectarian fanaticism, and, in response to that, the triumph of state fanaticism. But Luther was not so shallow as to have only instrumental reasons for fearing unsacramentality. I think the other thing that frightened him about that abyss was its sheer metaphysical emptiness. The ancient Greek heritage of deifying being made it impossible for Luther to see that the real absence of the body of Christ from our world may be, though negative, a positive negative.

I cannot help thinking that it was a major crisis when large segments of the Western church began in the sixteenth century to give up transubstantiation. Luther and Calvin insisted (in very different ways) that they were retaining "the real presence" of Christ in the eucharist. Yet the very fact that their ways of understanding that presence were so different from each other meant that the real eucharistic presence could no longer provide even the semblance of a sacrament of unity for Western Christendom. In spite of Luther's insistence that he was retaining the real presence, everything was different for Western Christendom after Karlstadt and others effectively challenged it in the early 1520s. The Western church had entered a dangerous new landscape.

This dangerous place of wilderness wandering, where the church must live as an alien exactly while proclaiming that danger is unnatural and that Ithaca is a peaceful and humane city, is where Christians have no choice but to dwell today. We live in Babylon, and we sing of Jerusalem. To call Babylon Jerusalem is to forget Jerusalem. We may think that our physical cathedrals are still mighty fortresses and that, as Christians, we are still custodians of unique sacramental authority in this Babylonian society, but they are not and we are not. Such prophets as T. S. Eliot and Paul Tillich, in their zest for the Middle Ages, seemed to be trying to reinstate a sacramentalism in which the church walls had not yet fallen down (but, even for Eliot, the church roof had been bombed in from above ["the dove descending breaks the air with flame of incandescent terror"] and, for Tillich, the roof had been blown out from inside by the intensity of the self-world ontology). Tillich and Eliot were trying to hang on to the church's walls. Long live Tillich and Eliot. But also long live such poets of the holy absence as Emily Dickinson, Herman Melville, and Wallace Stevens. For these poets, The Redeemer is everywhere and nowhere at the same time, and the everywhere and nowhere intensify each other. Strong's poetic monism puts the emphasis where it ought to be, it seems to me: on the ubiquity of Christ in the midst of the absence of Christ. Christ is absent from our sinfulness, except to keep suffering the consequences of it, paying the price for it, and with incredible graciousness carrying it away. But, as her poet, Christ is alive and present in that cosmos which is his bride and his body, present in the ecology, present in the chipmunk, present in the microbe, in the molecule, the atom, but also (and this is where—as in Nagarjuna—Buddhism's spirituality of absence is the key to Hinduism's spirituality of presence) Christ is present in the emptiness which fills the atom. This spirituality of emptiness is where Luther refused to go. But Luther's sacramental theory that Christ is everywhere is, like Strong's, really just the other side of Karlstadt's coin: that if Christ is physically everywhere in the cosmos, then Christ is physically nowhere in the cosmos.

It would have taken a Nagarjuna to show Luther that his universally present Christ is really (if he is truly universal and truly present) a universally absent Christ. And I really think a Nagarjuna could have convinced him of it. There would have been many costly *Anfechtungen*, but we would all have been much beter off if Luther had learned how close he really was to Karlstadt and Zwingli. But it was not to be, as we Calvinists say. Still, we can see what Luther did not have a Nagarjuna to show him. By basing non-dualism on vision, on poetic apprehension, on metaphor, and on faith (the substance of things hoped for, the evidence of things not seen), Strong gives a positive place to the category of emptiness, of The Zero, in both its tragic and its comic modes, just as Luther could have done if he had had the chance. (How the Lutherans will disagree with me on this, I fear!) Strong's Christ does not have a special place to láy his head. Instead, he claims every place and makes it his own.

In this way, salvation, for Strong, resembles Mahayana Buddhism's enlightenment in that salvation, like enlightenment, is not a removal from this secular, weighty world of ordinary understanding in which we dwell (not a removal from the wilderness wandering), but precisely a dwelling *in* this samsara (this wilderness) in such a way as to see, here today, in this very lack of completeness the completeness of nirvana in the mode of its absence. Being does not need to conquer non-being because non-being is no threat. If Christ will be Lord of the apocalypse (and only then will we see what it really means to say that he is Lord), then Christ is Lord of the now. The fullness of the apocalypse is compatible with the unfullness of the now. Indeed, it is the very unfullness of the now that gives the fullness of the apocalypse its holy opportunity to fulfill what needs fulfilling. Faith is not so much the fullness of our conceptions of God, then, as it is the emptiness with which we are no longer restless. Faith is the emptiness which we no longer anathematize, because the God who is not defeated by The All cannot be defeated by The Nothing either.

Meanwhile, neither comedy nor tragedy is enough without the other, neither dualism nor non-dualism, because, so far, these dualities are so trapped by our dualism (these mutualities are so trapped by our sin) that they are incapable of feeding each other as they should. Instead, the dualities appear to be in conflict with each other. But even though these visions are, taken in isolation, incomplete in themselves, we need them all the more now, between the times, for in the very absence of their reconciliation, tragedy and comedy, non-dualism and dualism, are emblems, anticipations of the final reunion of contraries. These arts and these religions are in their own way first fruits of them that sleep, promises and demands from the ultimate, reconciling future. They are what is left of the sacramental sense in a secularized universe, and it is incumbent upon us to understand the sacramental logic by which these arts testify to the presence of the Redeemer by testifying to his absence.

Just as it is easier by far to flip out than to flip back in, it is in fact easier to be a poet of the sacred than of the secular. As we learned in the 1960s during the theology of secularity, secularity rests upon certain specific religious assumptions. In Mahayana Buddhism, for example, it is one thing to seek one's own nirvana but quite another, ironically more spiritual and more secular thing, to postpone one's own nirvana until all sentient beings can achieve nirvana. The latter approach is more spiritual because it is is less selfish and more secular because it finds the real nirvana here in samsara when samsara is seen from the vantage point of a nirvana which is so real that we do not need to have it in order to let it shape this non-nirvana which is samsara. When we can let real nirvana in its present emptiness, its apparent unreality, guide and fill the emptiness of samsara, then samsara *is* nirvana. And then nirvana can graciously empty the fullness of samsara. We flip in rather than out.

Similarly(!), in ancient Israel, the challenge of daily life was to maintain the burden of a weighty religious skepticism. The gods and goddesses of field and plow, the sacred deities of sky and storm, of earth and water, all were supposed to be scornfully rejected by the believer in the living God of Israel. Giving up a god or goddess of field or plow has never been easy. For the Israelite, commanded to be skeptical of religious gobbledygook, all the normal ecstasies of a hierophantic exisence were to be demythologized. The living God was instead an invisible, ethical, awesome God of promise and demand whose history was a people-history rather than a place-history. But the Israelites *did* have a sacred place, did they not? Yes, but the whole point was that the place-history was to be subjected to the people-history, or else. That was why the sacred place was supposed to be so thoroughly subdued by the sacred people, not because the place was sacred in its own self or because the people were but because the people were called to be sacred by the God who dwells in light inaccessible, and he called the people to make the place sacred. Since God is holy, everything else is holy, not the other way around.

Fire and earthquake, sky and sea, earth and mountain, revealed the absence of this invisible God of the presence. To worship this terrifying God was not at all to deify *being* as an act of praise and thanksgiving but on the contrary to cut loose from every being less than he for the sake of attaching oneself to him in his invisibility and to his purposes in their transcendence of icon, image, and incarnation. The very heavens could declare him but could not contain him, and even the heavens declared him only because he declared himself through them. So, religious life in ancient Israel was a shockingly more secular life than was life in the worlds of Israel's neighbors. It is in this secular world, with its secular wisdom and arts, in the rough-and-tumble unsanctimonious politics of things like the Deuteronomic historians' account of David's life and death, that the purposes of God are to be ferreted out, one by one and in trial and error, with a confidence that there are many more false prophets than true prophets and that the false prophets are (as in all times and all places) both more attractive and more ecstatic.

In the Christian Middle Ages this dynamic, purpose-centered theology tended to get lost in the static container-model which Torrance has diagnosed for us. But even in the static model that dominanted medieval Christendom, the paradox of the secularity demanded by a holy God was evident. In his *Dante, Poet of the Secular World*, Erich Auerbach explained the religious assumptions that allowed Dante to be a consummate poet of the secular world in spite of the fact that Dante's fame is based on his poetry of the sacred worlds of hell, purgatory, and paradise.[1] Auerbach explained that the concept of *figura* allowed, and indeed required, Dante to be a poet of the secular world precisely as poet of the divine worlds. The characters Dante meets in death's other kingdom have the positions they do because of the *figura*, the figural correspondence, between That world and This world. What you do in This world with your ethical responsibility registers figurally in That world. And the registry is irreversible. Every moment, every act, every thought, in This world is linked by an exact correspondence to That world. Therefore, do not flip out. Be serious about this world. This secular world is where matters of eternal moment are being decided. Today's ethical decisions carry in them the weight of eternity. That makes you, if you are consistent, as (if ever anyone was) Dante was, a poet of the secular world.

Shakespeare is probably the world's most famous poet of the secular world. Nestled as he was between two such Obviously Theological Great Poets as Medieval Dante and Renaissance Milton, Shakespeare, who is always abiding our question, is as famous a theological riddle as is the smile of his fellow-Renaissance quintessence, the good Mona. In his comedies, what is the good Shakespeare smiling about? In our era, it is most commonly held that, whatever he was smiling about, it wasn't Our Lord and Savior Jesus Christ, and T. S. Eliot compared Shakespeare unfavorably to Dante because of the rag-tag character of Shakespeare's philosophy. But I think Augustus H. Strong was more luminous in his discussion of the riddle of theology and secularity in Shakespeare:

> I do not see how any one can read the tragedies without perceiving that Shakespeare is one of the greatest of ethical teachers. And what is true of these tragedies is true of his work in general, it wakens a response in the deepest heart of man. But not because the poet had any set purpose to be a moral teacher. All this is incidental. He aims only to

depict life, to show man to himself, to exhibit human nature with its
love, its hate, its hope, its fear. But all the more powerful is
Shakespeare's testimony to the supremacy of conscience in the moral
constitution of man.

The same remarks apply to Shakespeare's treatment of religion and
doctrine. He has not set himself to propound dogmas. Whether he was
Romanist or Protestant no one can surely tell; the most that we can say
is that he disliked Puritanism, and made it once or twice the subject of
a casual jest. Homer and Virgil, Dante and Milton, had each his heaven
and his hell, and each described without hesitation the unseen world.
But Shakespeare has no heaven and hell; he deals only with this present
life; even his ghosts and witches tell us nothing of the life beyond—they
are forbidden to tell the secrets of the prison house, and only intimate
that they "coud a tale unfold whose lightest word would harrow up the
soul" (*Hamlet* I, 5, 13). Our great dramatist is the poet of the secular and
not of the religious, of the temporal and not of the eternal.

Here is the limitation of his universality. As Scherer has said: "It is
on the boundaries of the invisible world that Shakespeare's vision fails."
But he has, notwithstanding, the most sane and level apprehension of
the relations of this life, and his testimony to Christian truth, like his
testimony to the ethical facts of remorse and retribution, is all the more
valuable because unintentionally given. Let us inquire what this
testimony is, and what doctrines of our faith derive confirmation from
it. In treating this portion of my theme I avail myself to some extent of
the references given so copiously in Bishop Wordsworth's excellent
book on *Shakespeare and the Bible*.

Though Shakespeare does not profess to teach theology, it is not
because he has no theology, nor because he regards theology as an
impossibility to man. He is not an agnostic. He distinctly maintains the
reality and the value, while he confesses the limitations, of our
knowledge of God and his relations to the universe.[2]

Strong goes on to argue that a moral and transcendent God is presupposed
in Shakespeare's dramatic world and that the human being is presupposed to
be created by and responsible to this living moral and gracious God. But
Shakespeare's focus is (we would say) as resolutely on the moral magnitude of
secular life as is Dante's or Zen's.

It seems to me that Shakespeare's sanctification of the secular is more
radical than Dante's in a way that parallels Hooker's radicalization of Aquinas's
eucharist. *The Winter's Tale* seems to me to presuppose a major change in the

concept of *figura* since Dante, and this change is reflected in Karlstadt's theology of eucharistic absence. Not that I think Shakespeare read Karlstadt! The point is that the change in eucharistic imagery epitomized by Karlstadt parallels the change in sacred-secular imagery epitomized by Shakespeare. If any individual had a major role in this shift, so typical of the age of Melanchthonian post-Lutheran pre-Calvinist humanism, it was, most ironically, Calvin himself! But influence is not the issue right now.

The shift in *figura* from Dante to Shakespeare (paralleling the shift from Aquinas to Hooker via Karlstadt) is: *figura* shifts from past to future and from an action of humanity to an action of God. In what follows, I will attempt to explain this shift and its importance.

In *The Winter's Tale*, as in Karlstadt, *figura* refers mainly not to the past but to the future and not to the ethics of human beings but to the ethics of God. In Dante, your status in the Next world is determined by the *figura* of your actions in This world. In Karlstadt, however, the eucharistic celebration is a re-enactment of Old Testament sacrificial ceremonies because the point the eucharist is making is that on his cross Christ fulfilled and thereby did away with all those Old Testament shadows, types, figures, and anticipations. So the eucharist, for Karlstadt, is not a presence of the sacrifice tradition. It is a celebration of *the absence* of that tradition, the end of it on Golgotha. Likewise, the eucharistic celebration is not about Christ's physical presence here on the altar today but about Christ's physical *absence* here on the altar today because *in the future* he will be here physically again, and then we shall no longer see in a glass darkly but face to face and shall know even as also we are known. *Now* Christ is physically in heaven. He is here with us in his spirit as he enters our spirits if we surrender enough in holy *Gelassenheit* (a word dear to the hearts of us Heideggerians) to let him enter our spirits and dwell in the ground (a word dear to us Tillichians) of our souls. There is an exact figural correspondence between the raising up of the Old Testament sacrifical animal and the raising up of Christ on his cross and then from his tomb and then in the ascension.

The other side of the *figura* will occur when the descent comes. It has already come in the Holy Spirit (and that is enough for us now—indeed, to treat the Spirit's presence as insufficient is rank ingratitude to God). But the day will come when the descent of Christ himself will occur. And the eucharist celebrates that future day, but *not as present*, only as future. To reverse the linearity of the time sequence is ingratitude to God and a destruction of the symbolism God has designed. (In my categories, it is to fly non-dualistically backward and to neglect the equally important dualistic flight forward.) We make a sacred *progress* in history, or else there is no history. We do not just keep going back to the past. The Old Testament sacrifices bear witness to their insufficiency exactly because of their frequent, seemingly endless, repetition. Those sacrifices were mute, figural cries for an end to the ever-repeated sacrificing. In Christ, that cry for a consummation was fulfilled. In Christ's death on the cross the sacrificial system came to culmination, fulfillment, and—graciously—an end. To perpetuate the sacrifice in our eucharistic symbolism is precisely to turn back the clock of salvation. It is to underestimate what I call the dualist demands of monotheism in favor of an over-emphasis on the non-dualist demands.

The Winter's Tale brings together the tragedies of transformation and of paradox which we examined in Chapter Three. It pursues the paradox theme in the Antigonean character Hermione. But *The Winter's Tale* is a tragi-comedy, a tragedy with a comedic ending, a romance, which studies the complementarity between tragic non-dualism and comedic dualism. Unlike Antigone's, Hermione's tragic "Here I Stand" is comedically vindicated through the action of the play, not just morally (as in tragedy), but linearly, in the flesh, on the stage, before our very eyes in her artful resurrection. Hermione's vindication is made possible by the tragedy of transformation which her husband undergoes. Boy eternal (I, ii, 64)[3] Leontes is a parodic Oedipus figure, not a Sphinx man like Oedipus, but close to it, a Lion (lyin') man and perhaps a Leo-natus, a Lion-born man; certainly, like Oedipus, a rash fool of a king, heedless of the gods, a ludicrously self-centered man for whom the answer is man and man only, nothing larger, nothing more, one who thought that any divine oracle would be putty in his hands.

When Leontes' manhood is threatened (by his own imagination), Boy Eternal goes into a destructive and self-destructive rage, trying to kill the very woman whose possible absence (in case she had fallen in love with Polixenes) had so terrified him that he wanted her dead. A man who so worshipped the presence of his wife that he could not love her enough to allow her any absence from his presence, Leontes is the typical male hero of a perverse tragedy of transformation—an Oedipus who cannot live with or without Jocasta, a Marduk who cannot live with or without Tiamat. Leontes lost his goddess. Her absence was good for him. It required him to start life over again. Only through lengthy repentance, in service (like Hercules) to a harsh and systematically humiliating school mistress, Paulina, does Leontes gradually grow up, so that at the end there can be a gracious restoration of much (not all) that had been so needlessly lost.

But even though Shakespeare makes us love Hermione, he does not so patronize her as to make her into either a goddess or a redeemer. Hermione is a woman of flesh and blood. She is graciousness incarnate, but she is not The Redeemer. The Redeemer is The Ultimate Artist, the Prospero of *The Winter's Tale*, the invisible, shadowy Sculptor (whom I enjoy calling God), the Lord of Paulina/Julio Romano, who uses both the penitence of Leontes and the art of Perdita as chisels with which to redeem the time, bringing organic life out of cold stone, spring out of winter, Hermione out of her unjust perdition.

What has happened to figura *in this story? It has shifted from past to future and from an action of humanity to an action of God.* In Dante, the moral turpitude of Leontes would have been the *figura* which would justifiably have placed Leontes in one of the grimmest *froda*-levels of hell. The point would have been an excellent one: do not act like Leontes. But, for Reformation Shakespeare, that advice, though important, is not the main point of the story. For Shakespeare, the main point of *The Winter's Tale* is that God does not act like Leontes.

Luther said in his famous Preface to the Latin edition of his works (1545) that what had terrified him as a young man was the righteousness of God.[4] What will become of me if there really is a God who is righteous and holds me accountable for being righteous too? What converted him, opening, Luther said, the gates of paradise to him, was the discovery that "the righteousness of God" did not mean the righteousness which God demands of Luther (at least not that only) but the righteousness God demands of himself. You and I may not succeed in obeying the laws propounded by Jesus, but the Gospel, the shock of recognition, is that God does. God loves his neighbor as himself and lays down his life for his friends. So the righteousness of God becomes the righteousness by which God judges Luther righteous on the basis of Christ's righteousness, not Luther's. The basis of Luther's goodness, of his hope, and of his very salvation, is, then, not in Luther but in God.

At this point Luther's Christianity seems to me much more compatible with the Buddhist concept of emptiness than with the Greek deification of being. What Luther discovers when God opens the gates of paradise to him is precisely his zerohood. To be sure, he discovers it through a tragic paradox which has gradually stripped away from him every shred of righteousness and even of "being itself" with which he could have come into God's presence as one who is properly attired to meet his maker. But this tragic paradox is after all transformative and comic, because it is precisely in his birthday suit that Luther meets his maker. Then Luther sees, not only how absurd had been the rags with which he had tried to cover himself in his maker's presence, but also how gracious were the masks with which his maker had covered his own nakedness. God comes to Luther clothed in the promises of Christ, and Luther comes to God clothed in the promises of Christ. It is the story of the grace of emptiness, of the absence of covers. Salvation, for Luther, is comedic exposé. The absence of Luther's worthiness, the emptiness of all that he can bring to God, is the path of salvation. The release comes, not from building a specious fullness of merits on that absence of merit, but exactly the opposite: emptying oneself of self-will so that all glory belongs in one's own consciousness to the only God to whom glory belongs in reality. Salvation is thus an enlightenment, an emptying of oneself into reality as it is. This is not identical with Buddhist enlightenment obviously, because, for the Christian, God in Christ is part of the inescapable situation of one's life. He cannot be transcended. But if this Buddhist-Luther approach to Christianity makes Jesus Christ look as much like a Zen master as he has previously looked like a Greek philosopher, this new *Verschmelzung* of hoizons cannot be all bad.

And if this approach makes Shakespeare and the other Reformers look somewhat Buddhist, so what? In *The Winter's Tale*, as in Karlstadt's eucharist, the *figura* has made a shift like Luther's: from what we human beings must do (though that is never forgotten) to what *God* does (and that alone makes it possible for us to do something of what we are to do). In Karlstadt's eucharist, we do no sacrifice at all, because the point is that *God* has already carried out the sacrifice. The eucharistic ceremony points quite literally to Christ himself, not to the bread, to what is *absent*, not to what is present. Christ is Christ by being invisible now. That apparent emptiness, that real absence, is the very mode of Christ's work. It is a blessing, not a curse.

In *The Winter's Tale*, The Invisible Sculptor will not be defeated by the folly of his creature, the lyin' King Lion Man. Instead, The Physically Absent Sculptor uses that rough stone as the intractable matter on which he will chisel penitence for sixteen years under Law-Woman Paulina's guidance, and he will fulfill the *figura* of Grace-Woman Hermione's entombment in stone to make it into an enwombment in grace. Hermione in her tomb-womb will not fall into everlasting death but will be properly born from above. She will grow like a flower out of rock, like spring out of winter, but not because of any power in her herself (for she is dead, absent), but only by the power of That Sculptor Who Dwells in Absence, the giver of every good and perfect gift.

Between Leontes and Hermione there had to be *a real absence* of sixteen long years if there was to be a real presence when the day of resurrection rolled around. To deny our experience of the absence of The Gracious One would be to deny our creaturehood and to deny the power of The Sculptor to sculpt invisibly. The Sculptor ascended into heaven because God said to. It is that way because God ordained that it should be that way. He is not here. He is risen. That absence is supposed to be comedic, something to rejoice about in the presence of the Spirit, whom he sent to be with us in the meantime (and what a mean time it has been). Blessed are those who have not seen and have still believed. So far, you and I have been called to live during the mean time, the dispensation of the absence.

Since we see through the glass darkly now, not face to face, to claim that the end has already come and Christ has already returned to our altars, is to depreciate both his future coming and his present absence. *The Winter's Tale* is about the light that shines in the darkness, but for us it is a light of imagination. It is a light of art (Perdita), a light of grace (Hermione), a light of nature and law (Paulina). Like the ancient Israelites, we do not yet see him that dwells in light inaccessible, for if we did, we would be blinded. Milton, like Homer and the Oedipus of Colonus, dwells in that epic world of physical blindness and cosmic insight. If we are called to go there, we must follow. But in the meantime (just as Northrop Frye used to say that we have not yet earned the right to be silent),[5] we have not yet earned the right to close our eyes in a vain quest for the physically invisible one. Our duty is to see the visible world in the emptiness which is sacred, the emptiness in which The Ascended One tells us to let him remain physically absent and physically invisible. His presence in the Spirit is enough for us now.

The medieval church's extension of the incarnation to itself was a misguided doctrine. If we could have seen what the Buddhists have seen, that non-being is part and parcel of being, that emptiness is what makes fullness possible, we would have been much better off. But our *horror vacui* prevented us from seeing the beauty of The Zero. Still, as Christian ideas are thought over by Asian philosophers in the coming decades, this expansion of insight will occur quite naturally. It will be a real liberation for us westerners when we will need to take neither the tragic path of bringing Christ down to our altars nor the comic path of rushing to a false, untimely apocalypse. We will, when we can see the absence in the presence and the non-being in the being, be able to see the tragedy in the comedy and the comedy in the tragedy, thereby letting the future belong, not to us (who so desperately want the Kingdom to Be Here Now, or think we do), but to God. If we can accept Christ's temporary physical absence, we will learn to give the apocalypse and the return of Christ back to God.

The apocalypse and the Kingdom belong to God, after all, not to us. That is what Milton learned only after the revolution had failed, after paradise had been lost, and he had passed, like hasty Oedipus, from physical vision to spiritual. But Shakespeare was called to live in this visible, unapocalyptic, secular world, where, as Eliot put it, our little light is dappled with darkness (which dappling is, after all, the negation process that makes vision possible). Shakespeare was the poet of this secular world, from which God appears to be absent. In the emptiness of this secularity Shakespeare is showing us the relentless work, graciousness, and morality of The Sculptor Who Remains Invisible. We must not fall into another *horror vacui* fit, filling the canvas with bogus cosmological, teleological, and ontological step-ladders to the god who would be less than God if he could be found at the top of a logical step-ladder.

On the contrary, we must, like Leontes, let art be art, let Perdita be found. Perdita, Artful Lady of the Lost, is an agent of The Invisible Sculptor, The Ultimate Gardener, The Anonymous Christ (though she does not know it, would find it quite hilarious and preposterous if we suggested it to her, and has no reason to know it yet), which means that Christ is present in the eucharist to the extent that the Lord loveth a cheerful metaphor. It is Perdita, Lady Art, who presides over the metaphor by which we say we can call Christ down to us physically from heaven. This calling down of the ascended Christ can indeed become a sin against the Holy Spirit if we literalize the activity, but as long as we realize that it is (as Zwingli saw) metaphor, the elaborate play of liturgy is harmless enough and is to be sumptuously affirmed. Long live High Church Metaphors! But Perdita uses very different metaphors, as well, to instruct us in making our gardens grow. Art can also see Christ as The Absent One. That is a sacred gift too. What we must learn is that it can be as holy to celebrate the absence of Christ from his eucharists as to celebrate his presence, not necessarily holier. But absence art is also capable of being holy art. And in our time the greatest art is absence art. We need to see The Invisible Sculptor guiding Perdita in that absence, so that we can know that, here too, grace's invisible work of holy grafting is marrying a gentler scion to the wildest stock to make conceive a bark of baser kind by bud of nobler race. In other words, "All shall be well," as Eliot put it, "and all manner of thing shall be well, by the purification of the motive in the ground of our beseeching."[6]

What does the proclamation of the absence of the body of Christ mean? It means, in *The Winter's Tale*, that The Invisible Sculptor has not yet finished the statue. The Ultimate Gardener has not yet finished gardening. This is the time *zwischen den Zeiten*, as, you will recall, we Barthians put it. The Sculptor is here in *figura* but not yet in trans*figura*. It is he that doth sculpt us and not we ourselves. The Celestial Sculptor is like a playwright in his own play, spiritually present everywhere, but physically absent, both filling the play and emptying it out. If The Playwright had not filled the play in the first place with himself, there would have been no play. But if he had not emptied it of himself, there would, again, have been no play. The Absent Playwright is giving others a chance to have their own exits and their entrances. Since, then, The Playwright both graciously is and graciously is not in the play, either/or is the wrong way to think about presence and absence, being and not being. As *zwischen den Zeiten* people, our watchword must be: "both already and not yet." Jesus Christ is both here and not here. We are living in the empty place, the real absence, between the tragedy and the comedy. In this time between, when the resurrection vision has not yet become flesh for us, as it has for our Lord, we must do what Saint Paulina says to do: "It is requir'd / You do awake your faith" (V, iii, 94-95).

So many theological interpretations of Shakespeare have been proffered across the centuries without moving us any closer to consensus on the topic of Shakespeare and religion that a good case can be made for abandoning the inquiry altogether. Still, I have already in this chapter made some wild claims about the theological (or a possible theological) meaning in *The Winter's Tale*, and it is proper for me to try to tell what I base these claims on. For the remainder of this chapter I propose to think about *The Winter's Tale* in the light of some hefty quotations from Richard Hooker's *Of the Laws of Ecclesiastical Polity*.

We shall begin with an examination of a discussion of grafting in Act IV of the play, a discussion which, I think, is as central to the soteriology of *The Winter's Tale* as is Paul's discussion of grafting in the epistle to the Romans. The situation in Act IV is that Hermione has supposedly been dead for sixteen years; Leontes has done penance for sixteen years; their old friend Polixenes has for the same time been dwelling in his own island kingdom of Bohemia in isolation from Leontes. The fact that Bohemia is not an island does not disturb our Shakespeare in this study of improbability which is *The Winter's Tale*. Nor is Shakespeare disturbed by the improbable fact that Paulina's elderly husband, Antigonus, had actually deposited Hermione's baby daughter for safe-keeping on Polixenes' island sixteen years previously. Leontes had decreed that the baby (to whom Hermione had given birth just before dying) should be killed or taken far away to be exposed to the elements. Antigonus (thinking it was better that he should die than that the baby should) had spent the last energies of his life trying to save the baby, and, having survived shipwreck and landed on the shore of Bohemia, was never to be heard from again ("Exit, pursued by a bear," Shakespeare's most famous, and most quintessentially tragi-comic, stage direction being the last information we have on poor Antigonus).

Polixenes, of course, is unaware that any little girl has been found on his shores, much less that the little girl is the banished daughter of Hermione and Leontes. The girl, now called Perdita by the aged shepherd who has found her, is reared by the shepherd in Bohemia as if she were his shepherdess daughter. Then, as if Shakespeare has not already thrown all canons of probability to the ocean winds, he introduces Act Four with the figure of old father Time. Time asks the audience to "impute it not a crime" that he slides over the passage of sixteen years in order to "leave the growth untried of that wide gap" (IV, i, 6-7). (Note once again the improbable and repetitive intrusion of the image of growth.) Time explains that Leontes has been for sixteen years grieving in solitude the death of his chaste wife and daughter as well as his son. Perdita has been living in Bohemia "now grown in grace / Equal with wondering." Time also pauses to note that King Polixenes has a son named Florizel (a fact which, in due time, will flower forth—isn't romance fun?—most improbably as grace continues to grow in the fertile vine of our plot).

For the central event of Act Four turns out to be, now that all mannerly distinguishment betwixt prince and beggar has been lost, the romance of princely Florizel and beggarly Perdita. However it happens (and how it happens is of course debatable in all this improbability), the mystery of Florizel's and Perdita's socially taboo attraction to each other proves to be the very mystery that heals the families of their parents. Yet both kings are ignorant of the mystery and (until the last possible moment) of their own healing. Grace (as exemplified by Hermione), Art (Perdita), and Nature (Paulina) are the agents which will in time heal the ignorant kings and their kingdoms, restoring the universe to its gracious moorings. Shakespeare does not allegorize his characters in the wooden way I have suggested, but it is fun to play with such allegorizations. Surely the garden-world of *The Winter's Tale* will tolerate such impish liberties. Shakespeare's own allegorization of Time in Act Four might suggest that he is inviting us to indulge in a bit of allegorical playfulness.

In any case, it is fitting that Time should introduce Act Four because this act is the celebration of time as an instrument of healing. Leontes and

Polixenes have suffered a fall which taints their progeny, but their progeny grow back into grace through a miracle of saving the Perdita that had been lost, and the restoration to grace works back up the generational line until the whole social cosmos is as improbably healed as it had been improbably put asunder. Yet, though time is the agent of grace, it is not the cause of grace. Time is at first the agent of perdition, for it makes possible the visitation of pusnishment upon both generations, even those individuals (like Hermione, Camillo, Paulina, Antigonus, Perdita, her foster father, and Florizel) who deserve no punishment. But in time time becomes, through no power of its own, the instrument of restoration. The crucial point is that Act Four presents a time which becomes an instrument of healing only because it is an instrument of the higher force of improbable (but natural) "growing."

It is not the time which records meaningless change that becomes an instrument of redemption but the time which permits growth, and the cause of nature's growth in this play is The Improbable itself, supernature's grace. Just as Shakespeare has at every point denied simple natural causality as the link among events in this play, so it is not a simple natural time and natural growth that are depicted as the agents of restoration but a time and growth somehow caught up, stretched forward by supra-time to their fruition. The nature which reconciles all the people who had become estranged from each other by the sin of Leontes is a nature (Paulina, you will recall) driven, redeemed, and fulfilled by grace (Hermione). The time and growth of the realm of probability must be, not overthrown, but overgrown, so that they can be transformed by a Gracious Improbability.

It is neither natural nor probable (though it is the essence of Love Stories) that Prince Florizel should be so strangely attracted to this shepherd girl as to say to Perdita in her beggarly clothes:

> These your unusual weeds to each part of you
> Do give a life; no shepherdess, but Flora
> Peering in April's front. This your sheep-shearing
> Is a meeting of the petty gods,
> And you the queen on't (IV, iv, 1-5).

Perdita chides the prince for dressing like a shepherd to woo her. Not so modestly rejoining that "the gods themselves, / Humbling their deities to love, have taken / The shapes of beasts upon them," Florizel says that he will not let his lusts burn hotter than his faith or his desires run before his honor. He intends to marry Perdita.

> For I cannot be
> Mine own, nor any thing to any, if
> I be not thine. To this I am most constant,
> Though destiny say no (IV, iv, 43-46).

Perdita, agreeable to the idea, beseeches lady Fortune to stand auspicious to it. Florizel, Perdita, and Perdita's foster-father, the shepherd, are holding a sheep-shearing festival to which King Polixenes and his faithful attendant Camillo are invited. When Perdita gives the noble guests some flowers to welcome them, a very important interchange ensues. Polixenes notes that he and Camillo are in the winter of their age, and hence it is appropriate for them to receive winter flowers. Perdita says that the fairest flowers there are at the moment between "summer's death" and "the birth of trembling winter" are "our carnations and streak'd gillyvors, / Which some call nature's bastards; of that kind / Our rustic garden's barren; and I care not / To get slips of them" (IV, iv, 81-85). Polixenes asks Perdita why she neglects such flowers, and she responds:

> For I have heard it said
> There is an art which in their piedness shares
> With great creating nature (IV, iv, 86-87).

This response seems to indicate that Perdita fears that the art of grafting is illegitimate because it seeks to compete with nature or because it corrupts nature. The piedness or variegation of creatures, Perdita implies, should be a power reserved for nature alone. The art of grafting illicitly steals nature's power of creation, putting it into human hands. Polixenes, however, teaches Perdita a truth about nature (a truth which he has not yet learned to apply to himself). Polixenes' fatherly gardening lesson will, in due time, come to fruition only when he is forced by improbable events beyond his control to apply it to himself. The speech on grafting is (like St. Paul's speech on grafting in the Epistle to the Romans) the key to the whole *commedia*.

> Say there be;
> Yet nature is made better by no mean
> But nature makes that mean: so, over that art
> Which you say adds to nature, is an art

> That nature makes. You see, sweet maid, we marry
> A gentler scion to the wildest stock,
> And make conceive a bark of baser kind
> By bud of nobler race. This is an art
> Which does mend nature, change it rather; but
> The art itself is nature (IV, iv, 88-96).

Perdita graciously accepts the instruction, and her teacher sums up by saying, "Then make your garden rich in gillyvors, / And do not call them bastards" (IV, iv, 98-99). Yet, as soon as he discovers that his own son, disguised in shepherd's weeds, is planning to marry this "prettiest low-born lass that ever / Ran on the green-sward," Polixenes flies into a Leontes-like rage, threatening to have Perdita's "beauty scratch'd with briers and made / More homely than thy state" (IV, iv, 438-9). Polixenes understands that in the world of nature a gentler scion can be married to the wildest stock to make conceive a bark of baser kind by bud of nobler race, but he does not understand that the same principle applies to human nature, especially his own.

Yet, in defense of Polixenes' indefensible behavior, we must note that he had not said that all grafting is good, only that grafting which is natural, which means that grafting which mends nature, changes it in such a way as to make it better, that grafting which fits in with nature, extending it and bringing it to its own perfection. Hence, we can generalize: for Polixenes, not all art is necessarily good, only that art which is "natural," bringing nature to nature's own perfection. This nature mended by an art which nurtures nature, *The Winter's Tale*, it seems to me, presents as More Than Nature: grace, though most paradoxically.

For now, we can at least say that Polixenes has described the nature of grace and the grace of nature without knowing it. He thinks he has only described nature. Only in due time will he discover that this self-mending power of nature is More Than Nature. Meanwhile, Camillo, the archetypal confidant, listens attentively as Florizel asks for his help in escaping as quickly as possible from the island of Bohemia with his beloved. Camillo, who (though he is temporarily alienated from the mad Leontes) is the very embodiment of faithfulness, is blessed with an uncanny ability to see into the good of things, even under the most improbable circumstances. At this moment, exactly when the future seems least floral for Florizel and most given up to perdition for Perdita, faithful Camillo (full of faith as he is) has a sense that all may yet be well.

Camillo has an intuition that his old master Leontes may now be repentant and just may be willing to harbor Polixenes' son, especially since Polixenes himself seems almost reborn in the features of the young man. Camillo says, as if in prophetic rapture:

> Methinks I see
> Leontes opening his free arms and weeping
> His welcomes forth; asks thee, the son, forgiveness,
> As 't were i' the father's person; kisses the hands
> Of your fresh princess; o'er and o'er divides him
> 'Twixt his unkindness and his kindness; the one
> He chides to hell, and bids the other grow
> Faster than thought or time (IV, iv, 560-7).

Our plot, which, like the morning-glory, is determined to grow as far as possible as fast as possible both vertically and horizontally, twists through many rustic beauties, including Autolycus (a Hermes figure), and various pastoral Dorcases and Mopsas, all of them adding with super-abundant richness to the imagery of growth, time, art, nature, the mending of nature, and the awesome presence of More Than Nature. It is tempting to pause to follow each turn of each tendril, but there is altogether too much richness for one book to do justice to. The main thread of the vine resumes just before Florizel and Perdita reach Sicilia, when Cleomenes, an attendant of King Leontes, renews the theme of penitence in speaking to the king.

Unlike Paulina, who had said sixteen years before that no penitence could ever begin to speak to the enormity of Leontes' misdeeds, Cleomenes thinks that Leontes should cease to blame himself and accept heaven's forgiveness:

> Sir, you have done enough, and have perform'd
> A saint-like sorrow. No fault could you make,
> Which you have not redeem'd; indeed, paid down
> More penitence than done trespass. At the last
> Do as the heavens have done, forget your evil;
> With them forgive yourself (V, i, 1-6).

In the ensuing scenes Leontes begins to move toward acceptance of the forgiveness proffered him. Florizel and Perdita present themselves to him. Leontes greets them with the love and joy Camillo had foreseen. In the course of the encounter Paulina and Leontes discover that the girl claiming to be

Florizel's sister is in fact the lost daughter of Leontes and Hermione. She looks exactly like her mother. As if this reunion had not been enough, Paulina offers in a celebrative gesture to let Leontes see in her home a statue which has been in the making for years. It is a statue of Leontes' departed wife.

By this time Polixenes and Camillo have arrived in search of Florizel and Perdita, and all of them accompany Leontes to Paulina's home to see the statue. Paulina carefully prepares the king for this encounter with an art that skillfully mocks nature. Although this artful statue is only a "dead likeness," Paulina urges, "...prepare / To see the life as lively mock'd as ever / Still sleep mock'd death. Behold! and say 't is well" (V, iii, 18-20). Leontes is stunned by the lifelikeness of the statue. Paulina explains that the artist has made the statue appear as Hermione would now have appeared had she lived for sixteen more years than she did. Maddened by the artwork, Leontes is possessed by a feeling that it is alive. Perdita bows to the statue to kiss its hand. Paulina apologizes to the king for causing him such agitation. She insists that she must draw the curtain around the statue before the king begins to imagine that it may move, but Leontes will not allow her to remove the apparition from his sight. When Leontes swears that the chisel has allowed this statue to breathe, he determines to kiss the statue, and Paulina prevents him. Either she must close the curtain now, or the group must be prepared for yet more amazement, and she must not be accused of using the assistance of wicked powers. All agree to stay. Paulina has the music begin, and the miracle occurs: "'Tis time; descend; be stone no more; approach" (V, iii, 99). Leontes sums up the play's fulfillment of art in nature in grace: "O, she's warm! / If this be magic, let it be an art / Lawful as eating" (V, iii, 109-111). Paulina introduces Perdita to her mother. Hermione again refers to grace in her restoration as she had at the beginning of her perdition: "You gods, look down / And from your sacred vials pour out your graces / Upon my daughter's head!" (V, iii, 121-3)

Yet Hermione's resurrection is but the first-fruits of the restored cosmos, the earnest of what is to come. All that had been lost has not yet been found. Hermione and Leontes have lost sixteen years. Their only son has died. Paulina's husband has died. All the major figures of the play have been severely stricken by their separation from one another. The healing has not removed the wounds. Redemption has begun, but, as Paulina knows, this is still the time *zwischen den Zeiten* (as we Barthians put it), between the total loss and the total restoration. Paulina rejoices in her lords' joys, but she herself must wait for her own. She says:

> Go together,
> You precious winners all; your exultation
> Partake to every one. I, an old turtle,
> Will wing me to some wither'd bough, and there
> My mate, that's never to be found again,
> Lament till I am lost (V, iii, 130-5).

Leontes understands Paulina's grief. He does not want her to leave, but he does not force her to stay. The pattern of restoration must proceed according to its own time. Leontes is at last no longer the slave of suddenness.

The finding of what had been lost, the unpredictable fulfillment of the one hope that had seemed so incapable of fulfillment that it was not worth hoping for—the achievement of forgiveness and the restoration to life of the dead—is the subject of *The Winter's Tale*, and it is the content of the Christian category of grace. The instrument of redemption is art in *The Winter's Tale*, but the cause that operates the instrument is unmistakably something more than art, just as the restored Hermione is something more than that statue which is the instrument of her restoration and just as Polixenes' winter flower is possible not only because of the art of grafting but also because that art is the instrument of the power which through nature betters nature.

In other words, art (Perdita) is the instrument that gives form to the working of nature (Paulina), but nature already has a fundamental level of form (law, order, pattern) even in its present fallen state before art does anything to it because of the living presence in nature's own home of what the world deems lost: grace (Hermione herself). So, though art gives form to nature, art is not the cause of nature's form but the tool used by that grace which continually forms nature and reforms it. Unless the art is one that, like grafting, is properly related to nature's own form-giving power (grace), it will be only the ape of nature at best and the rebellious upsetter of nature at worst. Therefore, art is not a free agent in giving form to nature but a natural agent, the servant of the higher form-giving power of grace. But art's servant-hood is ironically the key to art's freedom because only in this way does art participate in nature's freedom, which results from nature's participation in the freedom of "great creating nature," that art of grace which nurtures nature.

As Richard Hooker puts it, "every creature's limitation is according to his own kind, and therefore as oft as we note in them any thing above their kind, it argueth that the same is not properly theirs, but groweth in them from a cause more powerful than they are" (V, lv, 2).[7] This is the reasoning Polixenes,

Florizel, and Camillo use when they cannot help thinking that the lowly shepherdess Perdita must in fact be more than she appears to be, a noble in shepherdess's clothing, as it were (as indeed grace in nature in art is): "...nothing she does or seems / But smacks of something greater than herself, / Too noble for this place," says Polixenes of Perdita at the sheep-shearing festival (IV, iv, 157). Camillo calls her "the queen of curds and cream" (IV, iv, 161), and Florizel says that not only is she queenly but all her acts are queens (IV, iv, 146). Perdita demonstrates by means of her mastery of every art that she is more than nature appears to make her. Perdita uses art to improve her nature, and yet that is possible only because Perdita's real nature is in fact that of a queen, a superior nature, a new nature, in comparison with her fallen shepherdess state. It is "natural" for Perdita to be more than her apparent nature allows her to appear to be because by real nature Perdita is more than apparent nature allows her to appear to be. In that sense Perdita's grace is her nature; her nature is her grace; and the medium of connection between her grace and her nature is her art, her "great creating art," which, like a mother, nurtures nature. Perdita's art is a medium of connection between gods and mortals and therefore is also revelation. Through art The Lost One reveals the unlost grace of her actual nature which we in our lostness falsely think we have lost but which great greating nature (through the agency of Grace-Hermione, Nature-Paulina, and Faith-Camillo) has ensured that we have not lost.

A reality both beyond and within both art and fallen nature enables Perdita to practice her art in such a way as to improve her nature by restoring her true nature. Her new nature told the truth about Perdita's "lost" original nature. Hence grace works in this lost daughter of the king, never in opposition to nature or in spite of nature, but through nature from beyond nature. Grace does not do its work suddenly (as Leontes in his sin had wanted both truth and action to be sudden) but slowly, laboriously, intricately, in the real time of sixteen long years. And in this respect *The Winter's Tale*, though a comedy, is still a tragedy also. The finding of the Perdita that had been lost and the flowering of the Florizel that had almost been smothered were painful salvations. Much that had been lost has not yet been restored. Everything that was restored was restored only through agonizing separation, penitence, and long, tender, intricate growth. And although this restoration amounted to the fulfillment of true grace, nature, and faith, nevertheless, grace, nature, and faith had to be lost, and the human beings who had lost their grace, nature, and faith had to suffer from the consequences of their alienation before reason could be fulfilled through Divine Improbability and nature could be restored through

Gracious Art. The comedy of romance had to grounded in the tragedy of irony (as we Fryeeans say). To put the pain of *The Winter's Tale's* salvation story into a theological perspective, let us turn to an examination of the pain of salvation and its ironies in the soteriology of Richard Hooker.

For most Christian theologians, pride or selfishness has been the paradigm for sin, but Hooker sees the essence of sin as sloth. He stresses human beings' resistance to the working, forming, infusing, persevering, seeking, and transforming work of grace. Nature, for Hooker, is known by its works, but human beings in their fallen state often do not bother to work. Human beings prefer a lesser good to a greater good because they so often have not even had the enlightened self-interest to seek out the greater good. "For there was never sin committed," Hooker says, "wherein a less good was not preferred before a greater, and that wilfully;... There is not that good which concerneth us, but it hath evidence enough for itself, if Reason were diligent to search it out" (I, vii, 7). In the Appendix to Book V, written especially on grace in response to the Puritans, Hooker concludes yet more strongly: "So that our ignorance we must impute to our own slought [sic]...we study to deceive ourselves." In associating our lack of knowledge with our lack of diligence, Hooker is uncompromising: "...if God's special grace did not aid our imbecility, whatsoever we do or imagine would be only and continually evil" (V, App. I, 1).

It is clear in the light of such a passage that Hooker gives no credit to reason alone, much less to the will alone, for coming to understand something of nature's laws: for grace aids our imbecility. Without grace we would not even use our reason. "The search of knowledge is a thing painful; and the painfulness of knowledge is that which maketh the Will so hardly inclinable thereunto" (I, vii, 7). Just as Adam sinned through being too slothful to avoid negligence, so we are now cursed to finding the search for knowledge painful, even though Hooker agrees with Aristotle that human beings by nature love to know and to know more. Although we love to know, in our hatred of the work of learning we prefer a lesser good to our own greater good and hence remain ignorant. These obervations are not incidental for Hooker but central. For Hooker sees original sin always in terms of the refusal to work, to seek, to look up and recognize what is before our very eyes, and he sees grace always in terms of the aid to our imbecility, the power to work because it is the power which works in us, to make (as in Zen) what is directly in front of us obvious to us at last.

This emphasis on sin as sloth and grace as a working further explains why it is no foreign imposition on Hooker's thought when we argue that for Hooker, as much as for Shakespeare, the model of nature and art stands in significant analogy with the model of nature and grace. Yet it is an analogy of faith, not an analogy of being. Nature itself shows only nature itself. Beyond nature, there appears to be nothing. There is no necessary connection, no step ladder, between nature and More Than Nature in either the realm of grace or the realm of art. Whatever happens between Nature and More Than Nature is initiated and directed by More Than Nature. More Than Nature works on Nature by a process which, though quite reasonable in itself, appears to us to be Improbable, monstrously impossible.

Hooker frequently speaks of God as the workman of the universe, the artificer of man. When we compare these passages with his statements on the artist's relationship with his or her medium, we may note that two characteristics are always present: (1) there is stress on the presence of the artificer in his or her artwork; (2) there is much interest in the problem of intractable matter, the difficult, almost unworkable material that may at first glance seem to spoil the artificer's work but after all has clearly redounded by its very intractability to the greater glory of both the artificer and the work.

A stirling example of the stress on the presence of the artificer in the artwork is found in Book V:

> They which thus were in God eternally by their intended admission
> to life, have by vocation or adoption God actually now in them, as the
> artificer is in the work which his hand doth presently frame. Life as all
> other gifts and benefits groweth originally from the Father, and cometh
> not to us but by the Son, nor by the Son to any of us in particular but
> through the Spirit (V, lvi, 7; cf. I, iii, 4).

This life that "grows" from the Father, this grace that is transmitted from Father to Son, this indwelling of the Holy Spirit, is in no sense mechanical or automatic. It is a living, a growing, a transplanting, a dwelling, and when the gift of life is growing in the soul in grace, the process of grace's forming the virtues is itself far from mechanical or automatic. For Hooker, grace happens through the efforts of a God who works, a divine artificer. When Hooker speaks in Book I about the laws of nature, he points often to the obedience of the particulars to the scheme of the general, and yet he always emphasizes that the more freedom the creature possesses, the more difficult is that obedience. "See we not plainly that obedience of creatures unto the law of nature is the stay of the whole world?" (I, iii, 2). Yet in the very next passage Hooker shows us the peril in which this stay of the whole world stands. The divine artificer has rude and obstinate stuff with which to work when it comes to negligent humanity!

> Notwithstanding with nature it cometh sometimes to pass as with art. Let Phidias have rude and obstinate stuff to carve, though his art do that it should, his work will lack that beauty which otherwise in fitter matter it might have had (I, iii, 3).

In Book V, Hooker returns to the same theme in different words. It is an important point for him because Hooker is following Aquinas's practice of observing first the order of nature and then extrapolating to the necessity of an orderly artificer. Hooker, for all his intricate use of Augustine, still refuses to use the Augustinian innate ideas as windows onto divinity. Since he stresses the observation of nature's lawfulness as indispensable both in the interpretation of Scripture and in the individual's view of him or herself, Hooker must have some way of coping with the erratic in nature, the apparently futile. Does lawlessness come from a lawful God? Hooker's model of God as artificer and grace as a *working* provides the answer that it is nothing against the credit of an artificer if the material he or she works on resists his or her efforts to shape it. On the contrary, it is to the artificer's credit if he or she can do anything at all with difficult material. Hence, not only does nature have need of grace, but nature also needs art, in the sense of skilled working, in order to let its difficult materials be veritably beaten into shape. The most difficult and intractable of nature's materials, for Hooker, is slothful humanity. Hooker says in Book V about the credit due to the divine artificer in his sturggle with intractable humanity:

> If we leave Nature and look into Art, the workman hath in his heart a purpose, he carrieth in mind the whole form which his work should have, there wanteth not in him skill and desire to bring his labour to the best effect, only the matter which he hath to work on is unframable. This necessity excuseth him, so that nothing is derogated from his credit, although much of his work's perfection be found wanting (V, ix, 1).

But is Hooker's approach to nature and art really similar to that of Polixenes in the grafting passage? Polixenes speaks of nature itself as something that seems to have a power of its own to create. Perdita speaks of the "piedness" of nature, the variegation of it, as if it is a power native to nature itself. Is not

Hooker doing something very different when he employs his nature-art model in speaking of nature's creator, the divine artificer? It seems to me that even here Hooker is using the term "nature" and understanding the attributes of nature in very much the same way as Polixenes and Perdita do. Hooker also cites the variegation of nature as evidence of its creativity, and yet for him nature's creativity is necessarily evidence of God's creativity. Hooker traces with care the relationship (including profound differences) between his use of the artificer model and Plato's use of the demiurge model. One passage in particular from Book I deserves special examination:

> Although we are not of opinion therefore, as some are, that nature in working hath set before her certain exemplary draughts or patterns, which subsisting in the bosom of the Highest and being thence discovered, she fixeth her eye upon them, as travellers by sea upon the pole-star of the world and that according thereunto she guideth her hand to work by imitation (I, iii, 4),

(Hooker knows that such a Platonic approach could make the divine archetypes more important than the artificer and ultimately have the gnostic consequences against which the early church had so laboriously protected herself)

> ...nevertheless, forasmuch as the works of nature are no less exact, than if she did both behold and study how to express some absolute shape or mirror always before her; yea such her dexterity and skill appeareth, that no intellectual creature in the world were able by capacity and knowledge to do that which nature doth without capacity and knowledge; it cannot be but natue hath some director of infinite knowledge to guide her in all her ways. Who the guide of nature, but only the God of nature? 'In him we live, move, and are.' [Acts 17:28] ....nor is there any such art or knowledge divine in nature herself working, but in the Guide of nature's work (I, iii, 4).

Hooker and Shakespeare both, it seems to me, were opposing the image of a bifurcated universe, in which the fallen world is on one level and the world of grace is on a separate level. Instead, Hooker and Shakespeare are envisioning the cosmos more as a globe within a globe, the outer globe representing nature as we pereceive it with our ordinary senses and the inner globe representing grace, or the power of self-renewing nature. Art, as I am imagining it, might best be conceived in this vision not as another globe but as the working force, the energy, that keeps charging, like electricity (we would say), from grace through nature and renewing it, keeping it truly natural. Art, then, is, like time, the active agent of grace in grace's energetic renewal of nature. The best art seems most artless, most natural, most grace-ful, because it mocks nature as beguilingly as Julio Romano's art salvifically mocks Hermione. To carry this model yet further, it seems to me that art is operating in *The Winter's Tale* and in Hooker's theology much the way the Holy Spirit operates in Christian Trinitarian theory, linking grace and nature as the Holy Sprit links the Father and the Son in tri-unity, spreading the divine love throughout the universe, filling everything with God. Neither Hooker nor Shakespeare describes the grace-nature-art triad in Trinitarian terms. But, in a culture steeped in Christian discussion, triads often behave in Trinitarian ways. I think that is what is happening here, probably quite unconsciously.

As a symbol of resurrection, the statue of Hermione represents the entry of life eternal into temporal life. The important thing about the symbol is that it does not destroy nature but fulfills it. This art, this gracious magic, is a divine art which out-natures nature, and it can do this only because it comes into nature not from outside it but from the center and circumference of it, from the fullness and fulfillment of it. As grace, eternal life is the form of time, the ultimate shape of time from its inmost center to its outermost circumference. Eternity is the form-giving globe within the globe of time. Eternal life does not destroy time's linearity. (Sixteen years are still sixteen years.) But, by shaping time into a holy globe, eternal life heals the estrangement which time's linearity, its beside-each-other-ness, has forced upon human experience. As a saving circle, a saving globe, redeemed time shows us the end of things wrapped up in the beginning, the fulfillment in the commencement, the inner globe in the outer globe, the miraculous resurrection of mother Hermione precisely in the apparent perdition of daughter Perdita. As a saving circle, a saving globe, redeemed time (I would say) liberates linear time from dualism into duality. By redeeming time, grace reveals the positive of nature's negative.

The idea that grace redeems the soul by giving it the form of love is of course available to Hooker from the writings of Thomas Aquinas. Yet it seems to me that because of his particular ambience in Elizabethan art-nature theorizing, Hooker may be modifying Thomas's paradigm in an interesting way. Hooker says, with Thomas, that grace dwells in us through the Holy Spirit, and, with Thomas, Hooker uses the model of infusion for this relationship. But Hooker is more likely than Thomas to emphasize the difficulty of the work that grace accomplishes in working on our intractability. Hooker is as consistent as Thomas in his use of Aristotle's hylomorphic concept of substance, but while Thomas has so much reverence for grace that he assumes grace carries out its work of forming the soul just by its very presence, Hooker has so much suspicion of our intractability that he assumes grace must do more than simply be present in the soul if it is to give form to the soul.

For Hooker, grace must work relentlessly on our sloth, like Phidias hammer-and-chiselling away on his rock. Hence, I think we can say that, for both The Winter's Tale *and Richard Hooker, God is like a sculptor, and we are the stone into which God is continually breathing life and gradually pounding the form which was in fact already there but has been, to all appearances, lost. The form was already in the stone, not because of the stone, but because of the creative vision of the divine artificer, who put the form into the stone in the first place. And the form is created in the sculptor's own image, and in that respect the sculptor is inside the stone. The sculptor is both in the stone and not in it, both present and absent. The sculptor, like Michelangelo, is liberating his slaves' personhood from death to life as he gradually pounds the slaves out of the Promethean rock into the glorious liberty of the children of God.*

Hence we can ask, for both Hooker and Shakespeare: had Hermione really died, only to be brought back to life by sixteen years of hard work from the hand of Julio Romano or (just as improbably) had she been alive all along in the kingdom of the morally blind king, preserved in the home of Saint Paulina, the harsh school-mistress? The answer must be *both*. Hermione was dead to nature but alive to God. She was dead to life but alive to art. Hermione was hidden behind the stone of the tomb which her unjust husband had consigned her to but alive in the womb of the tomb, alive in the globe (grace) within the globe (nature), waiting until the time should be fulfilled; waiting until the Perdita who had been lost could be found and the Florizel who had been smothered could flower. So, in God, grace had been alive all along. Saint Paulina's penitential law had been the school-mistress leading us to the resurrected one. But all along God, our sculptor, had invisibly worked like a most energetic Phidias to make the whole thing happen. Simply being present was not enough for God. Yet when God worked so hard on our intractable nature, it was not because our intractability had any power over him and forced him to work. God could have accomplished everything in an instant, redeeming our nature by destroying it. Instead, God chose to work slowly and carefully, complicating everything like a long winter's tale that expands in every direction at once, because this was a more glorious way to accomplish his feat. In this slow and intricate way God was affirming our lives even when we had given up on them. God was ever so gradually extricating us from the destructive plots in which we had wrapped, tangled, and strangled ourselves. Nature reveals something of God by revealing God as working. In art, the human being is working within the concentric circles of God's working, as grafting artisans work by attuning themselves to nature's working, which itself is attuned to God's working. Thus, grace is grafted into humanity as the living Hermione is, as it were, grafted into the statue of Hermione, and what appears to be art (the imitation of Hermione) turns out to be grace (the restoration of Hermione). Nature and art are thus the vessels of grace within God's ordered pattern of creation, preservation, and redemption.

But how is grace so present in nature that it appears to be nature, not grace? How can both Shakespeare and Hooker speak at times as if "great creating Nature," not God, is the creator of nature? To explore this topic, we must investigate Hooker's concept of the participation of grace in nature. The key to the grace/nature relationship in Hooker is the art/nature relationship. As an example of Hooker's concept of God's participation, his real presence, in his creation there is no more forceful statement than the following:

> God hath his influence into the very essence of all things, without which influence of Deity supporting them their utter annihilation could not choose but follow....The Father as Goodness, the Son as Wisdom, the Holy Ghost as Power do all concur in every particular outwardly issuing from that one only glorious Deity which they all are....Therefore whatsoever we do behold now in this present world, it was enwrapped within the bowels of divine Mercy, written in the book of eternal Wisdom, and held in the hands of omnipotent Power, the first foundation of the world being as yet unlaid.
>
> So that all things which God hath made are in that respect the offspring of God, they are *in him* as effects in their highest cause, he likewise is *in them*, the assistance and influence of his Deity is *their life* (V, lvi, 5).

In specifically Christological passages Hooker explores more intricately this emphasis on the participation of God in his works and the participation of his works in him. For here Hooker stresses yet more the specifically salvific effect of this mutual inward participation. Hooker is not content with interpretations of our participation in Christ and Christ's in us which see this participation as only figurative:

> It is too cold an interpretation....The Church is in Christ as Eve was in Adam. Yea by grace we are every of us in Christ and in his Church, as by nature we are in those our first parents. God made Eve of the rib of Adam. And his Church he frameth out of the very flesh, the very wounded and bleeding side of the Son of man (V, lvi, 7).

This is the type of participational relationship which I think Shakespeare saw between nature and the creating power of nature in the grafting scene, between the dead Hermione and the restored Hermione, the lost Perdita and the found, the penitent Leontes and the forgiven. Without this mutual inward participation of the state of nature and the state of grace, both grace and nature are impossible. For Hooker, the gracious God and his fallen creatures are also related to each other through a state of mutual inward participation. This participation is summed up in Christ. In Christ God participates in us and we in God. But Christ's human nature is not fallen. It is a human nature that does not need salvation. It is salvation. Therefore, in describing the relation between human and divine in Christ, Hooker is concerned with the preservation of the separate integrity of the human nature and the divine nature. Hooker sums up the relationship between the human and divine natures of Christ as follows:

> Let us therefore set it down for a rule or principle so necessary as nothing more to the plain deciding of all doubts and questions about the union of natures in Christ, that of both natures there is a *co-operation* often, an *association* always, but never any mutual *participation*, whereby the properties of the one are infused into the other (V, liii, 3; V, liv, 10).

Hooker's concern in this passage is to avoid a collapsing into each other of the categories of divinity and humanity. Through Christ's work divinity and humanity have a mutual inward participation in each other, but that is only because of Christ's *work*. Hooker is giving us no monism by which divinity would actually be humanity and humanity would actually be divinity. On the contrary, divinity is different from humanity. There is a real presence of the one in the other, but this positive has a meaning only beacuse of its corresponding negative: that there is also a real absence of the one from the other. Humanity is not divinity. The link between them is work—the work of grace, the work of art, and the work of Christ.

When humanity is perfect, as in Christ, it remains humanity. In Christ, humanity often cooperates with divinity; it always associates itself with divinity, but the two are never infused into each other. The point is that we are not created to be God. We are created to be human. God's salvation does not destroy our humanity. God does not change our nature from humanity to divinity. On the contrary, God's salvation saves our humanity by fulfilling it, bringing it to its fruition precisely by bringing it *back* to its true humanity. To say this in Shakespearean terms, Hermione did not become a goddess. She became what she had been intended to be in the first place, a human being. Nor did Hermione become Julio Romano or Paulina. Her gracious sculptor brought Hermione back to exactly the person she had been created to be in the first place. Julio Romano-Paulina saved Hermione by restoring her, not by metamorphosing her. This is a way of saying that human destiny is excellent. Humanity is, in spite of its fall, most worthy of salvation. God made us worthy of salvation. We are made in the image of God.

Hence, when we have established that humanity is not destined to be divinity, even in Christ, it is possible to speak more precisely about the specific kind of "infusion" or "participation" between humanity and divinity which grace makes possible. In Christ, divinity and humanity maintain their separate dignities, as they must if the union between divinity and humanity is to be a union and not a confusion, and yet by the powerful work of God's grace in Christ a redemptive union (not confusion) of divinity with humanity occurs:

> Touching union of Deity with manhood, it is by grace, because there can be no greater grace shewed towards man, than that God should vouchsafe to unite to man's nature the person of his only begotten Son (V, liv, 3).

Hooker speaks in forceful terms of the thoroughness of this new union of divine and human:

> We have hitherto spoken of the Person and of the presence of Christ. Participation is that mutual inward hold which Christ hath of us and we of him, in such sort that each possesseth other by way of special interest, property, and inherent copulation (V, lvi, 1).

Yet Hooker is always careful to insist that this mutual inward hold is only possible because of the distinction of the two natures in Christ himself:

> The sequel of which conjunction of natures in the person of Christ is no abolishment of natural properties appertaining to either substance, no transition or transmigration thereof out of one substance into another, finally no such mutual infusion as really causeth the same natural operations or properties to be made common unto both substances; but whatsoever is natural to Deity the same remaineth in Christ uncommunicated unto his manhood, and whatsoever natural to manhood his Deity thereof is uncapable (V, liii, 1).

In summary, Hooker says: "To gather therefore into one sum all that hitherto hath been spoken touching this point, there are but four things which concur to make complete the whole state of our Lord Jesus Christ: his Deity, his manhood, the conjunction of both, and the distinction of the one from the other being joined in one" (V, liv, 10). This delicate balance serves as the model for Hooker's other descriptions of the nature of the relationship between divine and human: in nature, in humanity, and in the sacraments. Hooker is lucidly steering around one theological reef after another in these troubled waters. For example, on the question of the (Protestant) emphasis on justification-by-imputation versus the (Catholic) emphasis on sanctification-by-the-infusion-of-grace-as-a-*habitus*, Hooker, ever seeking his *via media*, refuses (quite hilariously—talk about comedic solutions to tragic problems!) to pit the one against the other:

> Thus we participate Christ partly by imputation, as when those things which he did and suffered for us are imputed unto us for righteousness; partly by habitual and real infusion, as when grace is inwardly bestowed while we are on earth, and afterwards more fully both our souls and bodies are made like unto his in glory (V, lvi, 11).

For Hooker refuses to consider the process of justification as an act which can be lifted out of the natural medium of time. Just as grace, for Hooker, cannot form the soul without the sort of incessant working upon intractable matter which Phidias performs upon stone, so God wills not to redeem without using the created instrument of time. Nature is fallen. An instantaneous restoration of nature would necessitate the instantaneous abolishing of nature, the approach (which I would call dualistic) that some of the more extreme Puritans took. But a restoration of nature which builds on nature's own fallen powers and instruments cannot abolish nature's instruments and cannot be instantaneous. Growth in grace, the formation of the *habitus* of grace within the soul, the infusion of supernatural power within the natural vessel of the human being: these require time. They build upon time to redeem time.

To conclude our consideration of the role of the art-nature paradigm in Hooker's Christology, we must ask whether his way of handling the conjunction-disjunction problem in the two natures of Christ has a parallel in his way of thinking about God's relation to nature and reason's relation to appetite. For in thinking about Christ we are not, Hooker always insists, thinking just about the abstract problem of two separate levels of being coming into conjunction but about the person of God coming into relationship with the person of that humanity which has rejected him. Hence Hooker's Christology does not stay on the metaphysical level of the two-natures problem but is graciously driven into the devotional realm of God's personal interaction with our recalcitrant souls. In disucssing the role of the Phidias model in Hooker's concept of grace, I have suggested that Hooker sees God as a Phidias working on the intractable matter of nature; grace as a Phidias working on the intractable matter of our soul; and reason as a Phidias working on the intractable matter of appetite. All three of these relationships are ultimately based, for Hooker, on the model of Christ's redemptive conjunction of divinity and humanity. The key to this conjunction in Christ is, as we have seen, the retention of a metaphysical distinction, a real absence, between the two poles of the relationship at the same time as there is a real *working* of the one pole on and in the other, a real presence.

A single sentence of remarkable scope in Book I reveals the centrality of the work-concept among such crucial categories as being, law, and perfection: "The being of God is a kind of law to his working: for that perfection which God is, giveth perfection to that he doth" (I, ii, 2). We can see something of the pattern of God's own being from our observation of God's working. The perfection of God's being gives perfection to what he does. Yet Hooker never says that we see perfection in the fallen vessels of this earth. The Phidias model is crucial. For just as Phidias cannot make a perfect statue with imperfect stone, so God wills not to make a perfect world out of imperfect matter. Yet the intractability of the matter redounds to the greater glory of the artificer. God uses imperfection for perfect purposes. God is not threatened by imperfection, nor is the perfection of his working hindered by it.

If therefore it be demanded, why God having power and ability infinite, the effects notwithstanding of that power are all so limited as we see they are: the reason hereof is the end which he hath proposed, and the law whereby his wisdom hath stinted the effects of his power in such sort that it doth not work infinitely, but correspondently unto the end for which it worketh, even "all things χρηστωσ [Sap. 8:1; 11:20] in most decent and comely sort," all things in "Measure, Number, and Weight" (I, ii, 3).

Therefore, Hooker does not use a naive cosmological argument for God's existence. For it is not enough to extrapolate from the observation of order in the creation surrounding us to the assumption that God's activity is orderly. This approach is insufficient because the nature in which we live is fallen. Our own sloth and negligence have done much to make God's purposes in nature appear to be disordered; our own reasoning power, exalted as it is above anything Travers and Cartwright believed it to be, is still twisted and sickened by our excessive appetite and faltering will. Therefore, Hooker presents a God known to us by his works, but at the same time the imperfection of the works around us must be measured according to the perfection of the ends for which God has ordained them. God tolerates, indeed uses, the imperfection of his natural vessels (ourselves) for his own perfect purposes. "Nor is the freedom of the will of God any whit abated, let or hindered, by means of this; because the imposition of this law upon himself is his own free and voluntary act" (I, ii, 6). God does not work in the world as (we would say) a machine works on its product. God's will is able to "stint" the ordinary laws of nature's operation for the sake of his own larger purposes.

Nature than which there is nothing more constant, nothing more uniform in all her ways, doth notwithstanding stay her hand, yea, and change her course, when that which God by creation did command, he doth at any time by necessity countermand (V, ix, i).

Hooker gives as an example of this alteration in nature's normal functioning "unloos[ing] the very tongues even of dumb creatures" (V, ix, 1). Is it possible that we are seeing latent nominalist patterns here? Is Hooker envisioning a level of existence which is ruled *de potentia ordinata*, in which we live and observe and use our reason and then on the other side, wholly transcendent to us and unkowable by us, the free realm of God's untrammeled and inexplicable activity *de potentia absoluta*? No, Hooker rules out any such bifurcation of God's activity. Indeed, Hooker is just as concerned to rule out this nominalist skepticism about human knowledge of the pattern of divine activity as he is to rule out an independent reason unaided by revelation: "They err therefore who think that of the will of God to do this or that there is no reason besides his will....not only according to his own will, but 'the Counsel of his own will' [Eph. 1:11]" does God rule (I, ii, 5).

Hence we may summarize Hooker's ideas about God's method of working in nature as follows:

1. God's being is a law unto his working: the perfection of God is transmitted as the perfection of his works;

2. innumerable works of God in our midst appear to be imperfect;

3. the first reason for this apparent imperfection is the intractability of the matter with which God chooses to work;

4. the second necessary consideration in regard to apparent imperfection is that God stints his own power to achieve purposes which he chooses to carry out not instantaneously but *in time*;

5. this stinting of God's activity is not to be seen as an imperfection in God, for it is by his own free will that God obeys the laws which he has ordained;

6. yet God's use of his own free will is itself not utterly untrammeled and unpredictable but according to *the counsel* of his will, the eternal Logos;

7. therefore, God uses reason to guide his will, which freely chooses to obey the laws of reason, which God himself has ordained, and yet since the ultimate ends for which the laws of reason were ordained by God cannot always be known by us, it may appear to us from time to time that God has made exceptions to the general laws of his working. But

8. these temporary apparent imperfections in God's acting are all subordinated to a perfect purpose; yet when they impinge on us, we are reminded of the limitation of our reason as compared with God's and the temporality of our existence as compared with God's eternity.

9.   Ends for us are not yet accomplished; yet God knows both the temporary incompleteness of all purposes and the final fulfillment of all ends. Hooker sums it up this way:

10.   "...unto the word of God, being in respect of that end for which God ordained it perfect, exact, and absolute in itself, we do not add reason as a supplement of any maim or defect therein, but as a necessary instrument, without which we could not reap by the Scripture's perfection that fruit and benefit which it yieldeth" (III, viii, 10).

Hooker's frequent insistence on the necessity of reason as the instrument with which we interpret Scripture has its basis in his assessment of the role of reasonableness in God's own activity. Reason is the counsel of God's will. God's will, like ours, is not made unfree by the laws which reason discerns because reason is followed on account of the free decision of will. Therefore, a reasonable law is the key to freedom. Hooker defines law in different ways in different contexts, but one of his most memorable definitions emphasizes its role as a pattern not only of our activity but also of God's: "That which doth assign unto each thing the kind, that which doth moderate the force and power, that which doth appoint the form and measure of working, the same we term a Law" (I, ii, 1). Hence, for Hooker, a law is not necessarily a prohibition. Much less is it something to be abolished by or held in dialectical tension with Gospel. Much less is law an inordinate demand upon the sinner. For Hooker, law is the pattern by which both God and we are able to choose to act freely. A good law is not the cancellation of reason in the face of authority but the grounding of authority upon reason. Indeed, our capacity to live according to the laws of reason is our chief retention of the image of God: our slothful unwillingness to live according to these laws is our chief obfuscation of God's image.

Man in perfection of nature being made according to the likeness of his Maker resembleth him also in the manner of working: so that whatsoever we work as men, the same we do wittingly work and freely; neither are we according to the manner of natural agents any way so tied, but that it is in our power to leave the things we do undone (I, vii, 2).

Hooker proceeds to outline his understanding of the structure of our various capacities. For the sake of illustrating the careful structure of his statement I will put the sentence into a schematic format and add italics and numbers:

1. *To choose*—is to will one thing before another. And

2. *To will*—is to bend our souls to the having or doing of that which they see to be good.

3. *Goodness*—is seen with the eye of the understanding. And

4. The light of the eye of the understanding—is *reason* (I, vii, 2).

Hooker concludes that "two principal fountains there are of human action[:] knowledge and will..." (I, vii, 2). Following the Phidias model, we may suggest that knowledge in Hooker's model has the duty of working to shape will, but knowledge alone cannot carry out such an active task, and therefore reason, the light of the understanding, the power to know, must work incessantly on our intractable will to drive it to choose the greater good over the lesser.

"Now if men had not naturally this desire to be happy," says Hooker, "how were it possible that all men should have it? All men have. Therefore this desire in man is natural" (I, xi, 4). But our will is slothful in seeking out what it most needs. Will does not exercise enough reason to differentiate between the evil which appears to be good and the true good which may not appear to be good: "For evil as evil cannot be desired: if that be desired which is evil, the cause is the goodness which is or seemeth to be joined with it. *Goodness doth not move by being, but by being apparent....*" (I, vii, 6; italics added). In the Appendix to Book V, Hooker says, "That which moveth man's will, is the *object* or thing desired. That which causeth it to be desired, is either true or apparent goodness: the goodness of things desired is either manifest by sense, gathered by reason, or known by faith" (V, App. 1, 9).

We have therefore a will, the nature whereof is apt and capable as well to receive the good as the evil; but sin is fraudulent, and beguileth us with evil under the shew of good: sloth breeding carelessness, and our original corruption sloth in the power of reason, which should discern between the one and the other (V, App. 1, 8).

But even though our will is both apt and capable to receive the good as well as the evil, aptness and capability are not the same thing. Hooker says to the Puritans: "You peradventure think aptness and ableness all one: whereas the truth is, that had we kept our first ableness, grace should not need; and had aptness been also lost, it is not grace that could work in us more than it doth in brute creatures" (V, App. 1, 1). We have not completely lost the image of God, even though Hooker can say in Book I: "But neither that which we learn of ourselves nor that which others teach us can prevail, where wickedness and malice have taken deep root" (I, x, 3). Still, despite the sickening power of wickedness and malice to pollute both our reason and our will, despite our lack of all "*ableness*" to be reasonable in the pursuit of our own happiness, still the *aptness* for goodness has not been entirely abolished, and here is a fertile field for the work of grace:

> ...Yea, whatsoever our hearts be to God and to his truth, believe we or be we as yet faithless, for our conversion or confirmation the force of natural reason is great. The force whereof unto those effects is nothing without grace. What then? To our purpose it is sufficient, that whosoever doth serve, honour, and obey God, whosoever believeth in Him, that man would no more do this than innocents and infants do, but for the light of natural reason that shineth in him, and maketh him apt to apprehend those things of God, which being by grace discovered, are effectual to persuade reasonable minds and none other, that honour, obedience, and credit, belong of right unto God (III, viii, 11).

Grace uses reason as Phidias uses his chisel to sculpt the intractable matter of sloth. Grace without reason would lead to the destruction of all that mighty workmanship of God, nature itself. But reason without grace would be unable to gain any hearing at all from our negligent will and our confused appetite.

> For whatsoever we have hitherto taught, or shall hereafter, concerning the force of man's natural understanding, this we always desire withal to be understood; that there is no kind of faculty or power in man or any other creature, which can rightly perform the functions allotted to it, without perpetual aid and concurrence of that Supreme Cause of all things (I, viii, 11).

The force of natural reason is great, but its powers are limited by our finitude as surely as they are aided by God's infinitude. "The book of this law we are neither able nor worthy to open and look into," Hooker says of our reason's power to know God's universal order. "That little thereof which we darkly apprehend we admire, the rest with religious ignorance we humbly and meekly adore" (I, ii, 5). Certainly our reason cannot be construed as a gift so powerful that it can dispute with God's reason. Our reason is entirely gift. Our reason is God's instrument for our benefit, not our instrument for rejecting his wisdom. "In matters which concern the actions of God, the most dutiful way on our part is to search what God hath done, and with meekness to admire that, rather than to dispute what he in congruity of reason ought to do" (III, xi, 21).

Self-seeking is a frequent cause of the sinful corruption of our reason, according to Hooker. But more frequent is simple negligence of our true self-interest. Malice and wickedness Hooker has pointed to as diseases of the soul which will sicken even its noblest faculties. But other, at first sight less insidious, ills beset our feeble souls as well: zeal and fear. It happens that Hooker believes the extremists of his own time were peculiarly beset by zeal and fear. In good Aristotelian fashion Hooker describes these ills as excesses of attributes which in moderation would have been good but in their extreme form are destructive: "Wherefore to let go this execrable crew, and to come to extremities on the contrary hand; two affections there are, the forces whereof, as they bear the greater or lesser sway in man's heart, frame accordingly the stamp and character of his religion; the one zeal, the other fear" (V, iii, 1). We do not need to go so far as to say that Shakespeare was in the character of Leontes allegorizing the Puritans of his day, although the excessive prudishness, squeamishness, and cowardice of Leontes, as in the case of that comically moralistic fool Malvolio, must have reminded a few in Shakespeare's audience of the Puritans who were incessantly agitating to have the theater closed down and all tom-foolery brought to an end once and for all. The figure of the zealous coward is familiar enough in any age, and it was the universality of the deadly effects of zeal and fear which must have struck both Hooker and Shakespeare. For both of them explore the ironic relationship between zeal and sloth not just in their own age but in the very make-up of humanity. Says Hooker:

> Zeal, except it be ordered aright, when it bendeth itself unto conflict with things either in deed, or but imagined to be opposite unto religion, useth the razor many times with such eagerness, that the very life of religion itself is thereby hazarded; through hatred of tares the corn in

the field of God is plucked up. So that zeal needeth both ways a sober guide (V, iii, 1).

Whether or not Shakespeare saw Leontes as a Puritan, it would be difficult to find any passage, either Elizabethan or modern, which so nearly approximates the wrong that zeal-crazed king did to his gracious wife. Furthermore, just as Leontes (like Othello and Malvolio in quite different contexts) is a victim not only of his zeal but also of the fear that fanned his zeal, so Hooker appends to his discussion of zeal some apt words about fear:

> Fear on the other side, if it have not the light of true understanding concerning God, wherewith to be moderated, breedeth likewise superstition. It is therefore dangerous, that in things divine we should work too much upon the spur of either zeal or fear. Fear is a good solicitor to devotion. Howbeit...[it] is of all affections (anger excepted) the unaptest to admit any conference with reason...(V, iii, 1).

Ironically, the Malvolio- and Leontes-figures in Shakespeare, like the Puritans in Hooker's description of them, are superstitious about the very qualities of soul which breed superstition: the affections. Whereas Leontes and the early Puritans used the affections of zeal and fear to attempt to drive out the affections that are not desirable, Hooker counselled that the affections must not be either driven out or manipulated but worked upon, nurtured, in an ordered effort to direct them toward devotion to God's purposes. Hence, just as Hooker refuses to drive art from the realm of grace, to drive nature from the pattern of redemption, to drive time from eternity, or to drive Christ's human nature from the God-man Jesus, so he also refuses to drive the affections from the rightly ordered soul. Zeal and fear in excess are the bane of reason, but the effort to eliminate the moderate forms of zeal and fear could arise only from a deeper and more dangerous zeal and fear that were themselves excessive. Therefore, Hooker retains the affections in his image of humanity, working upon them to let them in their disciplined maturity eventually reflect in our humanity the very image of God:

> In the powers and faculties of our souls God requireth the uttermost which our unfeigned affection towards him is able to yield. So that if we affect him not far above all things, our religion hath not that inward perfection which it should have, neither do we indeed worship him as our God (V, vi, 1).

The proper ordering of the affections, then, is part of our larger Christological concern: how is God present in nature and in our human nature? The answer of course can only be that God is graciously both absent and present, which, for Hooker, means present in such a way as to rescue us, to preserve and fulfill us, in spite of our rejection of our own humanity. God is in the process of rescuing, preserving, and fulfilling us in our reason, our will, and our affections. God is restoring his own image in all of them. He loves all of them. None of them needs to be, or should be, abandoned. All must be brought into disciplined and joyful conformity with God's will, and this is "a thing painful" because of our sloth. Being hammered into conformity with God's will means getting hit repeatedly by the terrible chisel of that Sculptor who pounds from both within and without. (A thing painful indeed.)

The most important aid which God gives us in our painful quest for the joy of his salvation is his church. The church mediates to us God's reasonable word and guides us in the difficult and time-consuming task of interpreting his word reasonably, and the church is the custodian of God's sacraments. If we are to understand how Hooker understands God's participation in us and our participation in God, there can be no more helpful resource than his discussion of the sacraments. It is not to our purpose in this context to discuss Hooker's sacramentology in detail, but we can look briefly at his understanding of sacramental presence and absence. As Hooker puts it: "...we are briefly to consider how Christ is present, to the end it may thereby better appear how we are made partakers of Christ both otherwise and in the Sacraments themselves" (V, lv, 1).

> Such as the substance of each thing is, such is also the presence thereof. Impossible it is that God should withdraw his presence from anything, because the very substance of God is infinite. He filleth heaven and earth, although he take up no room in either, because his substance is immaterial, pure, and of us in this world so incomprehensible, that albeit no part of us be ever absent from him who is present whole unto every particular thing, yet his presence with us we no way discern farther than only that God is present, which partly by reason and more perfectly by faith we know to be firm and certain" (V, lv, 3).

This theory of the infinity of deity's presence forms the basis of what at first appears to be a severe problem in Hooker's understanding of Christ's presence:

Which Deity being common unto him with none but only the Father and the Holy Ghost, it followeth that nothing of Christ which is limited, that nothing created, that neither the soul nor the body of Christ, and consequently not Christ as man or Christ according to his human nature can possibly be everywhere present....Wherefore Christ is essentially present with all things, in that he is very God, but not present with all things as man, because manhood and the parts thereof can neither be the cause nor the true subject of such presence (V, lv, 4).

Like Calvin, Hooker refuses to follow the Lutherans, who use the category of Christ's *corpus majestaticum* as a way through the dilemma:

The substance of the body of Christ hath no presence, neither can have, but only local....If his majestical body have now any such new property, by force whereof it may everywhere even in substance present itself, or may at once be in many places, then hath the majesty of his estate extinguished the verity of his nature (V, lv, 6).

It is in order to maintain the true humanity of Christ that Hooker insists on the unique importance of *local* presence in any discussion of Christ's presence. Hooker's Christology, as we have seen, insists that there is a mutual cooperation of the human and divine in Christ but never a confusion of the two, and, as Hooker sees it, this principle would be violated if he were to say that the majestical body of Christ has a substantial presence on earth, yet not a local presence. To hold such a view would, for Hooker, mean that there was something incomplete about the local, historical presence of Christ in the events of his birth, crucifixion, and resurrection. Hooker insists on a memorial presence. He finds a local presence or even a "majestical" substantial presence on earth of the ascended Christ both metaphysically and theologically incoherent. In V, lv, 7, Hooker presents a solution which seems calculated to raise further questions that demand consideration:

To conclude, we hold it in regard of the fore-alleged proofs a most infallible truth that Christ as man is not everywhere present....His human substance in itself is naturally absent from the earth, his soul and body not on earth but in heaven only...yet presence *by way of conjunction* is in some sort presence.

Hooker's elucidation of his category of "presence by way of conjunction" shows why our excursus above on his anthropology was necessary for a consideration of his sacramentology. For the analogy between the structure of our being and the structure of Christ's being makes possible the "presence by way of conjunction." Hooker's insistence that the will and the understanding are the chief fountains of human being comes to unexpected fruition in his doctrine of eucharistic presence:

> This government therefore he exerciseth both as God and as Man, as God by essential presence with all things, as man by cooperation with that which essentially is present. Touching the manner how he worketh as man in all things; the principal powers of the soul of man are the will and the understanding, the one of which two in Christ assenteth unto all things, and from the other nothing which Deity doth work is hid; so that by knowledge and assent the soul of Christ is present with all things which the Deity of Christ worketh (V, lv, 8).

Just as we order our affections by directing both our will and our understanding to the purposes of God, so Christ, as man, knows by understanding the purposes of God and by will carries them out. Thus God is present in Christ not by driving out the human natue of Christ (the qualities of will and understanding) but by working upon them, while they in turn cooperate with God. Hence Christ as human is finite and as God is infinite, and yet the finite in no sense contains the infinite, and the infinite does not destroy the finite.

Hooker can use Thomas's category of the effective presence of Christ in a way that in no sense conflicts with Thomas's image of the moon's effective presence in the tides. For example, in illustrating that no stint can be set to "the value or merit of the sacrificed body of Christ," stressing that it is "infinite in *possibility of application*," Hooker can say, "And even the body of Christ itself, although the definite limitation thereof be most sensible, doth notwithstanding admit in some sort a kind of infinite and unlimited presence likewise…, *a presence of force and efficacy* throughout all generations of men" (V, lv, 9). Yet Hooker's own fundamental illustration for the presence of God in Christ as well as the presence of Christ in the eucharistic celebration is not that of moon and tides but rather Phidias and the intractable stone. The moon is more present in the tides than Christ is present in Hooker's sacrament, for the moon cannot fail to be in the tides, and the tides cannot fail to respond to the moon's pulling, but Hooker's model makes more room for miscarriages in the mediation of grace, for the rock-like intractability of fallen humanity. I would say that just as Shakespeare has more room for tragedy in the Sophoclean sense than Dante did, so Hooker has more room for the failure of grace than St. Thomas did. They are not altogether dissimilar concepts after all. Hooker has a larger gap of empty, tragic irrationality in the God-human relationship than Thomas did. But Hooker sees this gap of empty irrationality not only as tragic but also (anachronistically, in the Shakespearean sense, it seems to me) as tragi-comic, as Shakespeare's late romances are both tragic and tragi-comic. For Hooker, the large tragi-comic gap of irrationality in the salvific process is more positive (Buddhist) than such a thing would be for Greekophile Thomas, who would not like it at all.

For Hooker, "The real presence of Christ's most blessed body and blood is not therefore to be sought for in the sacrament, but in the worthy receiver of the sacrament" (V, lxvii, 6). Hence, the real presence presupposes a real absence. Emptiness is the location of grace. Hooker is able to go so far as to say that the sacraments are "moral instruments" and to describe their work as that of "teaching." Is he reducing *sacramentum* to *exemplum*?

> Seeing therefore that grace is a consequent of sacraments, a thing which accompanieth them as their end, a benefit which he that hath receives from God himself the author of sacraments, and not from any other natural or supernatural quality in them, it may be hereby both understood that sacraments are necessary, and that the manner of their necessity to life supernatural is not in all respects as food unto natural life, because they contain *in themselves* no vital force or efficacy, they are not physical but *moral instruments* of salvation, duties of service and worship, which unless we perform as the Author of grace requireth, they are unprofitable (V, lvii, 4).

In an effort to reach a consensus on the bare minimum of commonly accepted sacramental doctrine, Hooker (doubtless knowingly) chooses a tenet whose acceptance was far from universal: "I can see on all sides at the length to a general agreement concerning that which alone is material, namely the *real participation* of Christ and of his life in his body and blood *by means of this sacrament*....no side denieth but that *the soul of man* is the receptacle of Christ's presence" (V, lxvii, 2). Any talk of the soul of man as the receptacle of Christ's presence was highly controversial in Elizabethan England and would, if proper qualifications had been omitted, have branded a theologian as leaning toward the subjectivist emphasis of the Puritans and spiritualists. Surely Hooker is careful to separate himself from these camps in all doctrines, including this one, but his concentrated effort to reach grounds of reconciliation with the Puritans, or at least the Calvinists, on the explosive issue of the eucharistic presence must be seen as purchased at the cost of a real departure from Aquinas.

It is a perilous balance that Hooker strives to maintain in his presentation of the mediation of Christ's grace to us. Speaking of the Pelagians and Semi-Pelagians, Hooker attempts yet again to show that neither sacraments alone nor human beings alone can bring us salvation:

> They knew no grace but external only, which grace inviteth, but draweth not: neither are we by inward grace carried up into heaven, the force of reason and will being cast into a dead sleep. Our experience teacheth us, that we never do any thing well, but with deliberate advice and choice, such as painfully setteth the powers of our minds on work: which thing I note in regard of *Libertines* and *Enthusiasts*, who err as much on the one hand, by making man little more than a block, as *Pelagians* on the other, by making him almost a god in the work of his own salvation (V, App. 1, 2).

Grace is mediated to us by a Christ who is present in the sacrament by way of conjunction, not in any sense (either local or majestical) by way of substance. Yet this presence by conjunction is not *only* presence by memorial, even though the locus of the presence is not in the sacrament itself but in the soul of the recipient. And even though grace dwells in the recipient's soul and not in the sacrament itself, still this event cannot occur outside the church, which is characterized by celebrating the sacrament according to the proper rules. Yet, (from a Thomist standpoint) subjectivity remains fatally predominant in Hooker's version of the *extra ecclesiam nihil salus est*. For Hooker grounds his version of the principle not on an authority handed down *directly* from God or from the Scriptures but rather on his characteristic basis of authority, that the best and wisest people of all times and places have accounted it so (*consensus gentium*). Hooker's hilariously down-to-earth, matter-of-fact, understated, outrageously English way of handling the *extra ecclesiam* doctrine is to resort to Ciceronian political theory: the sacraments cannot be efficacious outside the church because no one except the church considers them efficacious! Enough said! But this wonderful solution presupposes (although this is not Hooker's stated intention) that the efficacy of the sacraments is not only objective but also depends on the contribution made by the faith of the recipient and therefore is not fully objective in the Thomist (or Lutheran!) sense.

> Seeing that Sacraments therefore consist altogether in relation to some
> such gift of grace supernatural as only God can bestow, how should any
> but the Church administer those ceremonies as Sacraments which are
> not thought to be Sacraments by any but by the Church? (V, 1, 2).

Hence Hooker's argument for the exclusiveness of the church's power to
administer the sacraments efficaciously is different from that of both the
Roman Catholics and the Puritans of his day. Characteristically, it places
extraordinary emphasis on the cumulative judgment of wise people. There is no
reason to look for salvation outside the church because those outside the church
do not believe in the church's salvation anyway. This solution, at once
pragmatic and witty, is also characteristically filled with complex theoretical
assumptions and consequences. Presence by conjunction and efficacious
presence, then, which we have seen to be the keys to the relation between God
and nature, the relation between the human mind and the human appetites,
and the relation in the human being between soul and body, are also the keys
to Hooker's concept of the relation between Christ and the Christian in the
sacrament.

At the root of the concept of presence by conjunction is the concept of
efficacious presence. A controlling force attempts to control what seeks to
elude control in each of the instances enumerated above: Christ and Christian
in the sacrament, divine and human in Christ, God and nature, mind and
appetite, soul and body. For St. Thomas, the path to this control is through
harmony, moderation, balance, the sheer presence of the superior power in the
inferior vessel. For Hooker, as for Shakespeare, however, it seems that presence
is not enough. The absence of divinity from humanity requires that the method
of their reunion be the indefatigable hammering of the chisel of Phidias as he
works his intractable stone. When Phidias is finally present in his creation, it is
a presence more dominated by energy than by harmony, a presence more
uncertain and tense, more glorious and improbable, more tragic (I would say),
than that of Thomas's moon in the tides.

The stress Hooker puts on the difficulty of subjecting the body to the soul,
and the appetite (like the affections of zeal and fear) to reason, seems to be an
emphasis born of pain. Perhaps the pain of the long, slow English Reformation
influenced Hooker to include pain and work prominently in his soteriology. If
anything parallels this emphasis on the difficulty and importance of exhorting
the reason to summon up the tortured *energeia* of will to control the errant
appetites, it would be the thought of Hooker's very different countryman St.

Thomas More, as in his *Dialogue of Comfort against Tribulation*, who also had good reason to feel a bit exasperated by England's elephantine Reformation. Hooker says in the first book of his *summa* what he will say in various shades and tones throughout it: "The object of Appetite is whatsoever sensible good may be wished for; the object of Will is that good which Reason doth lead us to seek....Finally, Appetite is the Will's solicitor, and the Will is Appetite's controller...".(I, vii, 3).

> The soul then ought to conduct the body, and the spirit of our minds the soul (Eph.4:23). This is therefore the first Law, whereby the highest power of the mind requireth general obedience at the hands of all the rest concurring with it unto action (I, viii, 6).

There is no more cogent statement anywhere in the Laws of the meaning of "presence by conjunction" and "effective presence." A troubled, laborious presence it is. If it is divinely comedic at all, it is by way of most tragic comedy.

Finally, Hooker's sacramentology requires us to examine also the theme of time in the mediation of grace:

> The use of Sacraments is but only in this life, yet so that there they concern a far better life than this, and are for that cause accompanied with "grace which worketh Salvation." Sacraments are the powerful instruments of God to eternal life (V, 1, 3).

In passing, we may note Hooker's typical use of images of work, as in working Salvation, and power, as in the powerful instruments of God to eternal life. Our friend Phidias again! But what we are principally concerned with in *The Winter's Tale* is a resurrection, the ultimate work, the most improbable instance of power unto eternal life. In *The Winter's Tale*, some powerful instrument of the gods has, through error, growth, and redemption, been put into effect. And we have seen that the image of growth as chiefly exemplified in the grafter's art of nurturing nature through a transformation of nature into the realm of grace has been central to the play. The play is concerned, as Shakespeare's last plays all are in intense and explicit fashion, with the problem of time. In his early days, Shakespeare had presented time as a cormorant devouring life itself (*Love's Labour's Lost* I, i, 4). But in the last plays he is saying something different, emphasizing now time's restorative power. Even oblivion can be salutary in the late plays (as in later life). Penance extended over long years is a powerful instrument in Leontes' transformation: indeed, we can go so far as to say that Leontes' own penance is a powerful instrument in his wife's transformation to new life.

In Hooker's and Shakespeare's efforts to maintain, over against the early Puritans, the role of natural media in the mediation of grace, time is among the natural media that must be preserved. Just as Hooker insisted that reason is not abolished but redeemed by grace, so also time is not abolished but redeemed by a gracious eternity. Leontes abolished reason and found only zeal and fear; he abolished time in his willful effort to know all truth suddenly and found only death. Time, Leontes discovered later (too late, thought he), not only brings death (and hence can be hated and feared) but also forgiveness and restoration (and hence can be loved and welcomed). In the resurrection of Hermione, time does something more than Leontes had any right to expect it to do. Like the art of grafting, time allows in Hermione's restoration a power beyond nature, yet somehow the essence of nature (its center, we would say), to better nature. Time allows in Hermione's resurrection the rebirth of the loved one whom Leontes had thought for sixteen years that he would never see again.

Similarly, the discussions at the end of Book V on the calendar, on festivals, and fasts, are an integral part of Hooker's doctrine of grace, for in them Hooker elaborates a doctrine of sanctification by which time is not abolished; ends are not suddenly realized; time is redeemed, preserved, and fulfilled. "The sanctification of days and times is a token of that thankfulness and a part of that public honour which we owe to God for admirable benefits" (V, lxx, 1). A doctrine of time makes possible a doctrine of rest, just as workdays make possible holidays and motion makes an ending possible. Hooker's concept of the due measure of each thing within the hierarchy of measured things and motions is fundamental to his theory of movement and rest:

> Measure is that which perfecteth all things, because every thing is for some end, neither can that thing be available to any end which is not proportionable thereunto, and to proportion as well excesses as defects are opposite....every creature's limitation is according to his own kind, and therefore as oft as we note in them any thing above their kind, it argueth that the same is not properly theirs, but groweth in them from a cause more powerful than they are (V, lv, 2).

Natural agents may have supernatural causes and supernatural ends. Their natural movement may be toward some end which quite exceeds our reckoning. Persons are such instances of natural movement from supernatural origins to supernatural ends. Rest, then, the sacred pause in the laborious movement of time, is a means of sanctification for persons. Holy rest (I would say) is a flight backward to our original creation and forward to our new creation. "Festival solemnity therefore is nothing but the due mixture as it were of these three elements: Praise, and Bounty, and Rest" (V, lxx, 2).

> Rest is the end of all motion, and the last perfection of all things that labour. Labours in us are journeys, and even in them which feel no weariness by any work, yet they are but ways whereby to come unto that which bringeth not happiness till it do bring rest (V, lxx, 4).

"Labours in us are journeys": we have seen the importance to Hooker, as well as to Paulina, the midwife, of labors. In *The Winter's Tale*, it was by labors that Perdita came into the world, by labors that Hermione's death was atoned for, and by labors that Paulina preserved Hermione and/or caused her to be restored to life. The point is that labors are not completed in a night or a day but that, exactly as journeys in us, labors catch up our whole lives and give them whatever glimpse of eternity we may be able to obtain. But our labors arrive at their destinations only by the power of the God who works in us and only in that God's time. Just as all things are not restored at the end of *The Winter's Tale*, so the sacramental rest, as described by Hooker, is only a temporary rest foreshadowing the final rest.

> Grace, excluding possibility of sin, was neither given unto angels in their first creation, nor to man before his fall; but reserved for both till God be seen face to face in the state of glory, which state shall make it then impossible for us to sin, who now sin so often, notwithstanding grace, because the providence of God bestoweth not in this present life grace nearly so illustrating goodness, that the will should have no power to decline from it. Grace is not therefore here given in that measure which taketh away possibility of sinning, and so effectually moveth the will, as that it cannot (V, App. 1, 4).

And we may conclude by rejoicing in Hooker's unmodern refusal to glorify work for its own sake. Work is not only joyful and comic but also painful and tragic. A Protestant work ethic, which glorifies work as an end in itself, would be, for Hooker, an ungrateful rejection of that Holiday rest which God has prepared for his busy creatures. We post-Hookerian Sufi Buddho-Christians would add that the Holiday is, after all, the day for which and around which all the other days exist. Holiday is that sacred, so far unknown unplace full of that emptiness which makes it large enough for God himself to dwell in, that unplace where all the spokes of existence meet. For Hooker, as for us Sufi Buddho-Christians, this is the way the world ends, not with a bang or with a whimper, but with a Holiday.

This is also the way our exposition of Hooker ends, not with Hookerism but with some reflections on that Real Absence against which Hooker was not willing to completely close the door. For the only way to close the door was (as Cardinal Newman later saw) to go from Hookerism to Romanism. Hooker's sacrament, though filled like Luther's and Calvin's with metaphors of the non-metaphoricality of Real Presence, was after all even more metaphorical than theirs because, I have argued, the crux of Hooker's concept of salvific presence was artistic presence. To say that in Shakespearean, The Ultimate Gardener chose not to live without Perdita. The (not physically present) Gardener presides at his holy Sheep-Shearing Festival through his holy Perdita, Lady of the Arts. As Art Incarnate, Perdita learns how to be Lady of the Lost, nurturer of bastards.

Perdita had to be taught (by a philosopher-king who, without Perdita's help, could not even understand his own lecture enough to apply it to himself) that grafting is not an illegitimate art. Inasmuch as grafting simply mends and extends nature itself, it is nature that works through grafting, nature that nurtures the nurture of nature. "Do not call them bastards" (IV, iv, 98), those fruits of art's natural nurturing, even though "streak'd gillyvors" were produced by gardeners who combined other flowers through a grafting process to develop them. Our carnations and streak'd gillyvors, which seem unnatural in their origin, seem also unnatural in their death, apparently born only for perdition, when the year is growing ancient, not yet on summer's death or on the birth of trembling winter. Only if we understand the secret of winter (winter's tale) can we see that life is alive beneath winter's death (through no power of its own), and these false flowers, these bastards of nature, our carnations and streak'd gillyvors, are in fact pledges of that true life which comes from Beyond Nature, the life larger than death.

The world is full of such bastards, creatures whose original birth seemed to lead only to the stone of the tomb because of the sin which a wicked king let loose in the world. The poor bastards' mortality was not their individual fault, but only their collective fault, and their redemption, their grafting into the vine of immortality, of which Our Lord himself is the vinedresser, is not to their own credit but redounds only to the credit of their gracious Lord, who gives to us, not as we deserve, but only as he decrees. Our bastardy turns out to be part of that gracious nothingness of merit which we bring to the Lord. Our illegitimacy is our Lord's gracious opportunity to find us in our perdition, our moral and aesthetic infancy, and to become our provident shepherd, who claims nothing for himself but gives all to us, naming us Perdita, teaching us how to shear sheep and how to rejoice at Holiday festivals.

As Christ's Perditas, we are called to be ladies of the arts, ladies of the lost, ladies of the world's bastards. Our Florizel must put aside his princely robes for now. Florizel is absent as Florizel at our festival today. Florizel is in our midst as a beggar. Only art can allow us to see the prince in his absence, hidden beneath the beggar's garb. But that garb of lowliness is a mark of our prince's graciousness. God comes to us clothed only in the promises of Christ, and we come to God clothed only in those same promises. At this great Festival of Exchange, the Golgotha of total loss, all mannerly distinguishment betwixt prince and beggar must (tragically) be lost so that (comedically) we can learn what grace is, in a little theophany just right for us, made bearable by humility. It is requir'd we do awake our faith.

We must never forget or belittle the extent to which faith depends on Perdita, on art and imagination. As Strong put it:

> Since imagination, in its higher rational use, is a means of grasping truth not open to our senses, it is a most important coadjutor, if not a necessary instrument, of reason in its loftiest investigations. Neither mathematics nor morals can make known their highest truths to the man of no imagination. The dull plodder within the circle of material facts will discern no connections between them, and will have no science. Although God is apprehended not by imagination but by reason, yet imagination is a most important help to religion, and we may almost say that some men have not imagination enough to be religious.[8]

In the name of artful Perdita we must back off from three literalisms in particular which increase what Hooker called zeal and fear in religious matters: the literalism of Scripture, the literalism of altar, and the literalism of sword. Literalists of Scripture reduce The Invisible Gardener to a visible gardening manual, deifying the book and forgetting both its author and its hero. Literalists of the altar deny the metaphorical character of their songs of salvation, claiming, instead, that they have captured The Gardener in their holy bread and holy wine. Literalists of the sword are impatient with the slowness of the redemption which The Gardener brings. When they see their Lord threatened, they draw their sword when, instead, they should learn how, not to cut their opponent's ear off, but to speak into that ear. But that learning requires both time and art, more *froda* than *forza*. Those who spread their religion by the *forza* of sword lose their opportunity for the holy *froda* of dialogue and, instead, deny their Lord before the night is out.

Shakespeare, our poet of secularity, is not literally expounding Christian theology. Instead, Shakespeare is doing the work of a lowly hand-maiden of theology, mystically imitating theology outside the church doors, performing on his stage an analogue, a positive negative, of the mystery the priests are performing on their altars. Shakespeare is bequeathing to us the lesson which the Reformation taught Chrstendom, that the secular world, samsara, is not the denial of the sacred world, nirvana, but the negative of its positive, the positive of its negative, the emptiness of its fullness, the fullness of its emptiness. And, for that, we thank him. Shakespeare's philosophy may have been more beggarly than the great Dante's, but that does not keep Shakespeare from playing Perdita, Lady Of All Us Lost Bastards, at his Lord's Sheep-Shearing Festival.

Notes

Chapter 1. Christianity as a Dualistic Non-Dualism

1. Augustus Hopkins Strong, *Christ in Creation and Ethical Monism* (Philadelphia: Roger Williams Press, 1899), p. 1. Page numbers in parentheses in the text during the disucssion of Strong in this chapter will refer to this volume unless otherwise noted.

2. Augustus Hopkins Strong, *The Great Poets and Their Theology* (Philadelphia: The Griffith & Rowland Press, 1897) and *American Poets and Their Theology* (Philadelphia: The Judson Press, 1916). The former voume will be called *Great Poets* in the notes.

3. Strong discusses Christ and original sin in *Systematic Theology* (Philadelphia: The Judson Press, 1907), pp. 750–776 and 793–809.

4. H. Richard Niebuhr, *Christ and Culture* (New York: Harper & Brothers, 1951).

5. H. Richard Niebuhr, *Radical Monotheism and Western Culture* (New York: Harper & Row, 1960), pp. 28–31.

Chapter 2. Tragedy as Non-Dualism, Comedy as Dualism

1. Strong, *Great Poets*, pp. 169-170.

2. Northrop Frye, *The Critical Path: An Essay on the Social Context of Literary Criticism* (Bloomington: Indiana University Press, 1971).

3. Northrop Frye, *The Secular Scripture: A Study of the Structure of Romance* (Cambridge: Harvard University Press, 1976), pp. 65–188.

4. Paul Tillich, "The Two Types of Philosophy of Religion" (originally published in 1946), reprinted in: John Clayton, ed., Paul Tillich, *Writings in the Philosophy of Religion* (Berlin: Walter de Gruyter & Co., 1987), p. 289. Page numbers in parentheses in the text during the disussion of this essay are to this de Gruyter edition.

5. Paul Tillich, *Systematic Theology* (Chicago: University of Chicago Press, 1951ff.). Al-Ghazali's story can be found in: W. Montgomery Watt, *The Faith and Practice of al-Ghazali* (Lahore: Sh. Muhammad Ashraf, 1953).

6. Fazlur Rahman, *Islam*, 2nd ed. (Chicago: University of Chicago Press, 1979).

7. Gadjin Nagao, *The Foundational Standpoint of Madhyamika Philosophy* (Albany: State University of New York Press, 1989). Translated from Japanese by John P. Keenan.

8. Martin Luther, "Against the Heavenly Prophets in the Matter of Images and Sacraments, 1525," in: Conrad Bergendoff, ed., *Church and Ministry*, Vol. II, *Luther's Works*, American Edition, Vol. 40 (Philadelphia: Fortress Press, 1958). Part I translated from German by Bernhard Erling, Part II by Conrad Bergendoff.

9. Martin Luther, "Against the Robbing and Murdering Hordes of Peasants," in: Robert C. Schultz, ed., *The Christian in Society*, Vol. 3, *Luther's Works*, American Edition, Vol. 46 (Philadelphia: Fortress Press, 1967). Translated from German by Charles M. Jacobs. Revised by Robert C. Schultz.

10. Keiji Nishitani, *Religion and Nothingness* (Berkeley: University of California Press, 1982), p. 118. Translated from Japanese by Jan Van Bragt. I am grateful to Michael Monos for introducing me to Nishitani's work.

Chapter 3. Tragedy and Comedy in the Luther-Calvin Dialectic

1. Erich Auerbach, *Mimesis: The Representation of Reality in Western Literature* (Princeton: Princeton University Press, 1953). Translated from German by Willard R. Trask.

2. Northrop Frye, *A Natural Perspective: The Development of Shakespearean Comedy and Romance* (New York: Columbia University Press, 1965), pp. 1–2.

3. Northrop Frye, *Anatomy of Criticism* (Princeton: Princeton University Press, 1957).

4. H. Richard Niebuhr, *op. cit.* See Chap. 1, n. 4.

5. Niebuhr argued that Thomas belongs in the "Christ Above Culture" category (*Christ and Culture*, pp. 116–148). I have argued that he belongs also on the transformationist side of a paradox/transformationist arch in "The Paradigm of Aristotelian Tragedy in the Theology of Thomas Aquinas" in: Nancy van Deusen and Alvin E. Ford, eds., *Paradigms in Medieval Thought Applications in Medieval Disciplines: A Symposium* (Lewiston, N. Y.: The Edwin Mellen Press, 1990), pp. 111-125.

6. A good introduction to Torrance's thought is: Thomas F. Torrance, *The Christian Frame of Mind: Reason, Order, and Openness in Theology and Natural Science* (Colorado Springs: Helmers & Howard, 1989).

Chapter 4. On Not Swallowing a Metaphor: Karlstadt's Eucharistic Radicalism in 1523-24

1. Ronald J. Sider, *Karlstadt's Battle with Luther: Documents in a Liberal-Radical Debate* (Philadelphia: Fortress Press, 1978). During Luther's absence from Wittenberg in late 1521 and early 1522, Karlstadt was, more than any other single individual, in charge of the Reformation in Wittenberg. The extent of Karlstadt's responsibility for the iconoclastic riots that occurred during that time has been debated ever since. In any event, Luther held him responsible, and after Luther's return to Wittenberg in March of 1522, Karlstadt was forced to stand in the background. In 1523, Karlstadt moved to Orlamünde, a village in Thuringia, where he took charge of the local church (from which he had previously received an income *in absentia*). He served the church as pastor, farmed for a living, dressed as a peasant, associated on a daily basis with the common people, and identified himself as "a new layman." Karlstadt also became associated with Thomas Müntzer. In September of 1524, the authorities banished Karlstadt from electoral Saxony, thus making it necessary for him to leave his young, pregnant wife in Orlamünde. When, in early 1525, Karlstadt promised to remain silent about the eucharist, he was re-admitted to Saxony, arriving on Luther's doorstep as a refugee just after Luther's wedding. Karlstadt remained silent about the eucharist until 1527, when he again spoke up, eventually leaving Saxony for Basel. Karlstadt lived until 1541.

For an account of these events in their larger historical context see George Huntston Williams, *The Radical Reformation* (Philadelphia: The Westminster Press, 1962). I discussed Karlstadt's eucharistic theology and the controversy surrounding it in: "The Coherence of Andreas Bodenstein von Karlstadt's Early Evangelical Doctrine of the Lord's Supper: 1521–1525" (Ph.D. dissertation: Hartford, Connecticut: Hartford Seminary Foundation, 1973). The dissertation is available from University Microfilms in Ann Arbor, Michigan.

2. Gordon Rupp, *Patterns of Reformation* (Philadelphia: Fortress Press, 1969), pp. 141-2.

3. *Ibid.*, p. 142.

4. *Ibid.* See also Hermann Barge, *Andreas Bodenstein von Karlstadt*, 2 vols. (Leipzig: Friedrich Brandstetter, 1905). Barge discusses his judgment that *Von dem Priesterthum* contains a denial of Christ's physical eucharistic presence in Vol. II on p. 151. Barge and E. Freys provided a list of Karlstadt's treatises, along with the data on their places and times of publication and their later availability in major libraries in: Hermann Barge and E. Freys, eds., "Verzeichnis der gedruckten Schriften des Andreas Bodenstein von Karlstadt," *Zentralblatt für Bibliothekswesen*, XXI (1904), 153-179, 209-243, 305-331. The Karlstadt treatises I am discussing in this chapter, along with their identification numbers in the Barge-Freys "Verzeichnis," are: *Von dem Priesterthum und opffer Christi* (Jena, December 29, 1523, "Verzeichnis" #112); *Ob man mit heyliger schrifft erweysen müge, das Christus mit leyb, blut und sele im Sacrament sey* (Basel, October-November, 1524, "Verzeichnis" #124); *Dialogus oder ein gesprechbüchlin Von dem grewlichen unnd abgöttischen missbrauch, des hochwirdigsten Sacraments Jesu Christi* (Basel, October-November, 1524, "Verzeichnis" #126; included in: Erich Hertzsch, ed., *Karlstadts Schriften aus den Jahren 1523–1525* [Neudrucke deutscher Literaturwerke des 16. und 17. Jahrhunderts, No. 325, Halle (Saale): Max Niemeyer, 1956-1957], Vol. II, pp. 5–49); *Auszlegung dieser wort Christi. Das ist meyn leyb, welcher für euch vergossen würt. Luce am. 22. Wider die einfeltige unnd zwyfeltige papisten, welche soliche wort, zy einem abbruch des kreützes Chrsti brauchen* (Basel, October-November, 1524, "Verzeichnis" #129); *WIder die alte un newe Papistische Messen* (Basel, October-November, 1524, "Verzeichnis" #131); *Von dem wider christlichen missbrauch des hern brodt und kelch. Ob der glaub in das sacrameent, sünde vergäbe, und ob das sacrament eyn arrabo, oder pfand sey der sünde vergäbung. Auszlegung dess. xi. Capit. in der j.*

Epistel Pauli zu den Corinthiern von des hern abentmal (Basel, October-November, 1524, "Verzeichnis" #135).

6. Karlstadt, *Von abtuhung der Bylder, Und das keyn Betdler unther den Christen seyn sollen* (Wittenberg, January, 1522, "Verzeichnis" #88). Included in: Hans Lietzmann, ed., *Von Abtuhung der Bilder und das keyn Bedtler unther den Christen seyn sollen, 1522, und die Wittenberger Beutelordnung*, Kleine Texte für theologische und philologische Vorlesungen und Übungen, Vol. LXXIV (Bonn: Marcus und Weber, 1911).

7. See Sacvan Bercovitch, *The Puritan Origins of the American Self* (New Haven: Yale University Press, 1975). See also Bercovitch's *The American Jeremiad* (Madison: The University of Wisconsin Press, 1978) and the following volumes edited by Bercovitch: *Typology and Early American Literature* (Boston: The University of Massachusetts Press, 1972); *The American Puritan Imagination: Essays in revaluation* (Cambridge: Cambridge University Press, 1974); and *Reconstructing American Literary History* (Cambridge, Mass.: Harvard University Press, 1986)

Chapter 5. The Real Absence in the Soteriologies of Richard Hooker and *The Winter's Tale*

1. Erich Auerbach, *Dante: Poet of the Secular World* (Chicago: University of Chicago Press, 1961). Translated from German by Ralph Manheim.

2. Strong, *Great Poets*, pp. 193-4.

3. Quotations are from the edition of *The Winter's Tale* edited by Frederick E. Pierce in "The Yale Shakespeare" (New Haven, Yale University Press, 1918).

4. Martin Luther, "Preface to the Complete Edition of Luther's Latin Writings, 1545" in: Lewis W. Spitz, ed., *Career of the Reformer*, Vol. IV, *Luther's Works*, American Edition (Philadelphia: Fortress Press, 1960). Translated from Latin by Lewis W. Spitz, Sr.

5. Northrop Frye, *The Secular Scripture*, p. 188.

6. T. S. Eliot, "Little Gidding," *Collected Poems 1909–1962* (New York: Harcourt, Brace & World, Inc., 1970), pp. 206–7.

7. Richard Hooker, *Of The Laws of Ecclesiastical Polity*, in: John Keble, ed., *The Works of that Learned and Judicious Divine Mr. Richard Hooker*, 7th ed. (Oxford: Clarendon Press, 1888). W. Speed Hill has directed the publication of a new edition of Hooker's works, but I hope Dr. Hill and the kindly reader will forgive me for sticking to my Keble (as I also stick to the King James Version of the English Bible). There is perhaps no excuse for it, but I am too old to change. I think Hooker would forgive such flamboyant conservatism, but I *know* Keble would. So I hope you will too.

8. Strong, *Great Poets*, p. 169.

Index of Names